P9-CJH-139

PENGUIN CLASSICS

# THE RIG VEDA

ADVISORY EDITOR: BETTY RADICE

WENDY DONIGER O'FLAHERTY was born in New York in 1940 and trained as a dancer under George Balanchine and Martha Graham before beginning the study of Sanskrit at Radcliffe College in 1958. She holds doctoral degrees in Indian literature from Harvard and Oxford Universities, and is now Professor of the History of Religions and Indian Studies in the Divinity School at the University of Chicago. Her publications include *Women, Androgynes, and Other Mythical Beasts*, *Asceticism and Eroticism in the Mythology of Śiva*, *The Origins of Evil in Hindu Mythology* and *Karma and Rebirth in Classical Indian Traditions* as well as numerous articles on Indian history, literature, and mythology. She has also translated *Hindu Myths* for the Penguin Classics.

# THE RIG VEDA

## *An Anthology*

---

ONE HUNDRED AND EIGHT HYMNS,
SELECTED, TRANSLATED AND ANNOTATED
BY WENDY DONIGER O'FLAHERTY

PENGUIN BOOKS

PENGUIN BOOKS

Published by the Penguin Group
27 Wrights Lane, London W8 5TZ, England
Viking Penguin Inc., 40 West 23rd Street, New York, New York 10010, USA
Penguin Books Australia Ltd, Ringwood, Victoria, Australia
Penguin Books Canada Ltd, 2801 John Street, Markham, Ontario, Canada L3R 1B4
Penguin Books (NZ) Ltd, 182–190 Wairau Road, Auckland 10, New Zealand

Penguin Books Ltd, Registered Offices: Harmondsworth, Middlesex, England

This selection first published in this translation 1981
5 7 9 10 8 6

Copyright © Wendy Doniger O'Flaherty, 1981
All rights reserved

Made and printed in Great Britain by
Richard Clay Ltd, Bungay, Suffolk
Set in Monotype Garamond

Except in the United States of America,
this book is sold subject to the condition
that it shall not, by way of trade or otherwise,
be lent, re-sold, hired out, or otherwise circulated
without the publisher's prior consent in any form of
binding or cover other than that in which it is
published and without a similar condition
including this condition being imposed
on the subsequent purchaser

*For*

*Tatyana Yakovlena Elizarenkova*

*and*

*Frits Staal*

# *Contents*

CONTENTS

## *Introduction*

THIS is a book for people, not for scholars. Real scholars will read the *Rig Veda* in Sanskrit; would-be scholars, or scholars from other fields, will fight their way through the translations of Geldner (German), Renou (French), Elizarenkova (Russian) and others;* they will search the journals for articles on each verse, and on each word;† they will pore over the dictionaries and the concordances.‡ But there is so much in the *Rig Veda* to interest and excite non-Vedists; it seems a shame to let it go on being the treasure of a tiny, exclusive group, hidden as it is behind the thorny wall of an ancient and cryptic language. There are several good reasons why it has remained hidden for so many years: it is so long (1,028 hymns, each averaging about ten verses) that a complete translation is a daunting prospect;§ and it is so complex that most serious translations have been rendered unreadable by critical apparatus.

Yet, this need not be so. One need not read *all* of the *Rig Veda* to enjoy its beauty and wisdom; and since the text is itself an anthology of separate, individually complete hymns, a selection destroys no continuity of the original. Moreover, despite its awesome and venerable reputation, the *Rig Veda* proves surprisingly accessible when one has a little help from one's friends. By standing upon the shoulders of the many

* See Appendix 3 for a bibliography of translations into European languages.

† See Appendix 4 for a bibliography of articles pertaining to each translated hymn.

‡ See Appendix 2 for a bibliography of dictionaries and concordances.

§ It did not daunt Geldner, Wilson, and Griffith (nor Renou, whose translation was almost complete at the time of his death), but these works are awkward to read and often totally misleading; it does not daunt Stanley Insler, but his projected complete translation is still far from complete.

giants (and pygmies) in the long academic procession of Vedists, I have tried to construct a translation that is sound but readable;* by using the available scholarship, I have tried to make the best educated guess on the many problematic points; and by citing this scholarship in the bibliographies, I invite the would-be scholar to make a better guess. For although this is not a book *for* scholars, it is a book *from* scholars, from the many painstaking Indian commentators (Yāska, Śaunaka, Sāyaṇa and lesser figures) and European interpreters (beginning with Max Müller) who were driven by a sharp need to fathom this fascinating work.

Having resolved upon a working method, it was necessary to rationalize a selection. My field was automatically limited by the realization that I would be forced to exclude all the hymns that I could not decipher (or that I could only render intelligible by means of a commentary too complex for the present purpose) and that I would indulge myself by excluding all those that I found boring. This is certainly not a 'representative' anthology of the *Rig Veda* except in the sense that it is representative of my taste and of the taste of those scholars whose works I have so shamelessly plundered; it is the product of serendipity and hot tips from my friends and colleagues, living and long dead. It is a selection of what I have found to be beautiful, interesting, and profound in the *Rig Veda*, following the leads of my elders and betters. In number, these 108 (a holy number in India)† hymns are ten per cent of the whole collection, roughly the size of one of the ten books. These are the hymns that I have come across and loved, that scholars whom I respect have found most worthy of study, that later Hindus have made use of in building their religious ideas. Idiosyncratic and eclectic, it may yet serve as

* Of the existing English translations, some are complete but unsound (Wilson, Griffith), some incomplete and unsound (Max Müller, P. Lal), some incomplete but sound (Macdonell, Panikkar), but only Panikkar could be called readable, and his is a strongly slanted selection and rendition.

† There are 108 classical *Upaniṣads*, 108 *bhakti* prayers, etc.

an introduction to a significant number of hymns in many diverse veins. Many of these centre upon mythology, which interests me most; many delve into philosophy (and therefore come from the latest books of the *Rig Veda*, the first and last), which has interested students of Indian thought most; many explore the symbolism and mechanism of Vedic ritual, which has interested historians of religion most; many are included for the sake of the light they shed on details of daily life, which interests historians and sociologists most, and many for the sake of their poetry.

I have kept the notes to a minimum, and avoided the tautological type entirely ('This is the name of a sage', 'Here the hymn switches from the singular to the plural'), for these seem to me mere automatic reflexes and conventions into which translators often lapse, like hosts showing their guests a new house ('This is the kitchen,' 'This is the bedroom'). I have also resisted, often with great difficulty, the powerful temptation to explain the *Rig Veda* by looking backward or forward, to draw upon the ancient Indo-European civilization out of which it grew or to show how Vedic ideas developed in post-Vedic India. Such explanations are fascinating and often useful, but they would have doubled the length of my notes and would, in any case, have distracted the reader from the particular moment in time when these hymns were composed, the moment that I strove to capture in my translations.

The skeletal nature of the critical apparatus is also intended to spare the reader a painful and confusing glimpse behind the curtain into the translator's messy workshop, to gloss over a number of the agonized (and often unsatisfying) decisions that were necessary in rendering the Sanskrit into a comprehensible form of English. The magnitude of the problem faced by the translator of the *Rig Veda* is immediately evident from the disgruntled mumblings, apologies, and *cris de cœur* that slip out of the notes in the extant translations – 'This hymn is one of the most obscure in the whole *Rigveda*'; 'I can make no sense at all of the second line'; '*mot inconnu*'; '*Ein dunkles Lied*'; '*Nicht ganz klar*'. Translation should be exempt from fault-finding, but it is hard to resist the temptation to wonder where the obscurity comes into play along the long, fragile thread that connects the original with the translation. Is it an obscure transmission, or an obscure reception?

In many places, a difficult idea is couched in simple language; in others, a simple idea is obscured by difficult language. Every translator has encountered the latter problem, and such instances occur frequently in the *Rig Veda*, but so do instances of the opposite type: several hymns are simple enough to translate, but impossible to understand. The linguistic problem in both cases is intriguing, if we try to separate idea from language, structure from vocabulary. In the first instance, the language may be intrinsically difficult (dense, complex, and esoteric even for the people of its own time), difficult to people of another time (because of archaisms, *hapax legomena*, discontinued usages), or difficult because we have lost the thread of the underlying idiom. In the second instance, how can we know that we are in fact translating correctly and not merely unconsciously simplifying complex ideas?* Almost a century ago, Abel Bergaigne pointed out that one must make a choice between simplifying the Vedic lexicon and thereby dealing with more complex ideas, or complicating the lexicon in order to simplify Vedic ideas.† Although Bergaigne inclined to the former method (and many Vedists today still follow him), my own feeling is that Vedic words are more complex than Vedic contexts; that to seek various English equivalents for single words along a broad spectrum of linked concepts is ultimately more productive than to seek to boil down such a term into a single neutral word that can be plugged into any context. Poetic applications even of basic terms always retain a certain measure of ambiguity, but this cannot be captured by a compromise gloss.

How can we understand the words if we do not understand the meaning behind them? Here one is reminded of Samuel

* I am indebted to David Grene for this clarification.

† Abel Bergaigne, 'Etudes sur le lexique du Rig-Veda', *Journal asiatique*, October-November-December 1883, pp. 468–74.

Johnson's criticism of a colleague: 'He has too little Latin; he takes the Latin from the meaning, not the meaning from the Latin.' To some degree, we all do take the Sanskrit from the meaning, especially where the words themselves are difficult. And to this extent, we cannot translate a hymn in 'simple language', either, if we do not understand it. Nor can we write something that we know to be obscure; if what we write is obscure by accident, that is another matter, but we must think we understand an obscure poem in order to translate it.

In some cases, a linguistically simple phrase contains a thought that might be explained by a long footnote, but often such a note cannot be written with any confidence. The phrase, 'We have become immortal', for example, is linguistically straightforward; few would challenge the plain English rendering. But what does it mean? What did they mean by immortality? Surely not eternal life, but what kind of afterlife? Questions of this sort may begin to be answered when one undertakes a thorough study of Vedic religion and philosophy (a subject on which far too many books have been written, and one to which this volume will not add);* but even then the hymn remains tantalizingly obscure. What does it mean? It means what it says. This is a book of questions, not a book of answers; and, to paraphrase Gertrude Stein, 'What is the question?' must always be our starting-point – and often our finishing-point as well.

The notes, therefore, provide only enough glosses to allay the reader's suspicion that something important may be missing or that something is wrong with the verse; scholarly material ('This also occurs in the Avesta') has been used only when the verse makes no sense at all without it. This austerity in commentary may often puzzle the reader. Good. The hymns are meant to puzzle, to surprise, to trouble the mind; they are often just as puzzling in Sanskrit as they are in English. When the reader finds himself at a point where the sense is unclear (as long as the language is clear), let him use

* See Appendix 2 for a selection of such books.

his head, as the Indian commentators used theirs; the gods love riddles, as the ancient sages knew, and those who would converse with the gods must learn to live with and thrive upon paradox and enigma.

The riddles in the *Rig Veda* are particularly maddening because many of them are *Looking Glass* riddles ('Why is a raven like a writing desk?'): they do not have, nor are they meant to have, answers. They are not merely rhetorical, but are designed to present one half of a Socratic dialogue through which the reader becomes aware of the inadequacy of his certain knowledge. This deliberate obfuscation of issues that are in any case intrinsically unfathomable sometimes seems to add insult to injury; one feels that the hymns themselves are mischievous translations into a 'foreign' language. Like the Englishman who announced that he preferred English to all other languages because it was the only language in which one said the words in the order that one thought of them, one feels that the *Rig Veda* poets are not saying the words in the order that *they* thought of them, let alone the order that we would think of them.

An example of this is the complexity of tenses and references to past and present. Sometimes the poet slips from the present to the past in the traditional way, collapsing the mythical past and the ritual present together: Indra, do now what you did in the past. But sometimes the poet deliberately invokes or highlights a paradox of time: Aditi gave birth to Dakṣa, and Dakṣa gave birth to Aditi. These cognitive paradoxes, underscored by grammatical inconsistencies in tense, draw the reader into the timeless world of the myth and ritual.

Another, related, form of deliberate confusion is the use of mutually illuminating metaphors. Certain concerns recur throughout the *Rig Veda*: the themes of harnessing and unharnessing (yoking cattle, controlling powers), which shift in their positive or negative value (sometimes harnessing is good, sometimes bad); the closely related theme of finding open space and freedom, always a positive value, in contrast with being hemmed in and trapped (suffering from the anguish of *aṃhas*, a 'tight spot', constriction and danger); and the fear of being hated and attacked (by the gods, or by other human beings). These are linked to other constellations of images: conflict within the nuclear family and uneasiness about the mystery of birth from male and female parents; the preciousness of animals, particularly cows and horses; the wish for knowledge, inspiration, long life, and immortality; awe of the sun and the rain and the cosmic powers of fertility. The problem arises when one tries to determine which of these are in the foreground and which in the background of a particular hymn: are the cows symbolic of the sun, or is the sun a metaphor for cows? The careless or greedy exegete finds himself in danger of rampant Jungianism: everything is symbolic of everything else; each is a metaphor for all of the others. The open-minded interpreter will sit back and let the images come to him; when asked to pinpoint the central point of a particular verse, he will fall back upon the traditional catch-all of the short-answer questionnaire: all of the above.

In places the metaphors are incomplete or jagged, the language elliptic or dense; I have not tried to smooth these places out or simplify them. An eloquent defence of this approach to translation appears in David Grene's review of Robert Lowell's translation of Aeschylus's *Oresteia*, a trilogy whose extraordinarily rich poetry may have rendered it difficult even for an Athenian audience at first hearing:

> The temptation to a modern translator in such a matter is either to cut or to substitute a kind of poetry that is more acceptable. But Aeschylus was like that, and perhaps we ought to settle for the strangeness and roughness of a literal rendering. There was a creative poet there whose images and metaphors were his own and no one else's, and if we brood over them even in their bare bones we may learn more about poetry than by trying to make them over in our own terms.*

I have tried to find the bare bones of the Vedic verses and clothe them with as few scholarly veils as possible.

* From a review in *The New York Times*, Sunday Book Review section. 8 April 1979, p. 43.

There is yet another, related ambiguity which will plague the reader of this translation, and one that I cannot resolve. Some of the poetry works as poetry even in English; some of it does not. When it does not, the break may occur at any of several points along the line. One tends to think that it occurs at the point of translation (following the ancient observation that a translation is like a woman: if it is beautiful, it cannot be faithful; and if it is faithful, it cannot be beautiful), and there are many verses in this collection that I love in the Sanskrit and am bothered by in the best rendition that I could produce. But there are other obstacles to the poetry, places where complex ritual vocabulary or highly abstract philosophical arguments interfere (to our ears, though not necessarily to those of the ancient audience) with the power of the poetry. Perhaps the single factor that tends to interfere most with the poetry throughout the *Rig Veda* is the fragmentary quality of the work. Not only is each hymn a separate statement (though some work well together, like 4.26–7), but each verse stands on its own and often bears no obvious relationship with the verses immediately preceding and following it; indeed, each line of a two-line verse – and sometimes each half-line – may contain a thought not only grammatically distinct from what surrounds it but different in tone, imagery, and reference. This discontinuity – which is, ironically, the one continuous thread in the *Rig Veda*, the one universal semantic feature – tends to produce a kind of poetry that can be overpowering in the intensity of the separate forces that it juxtaposes but disconcerting to anyone looking for a sustained mood. It also tends to obscure the narrative flow of the stories hidden behind the hymns, for the *Rig Veda* has no true mythology; it is written out of a mythology that we can only try to reconstruct from the Rig Vedic jumble of paradoxes heaped on paradoxes, tropes heaped on tropes.*

Yet one does sense a solid mythological corpus behind the hymns, for one hymn may refer obliquely to a story that is

* These ideas arose from conversations with Boris Ogibenin and Jan Heesterman.

told fully in another hymn, which makes us suspect that other oblique phrases may in fact allude to texts widely known at the time of the *Rig Veda* though lost to us now. This suspicion is strengthened by other, fuller variants of such thumbnail episodes that we encounter in other Indo-European mythologies and in the texts of later Hinduism.

There are, nevertheless, times when, I suspect, the Vedic poet himself fails to carry off what he intends (after all, why should we expect *any* poet to remain first-rate for over 1,000 hymns, let alone a motley group of ancient sages?), or, finally, when the poem is not poetry in the modern sense at all, and we do it a disservice to look for modern poetic qualities in it.* This being so, the reader is advised to be as open to the words as possible, letting them move him when they can, and not trying to wrench from them a kind of poetry that they cannot yield.

While we are still in the mood for apologies and laying it on the line, let me say that for this volume I have retranslated several hymns used in my earlier publications, and the alert reader will notice massive differences between the two versions. I have learned a lot about the *Rig Veda* in the intervening years and I hope to continue to do so; translations made ten years from now would probably be equally different from these, and with good reason. Translators are, to paraphrase Charles Long, painters rather than photographers, and painters make mistakes. Translators should, I think, be allowed to make their guesses out loud, treating their own earlier attempts like old wills: I hereby revoke and declare null and void, all previous translations . . . In the present instance, most of these mistakes will probably occur in places where the text is so vague or obscure that one is given the choice either to hedge (to say nothing unequivocal) or to go for broke: to figure out what it most probably means, and to say that. For

* For a straightforward discussion of these problems, see David Grene's introduction to *Most Ancient Verse*, a volume of translation, from Babylonian and Egyptian poetry by Thorkild Jacobsen and John A. Wilson (Chicago, Ill., University of Chicago Press, 1948).

example, when a god is said to be 'man-gazed' (*nṛ-cakṣas*) does it mean that he gazes at men or that his eye is like that of a man? In the contexts in which it occurs, the former seems more likely to me, and that is how I have translated it; years from now it may turn out that the term does, in fact, mean that his eye is like that of a man; I would rather live with that possibility than leave the reader in the lurch with a hedged 'man-gaze'.

Idiosyncratic as this collection is, it is nevertheless in many senses a collaboration. I owe, first of all, a great debt to my predecessors in the field of Vedic scholarship, in particular to Renou, Geldner, Grassmann, and the medieval commentator Sāyaṇa, who is, for all his sins, someone good to be able to argue with about the meaning of a Vedic hymn. I owe a more immediate debt to my potential successors in the field, my students, who have helped me puzzle out many a recalcitrant verse: my students in Berkeley (Gar Emerson Kellom, Charles Pain, Elizabeth Read Kenney, Linda Blodgett Sparrowe) and in Chicago (Ralph Strohl, Catherine Bell, Gary Ebersole, Vicki Kirsch, Barry Friedman, and Susan Turk). In particular, I must thank William Kalley Mahony and Brian K. Smith, who did much of the work for the bibliographies; Ralph Strohl, who helped me with the index; and Martha Morrow, who retyped much of the text with unflagging enthusiasm.

I never would have undertaken this project without the help of Frits Staal, who worked with me for the first year, until his other commitments and the daunting distance between Chicago and Berkeley reduced this to a one-person project; I owe him thanks not only for the start he gave me in Vedic bibliography and the hymns that he taught me to appreciate, but especially for his joyous and stylish support throughout. To A. K. Ramanujan I owe thanks not only for his continuous warm support of my work but also for the simple but apocalyptically helpful suggestion that it was useful to translate *part* of the *Rig Veda* if one lacked the *Sitzfleisch* for the whole thing. David Grene generously allowed me to tap his great expertise as a translator, and his great innocence of things Vedic, to act as the perfect guinea-pig; I am grateful to him for the care he has taken in reading through an early draft and responding so frankly and sensitively to it. Last of all, I owe an inexpressible debt of gratitude to my friend and colleague Tatyana Yakovlena Elizarenkova, for her help, for the brilliant example set by her own *Rig Veda* translations (which always made more *sense* to me than those of anyone else), and for her encouragement. When I first wrote to her of this project she replied, 'Let the two of us dig the mysterious old *Rig Veda* from both sides, I from Russia and you from America, and perhaps we will meet in the middle.' I doubt that any of us has come near to the molten centre of this rich and secret book, but perhaps by digging at it from all sides, each of us will mine a treasure worth labouring for. I lay mine at the feet of the reading public.

## 8.30 *To All the Gods*

1 Not one of you, gods, is small, not one a little child; all
of you are truly great.
2 Therefore you are worthy of praise and of sacrifice, you
thirty-three gods of Manu, arrogant and powerful.
3 Protect us, help us and speak for us; do not lead us into
the distance far away from the path of our father Manu.
4 You gods who are all here and who belong to all men,
give far-reaching shelter to us and to our cows and horses.

# CREATION

THE *Rig Veda* refers glancingly to many different theories of creation. Several of these regard creation as the result – often apparently a mere by-product – of a cosmic battle, such as those mentioned in the hymns to Indra, or as a result of the apparently unmotivated act of separating heaven and earth, an act attributed to several different gods. These aspects of creation are woven in and out of the hymns in the older parts of the *Rig Veda*, books 2 through 9. But in the subsequent tenth book we encounter for the first time hymns that are entirely devoted to speculations on the origins of the cosmos.

Some of these hymns seek the origins of the existence of existence itself (10.129) or of the creator himself (10.121). Others speculate upon the sacrifice as the origin of the earth and the people in it (10.90), or upon the origins of the sacrifice (10.130, 10.190). Sacrifice is central to many concepts of creation, particularly to those explicitly linked to sacrificial gods or instruments, but it also appears as a supplement to other forms of creation such as sculpture (10.81–2) or anthropomorphic birth (10.72).

## 10.129 *Creation Hymn (Nāsadīya)*

This short hymn, though linguistically simple (with the exception of one or two troublesome nouns), is conceptually extremely provocative and has, indeed, provoked hundreds of complex commentaries among Indian theologians and Western scholars. In many ways, it is meant to puzzle and challenge, to raise unanswerable questions, to pile up paradoxes.

*1* There was neither non-existence nor existence then; there was neither the realm of space nor the sky which is beyond. What stirred?[1] Where? In whose protection? Was there water, bottomlessly deep?

*2* There was neither death nor immortality then. There was no distinguishing sign[2] of night nor of day. That one breathed, windless, by its own impulse. Other than that there was nothing beyond.

*3* Darkness was hidden by darkness in the beginning; with no distinguishing sign,[2] all this was water. The life force that was covered with emptiness, that one arose through the power of heat.[3]

*4* Desire came upon that one in the beginning; that was the first seed of mind. Poets[4] seeking in their heart with wisdom found the bond of existence in non-existence.

*5* Their cord[5] was extended across. Was there below? Was there above? There were seed-placers; there were powers.[6] There was impulse beneath; there was giving-forth above.

*6* Who really knows? Who will here proclaim it? Whence was it produced? Whence is this creation? The gods came afterwards, with the creation of this universe.[7] Who then knows whence it has arisen?

*7* Whence this creation has arisen – perhaps it formed itself, or perhaps it did not – the one who looks down on it, in the highest heaven, only he knows – or perhaps he does not know.

NOTES

1. The verb is often used to describe the motion of breath. The verse implies that the action precedes the actor.

2. That is, the difference between night and day, light or darkness, or possibly sun and moon.

3. *Tapas* designates heat, in particular the heat generated by ritual activity and by physical mortification of the body.

4. *Kavi* designates a poet or saint.

5. Possibly a reference to the 'bond' mentioned in verse 4, or a kind of measuring cord by which the poets delimit – and hence create – the elements.

6. Through chiasmus, the verse contrasts male seed-placers, giving-forth, above, with female powers, impulse, below.

7. That is, the gods cannot be the source of creation since they came after it.

## 10.121 *The Unknown God, the Golden Embryo*

This creation hymn poses questions about an unnamed god (whom Max Müller first dubbed Deus Ignotus); later tradition (beginning with the subsequent appending of the final verse of this hymn, a verse that ends with a phrase used to conclude many other *Rig Veda* hymns) identified this god with Prajāpati and made the question in the refrain (who?) into an answer: 'Who' (Ka) is the name of the creator, a name explicitly said, in later texts, to have been given to Prajāpati by Indra (as agnostics are sometimes accused of praying 'to whom it may concern'). But the original force of the verse is speculative: since the creator preceded all the known gods,[1] creating them, who could he be? In verse 7, he seems to appear after the waters; in verse 9, the waters appear from him. They are born from one another, a common paradox.[2]

The creator in this hymn is called Hiraṇyagarbha, a truly pregnant term. It is a compound noun, whose first element means 'gold' and whose second element means 'womb, seed, embryo, or child' in the *Rig Veda* and later comes to mean 'egg'; this latter meaning becomes prominent in the cosmogonic myth of the golden egg that separates, the two shells becoming sky and earth, while the yolk is the sun.[3] In the present hymn, the compound functions straightforwardly: the god *is* the golden embryo or seed. Later, it is glossed as a possessive compound: he is the god who (more anthropomorphically) *possesses* the golden seed or egg. Sāyaṇa suggests that the compound may be interpreted possessively even here, making it possible to include several levels of meaning at once – 'he in whose belly the golden seed or egg exists like an embryo'. This seed of fire is placed in the waters of the womb; it is also the embryo with which the waters become pregnant (v. 7). So, too, Agni is the child of the waters but also the god who spills his seed in the waters. These are interlocking rather than contradictory concepts; in the late Vedas, the father is specifically identified with the son. Furthermore, the egg is both a female image (that which is fertilized by seed and which contains the embryo that is like the yolk) and a male image (the testicles containing seed). Thus the range of meanings may be seen as a continuum of androgynous birth images: seed (male egg), womb (female egg), embryo, child.

*1* In the beginning the Golden Embryo arose. Once he was born, he was the one lord of creation. He held in place the earth and this sky.[4] Who is the god whom we should worship with the oblation?

*2* He who gives life, who gives strength, whose command all the gods, his own, obey; his shadow is immortality – and death.[5] Who is the god whom we should worship with the oblation?

*3* He who by his greatness became the one king of the world that breathes and blinks, who rules over his two-footed and four-footed creatures – who is the god whom we should worship with the oblation?

4 He who through his power owns these snowy mountains, and the ocean together with the river Rasā,[6] they say; who has the quarters of the sky as his two arms [7] – who is the god whom we should worship with the oblation?

5 He by whom the awesome sky and the earth were made firm, by whom the dome of the sky was propped up, and the sun, who measured out the middle realm of space [8] – who is the god whom we should worship with the oblation?

6 He to whom the two opposed masses looked with trembling in their hearts, supported by his help,[9] on whom the rising sun shines down – who is the god whom we should worship with the oblation?

7 When the high waters came, pregnant with the embryo that is everything, bringing forth fire, he arose from that as the one life's breath of the gods. Who is the god whom we should worship with the oblation?

8 He who in his greatness looked over the waters, which were pregnant with Dakṣa,[10] bringing forth the sacrifice, he who was the one god among all the gods – who is the god whom we should worship with the oblation?

9 Let him not harm us, he[11] who fathered the earth and created the sky, whose laws are true, who created the high, shining waters. Who is the god whom we should worship with the oblation?

10 O Prajāpati, lord of progeny, no one but you embraces all these creatures. Grant us the desires for which we offer you oblation. Let us be lords of riches.

## NOTES

1. Cf. 10.129.6. Here and throughout these notes, numbers without a designated text refer to Rig Vedic hymns translated in this volume.

2. Cf. the birth of Dakṣa and Aditi from one another in 10.72.4.

3. Cf. 10.82.5–6.

4. This traditional cosmogonic act is often credited to Viṣṇu, Varuṇa, Indra, and other gods.

5. This may refer to the world of gods and the world of humans, or it may have some subtler and darker metaphysical significance.

6. The river Rasā surrounds heaven and earth, separating the dwelling-place of men and gods from the non-space in which the demonic powers dwell. Cf. 10.108.2.

7. A reference to the cosmic giant, Puruṣa (cf. 10.90), whose arms are in that part of space which the four cardinal directions span.

8. This act of measuring out space, closely connected with the propping apart of sky and earth (cf. v. 1), is also attributed to Viṣṇu and Varuṇa, who are said to set up the sun and then to measure out a space for him to move through, a space which (unlike sky and earth) has no finite boundaries. The sun itself also functions both as a prop to keep sky and earth apart and as an instrument with which to measure space. Cf. 1.154.1 and 1.154.3.

9. This verse presents an image on two levels. The two opposed masses are armies, the polarized forces of gods and demons (Asuras) who turn to the creator for help (as in 2.12.8). But they also represent the parted sky and earth, who seek literal 'support' (the pillar to keep them apart). The images combine in a metaphor suggesting that sky and earth themselves form a phalanx in the fight between gods and demons.

10. Dakṣa represents the male principle of creation and is later identified with Prajāpati. As the embryo of the waters, he is identified with the seed or fire (v. 7), the latter then explicitly defined in this verse as the sacrifice, or sacrificial fire. Sacrifice is often an element in primeval creation (cf. 10.90.6–9).

11. In this verse, the abstract tone vanishes and the poet lapses back into a more typical Vedic fear (and particularly typical of book 10), the fear of a personified, malevolent god.

## 10.90 *Puruṣa-Sūkta, or The Hymn of Man*

In this famous hymn, the gods create the world by dismembering the cosmic giant, Puruṣa, the primeval male who is the victim in a Vedic sacrifice.[1] Though the theme of the cosmic sacrifice is a widespread mythological motif, this hymn is part of a particularly Indo-European corpus of myths of dismemberment.[2] The underlying concept is, therefore, quite ancient; yet the fact that this is one of the latest hymns in the *Rig Veda* is evident from its reference to the three Vedas (v. 9) and to the four social classes or *varṇas* (v. 12, the first time that this concept appears in Indian civilization), as well as from its generally monistic world-view.

*1* The Man has a thousand heads, a thousand eyes, a thousand feet. He pervaded the earth on all sides and extended beyond it as far as ten fingers.

*2* It is the Man who is all this, whatever has been and whatever is to be. He is the ruler of immortality, when he grows beyond everything through food.[3]

*3* Such is his greatness, and the Man is yet more than this. All creatures are a quarter of him; three quarters are what is immortal in heaven.

*4* With three quarters the Man rose upwards, and one quarter of him still remains here. From this[4] he spread out in all directions, into that which eats and that which does not eat.

*5* From him Virāj[5] was born, and from Virāj came the Man. When he was born, he ranged beyond the earth behind and before.

*6* When the gods spread[6] the sacrifice with the Man as the offering, spring was the clarified butter, summer the fuel, autumn the oblation.

*7* They anointed[7] the Man, the sacrifice[8] born at the beginning, upon the sacred grass.[9] With him the gods, Sādhyas,[10] and sages sacrificed.

*8* From that sacrifice[8] in which everything was offered, the melted fat[11] was collected, and he[12] made it into those beasts who live in the air, in the forest, and in villages.

*9* From that sacrifice in which everything was offered, the verses and chants were born, the metres were born from it, and from it the formulas were born.[13]

*10* Horses were born from it, and those other animals that have two rows of teeth;[14] cows were born from it, and from it goats and sheep were born.

11 When they divided the Man, into how many parts did they apportion him? What do they call his mouth, his two arms and thighs and feet?

12 His mouth became the Brahmin; his arms were made into the Warrior, his thighs the People, and from his feet the Servants were born.[15]

13 The moon was born from his mind; from his eye the sun was born. Indra and Agni came from his mouth, and from his vital breath the Wind was born.

14 From his navel the middle realm of space arose; from his head the sky evolved. From his two feet came the earth, and the quarters of the sky from his ear. Thus they[16] set the worlds in order.

15 There were seven enclosing-sticks[17] for him, and thrice seven fuel-sticks, when the gods, spreading the sacrifice, bound the Man as the sacrificial beast.

16 With the sacrifice the gods sacrificed to the sacrifice.[18] These were the first ritual laws.[19] These very powers reached the dome of the sky where dwell the Sādhyas,[10] the ancient gods.

## NOTES

1. Cf. the horse as the primeval sacrificial victim in 1.162 and 1.163.

2. The dismemberment of the Norse giant Ymir is the most striking parallel, but there are many others.

3. This rather obscure phrase seems to imply that through food (perhaps the sacrificial offering) Puruṣa grows beyond the world of the immortals, even as he grows beyond the earth (v. 1 and v. 5). He himself also transcends both what grows by food and what does not (v. 4), i.e. the world of animate and inanimate creatures, or Agni (eater) and Soma (eaten).

4. That is, from the quarter still remaining on earth, or perhaps from the condition in which he had already spread out from earth with three quarters of his form.

5. The active female creative principle, Virāj is later replaced by Prakṛti or material nature, the mate of Puruṣa in Sānkhya philosophy.

6. This is the word used to indicate the performance of a Vedic sacrifice, spread or stretched out (like the earth spread upon the cosmic waters) or woven (like a fabric upon a loom). Cf. 10.130.1–2.

7. The word actually means 'to sprinkle' with consecrated water, but indicates the consecration of an initiate or a king.

8. Here 'the sacrifice' indicates the sacrificial victim; they are explicitly identified with one another (and with the divinity to whom the sacrifice is dedicated) in verse 16.

9. A mixture of special grasses that was strewn on the ground for the gods to sit upon.

10. A class of demi-gods or saints, whose name literally means 'those who are yet to be fulfilled'.

11. Literally, a mixture of butter and sour milk used in the sacrifice; figuratively, the fat that drained from the sacrificial victim.

12. Probably the Creator, though possibly Puruṣa himself.

13. The verses are the elements of the *Rig Veda*, the chants of the *Sāma Veda*, and the formulas of the *Yajur Veda*. The metres often appear as elements in primeval creation; cf. 10.130.3–5 and 1.164.23–5.

14. That is, incisors above and below, such as dogs and cats have.

15. The four classes or *varṇas* of classical Indian society.

16. The gods.

17. The enclosing-sticks are green twigs that keep the fire from spreading; the fuel sticks are seasoned wood used for kindling.

18. The meaning is that Puruṣa was both the victim that the gods sacrificed and the divinity to whom the sacrifice was dedicated; that is, he was both the subject and the object of the sacrifice. Through a typical Vedic paradox, the sacrifice itself creates the sacrifice.

19. Literally, the *dharmas*, a protean word that here designates the archetypal patterns of behaviour established during this first sacrifice to serve as the model for all future sacrifices.

## 10.130 *The Creation of the Sacrifice*

The image of weaving the sacrifice (cf. 10.90.15) is here joined with explicit identifications of ritual and divine, ancient and present, elements of the sacrifice.

*1* The sacrifice that is spread out with threads on all sides, drawn tight with a hundred and one divine acts, is woven by these fathers as they come near: 'Weave forward, weave backward,' they say as they sit by the loom that is stretched tight.

*2* The Man[1] stretches the warp and draws the weft; the Man has spread it out upon this dome of the sky. These are the pegs, that are fastened in place; they[2] made the melodies into the shuttles for weaving.

*3* What was the original model, and what was the copy, and what was the connection between them? What was the butter, and what the enclosing wood?[3] What was the metre, what was the invocation, and the chant, when all the gods sacrificed the god?[4]

*4* The Gāyatrī metre[5] was the yoke-mate of Agni; Savitṛ joined with the Uṣṇi metre, and with the Anuṣṭubh metre was Soma that reverberates with the chants. The Bṛhatī metre resonated in the voice of Bṛhaspati.

*5* The Virāj[6] metre was the privilege of Mitra and Varuṇa; the Triṣṭubh metre was part of the day of Indra. The Jagatī entered into all the gods. That was the model for the human sages.[7]

*6* That was the model for the human sages, our fathers, when the primeval sacrifice was born. With the eye that is mind, in thought I see those who were the first to offer this sacrifice.

*7* The ritual repetitions harmonized with the chants and with the metres; the seven divine sages harmonized with the original models. When the wise men looked back along the path of those who went before, they took up the reins like charioteers.

NOTES

1. Puruṣa, as in 10.90.
2. The gods who first performed the sacrifice. Cf. 10.90.14.
3. Cf. 10.90.15.
4. The circular sacrifice of the god to the god, as in 10.90.6, 10.81.5–6.
5. The metres alluded to in 10.90.9 are here enumerated and associated with particular gods.
6. Virāj, a female cosmic principle in 10.90.5, is here merely a metre.
7. Sages (*ṛṣis*) are seers as well as poets.

## 10.190 *Cosmic Heat*[1]

*1* Order[2] and truth were born from heat as it blazed up. From that was born night; from that heat was born the billowy ocean.

*2* From the billowy ocean was born the year, that arranges days and nights, ruling over all that blinks its eyes.[3]

*3* The Arranger has set in their proper place the sun and moon, the sky and the earth, the middle realm of space, and finally the sunlight.

NOTES

1. *Tapas*, the heat produced by the ritual activity of the priest, is equated with the primeval erotic or ascetic heat of the Creator.
2. *Ṛta*, cosmic order. Truth (*satya*) is, like *ṛta*, also a term for reality.
3. For blinking as a sign of a living creature, cf. 10.121.3.

## 10.81–2 *The All-Maker (Viśvakarman)*

These two hymns to the artisan of the gods speculate on the mysterious period of the ancient past, now veiled from the priests of the present (10.81.1 and 10.82.7). The Creator is imagined concretely as a sculptor (10.81.2), a smith (10.81.3), or as a woodcutter or carpenter (10.81.4), but also as the primeval sacrificer and victim of the sacrifice (10.81.1, 10.81.5–6, 10.82.1), assisted by the seven sages (10.81.4, 10.82.2 and 10.82.4). Finally, he is identified with the one who propped apart sky and earth (10.81.2–4, 10.82), the one who inspires thought (10.81.7) and answers questions (10.82) but is himself beyond understanding (10.82.5 and 7).

10.81

*1* The sage, our father, who took his place as priest of the oblation and offered all these worlds as oblation, seeking riches through prayer, he entered those who were to come later, concealing those who went before.[1]

*2* What was the base,[2] what sort of raw matter was there, and precisely how was it done, when the All-Maker, casting his eye on all, created the earth and revealed the sky in its glory?

*3* With eyes on all sides and mouths on all sides, with arms on all sides and feet on all sides, the One God created the sky and the earth, fanning them with his arms.[3]

*4* What was the wood and what was the tree from which they[4] carved the sky and the earth? You deep thinkers, ask yourselves in your own hearts, what base did he stand on when he set up the worlds?

*5* Those forms of yours that are highest, those that are lowest, and those that are in the middle, O All-Maker, help your friends to recognize them in the oblation. You who follow your own laws, sacrifice your body yourself, making it grow great.[5]

*6* All-Maker, grown great through the oblation, sacrifice the earth and sky yourself. Let other men go astray all around;[6] let us here have a rich and generous patron.

*7* The All-Maker, the lord of sacred speech, swift as thought – we will call to him today to help us in the contest. Let him who is the maker of good things and is gentle to everyone rejoice in all our invocations and help us.

10.82

1 The Father of the Eye,[7] who is wise in his heart, created as butter[8] these two worlds that bent low. As soon as their ends had been made fast in the east, at that moment sky and earth moved far apart.

2 The All-Maker is vast in mind and vast in strength. He is the one who forms, who sets in order, and who is the highest image. Their[9] prayers together with the drink they have offered give them joy there where, they say, the One dwells beyond the seven sages.

3 Our father, who created and set in order and knows all forms, all worlds, who all alone gave names to the gods, he is the one to whom all other creatures come to ask questions.

4 To him the ancient sages together sacrificed riches, like the throngs of singers who together made these things that have been created, when the realm of light was still immersed in the realm without light.[10]

5 That which is beyond the sky and beyond this earth, beyond the gods and the Asuras[11] – what was that first embryo that the waters received, where all the gods together saw it?[12]

6 He was the one whom the waters received as the first embryo, when all the gods came together. On the navel of the Unborn was set the One on whom all creatures rest.[13]

7 You cannot find him who created these creatures; another[14] has come between you. Those who recite the hymns are glutted with the pleasures of life;[15] they wander about wrapped up in mist and stammering nonsense.

## NOTES

1. The early stages of creation remain in shadow, perhaps because the All-Maker destroyed them by sacrificing them and then prayed anew for the materials of creation.

2. The question, to which verse 4 returns, is the problem of

what the primeval sculptor stood on before there was anything created.

3. Though he has arms on all sides, here the anthropomorphic smith has two arms and 'wings', probably the feathers used to fan the forge. Cf. 9.112.2.

4. The assistants of the Creator, perhaps the seven sages (cf. 10.82.2 and 10.82.4).

5. Here and in the next verse, the Creator is both the sacrificer and the sacrificial victim, as Puruṣa is in 10.90.16.

6. Here, and in 10.82.7, the enemies of the poet in the contest are mocked.

7. That is, creator of the sun.

8. Butter is symbolic of primeval chaotic matter, the seed of the creator, and the sacrificial oblation. The creator churns chaos. Cf. 4.58 for butter.

9. The wishes and sacrifices of the first sacrificers, the pious dead, are fulfilled in heaven.

10. Day and night separated, like sky and earth.

11. The Asuras are the ancient dark divinities, at first the elder brothers and then the enemies of the gods (Devas).

12. For the embryo, cf. 10.121.1 and 10.121.7.

13. The navel is the centre of the wheel; cf. 1.164.13, 1.164.48.

14. Another creator has come between you, or, more likely (for the noun is neuter), another thing – ignorance – has come inside you as an obstacle; or a bad priest (such as are mentioned in the second half of the verse) has obscured the way to the gods.

15. A double meaning here: the priests are glutted with the life they have stolen from the sacrificial beast and with the high life of luxury they have bought with their undeserved fees. Here the poet speaks of his priestly enemies, who do not understand the meaning of the sacrifice. The mist is both the miasma of their clouded minds and the smoke from the useless sacrifice.

## 10.72 *Aditi and the Birth of the Gods*

This creation hymn poses several different and paradoxical answers to the riddle of origins. It is evident from the tone of the very first verse that the poet regards creation as a mysterious subject, and a desperate series of eclectic hypotheses (perhaps quoted from various sources) tumbles out right away: the 'craftsman' image (the priest, Brahmaṇaspati or Bṛhaspati, lord of inspired speech); the philosophical paradox of non-existence;[1] or the paradox of mutual creation (Aditi and Dakṣa, the female principle of creation or infinity and the male principle of virile efficacy, creating one another)[2] or contradiction (the earth born from the crouching divinity and then said to be born from the quarters of the sky).

At this point, the speculations give way to a more anthropomorphic creation myth centring upon the image of the goddess who crouches with legs spread (Uttānapad); this term, often taken as a proper name, designates a position associated both with yoga and with a woman giving birth, as the mother goddess is often depicted in early sculptures: literally, with feet stretched forward, more particularly with knees drawn up and legs spread wide. Since she is identified with Aditi, the hymn moves quickly to the myth of Aditi and Dakṣa (in which the paradox of mutual creation is given incestuous overtones) and the creation of gods and men.

The creation of the universe out of water (vv. 6–7) and the rescuing of the sun from the ocean (v. 7) are well-known Vedic images that move the hymn back to the cosmic level, from which it then returns to anthropomorphism and to the myth of Aditi, when the sun reappears as Mārtāṇḍa, whose birth from Aditi is the subject of the final two verses.

*1* Let us now speak with wonder of the births of the gods – so that some one may see them when the hymns are chanted in this later age.[3]

*2* The lord of sacred speech, like a smith, fanned them together.[4] In the earliest age of the gods, existence was born from non-existence.[5]

*3* In the first age of the gods, existence was born from non-existence. After this the quarters of the sky were born from her who crouched with legs spread.

*4* The earth was born from her who crouched with legs spread, and from the earth the quarters of the sky were born. From Aditi, Dakṣa was born, and from Dakṣa Aditi was born.[6]

5 For Aditi was born as your daughter, O Dakṣa, and after her were born the blessed gods, the kinsmen of immortality.

6 When you gods took your places there in the water with your hands joined together, a thick cloud of mist[7] arose from you like dust from dancers.

7 When you gods like magicians[8] caused the worlds to swell,[9] you drew forth the sun that was hidden in the ocean.

8 Eight sons are there of Aditi, who were born of her body. With seven she went forth among the gods, but she threw Mārtāṇḍa,[10] the sun, aside.

9 With seven sons Aditi went forth into the earliest age. But she bore Mārtāṇḍa so that he would in turn beget offspring and then soon die.

## NOTES

1. Cf. 10.129.1.

2. Cf. Puruṣa and Virāj in 10.90.5.

3. The idea of 'seeing' the births of the gods may refer not to being actually present at that early time but rather to the poet's gift of 'seeing' mythic events by means of his inspired vision.

4. 'Them' must refer to the two worlds, heaven and earth, rather than to the gods; the lord of sacred speech is here regarded as responsible for manual rather than spiritual creation.

5. Cf. 10.129.1.

6. Sāyaṇa remarks that Yāska's *Nirukta* 11.23 states that by the *dharma* of the gods, two births can be mutually productive of one another.

7. 'Mist' or 'dust' refers to the atomic particles of water, a mist that plays an important part in creation by virtue of its ambivalence, half water and half air, mediating between matter and spirit. Thus the steam rising from the asceticism of the Brahmacārin in the water (cf. 10.129.3–4) or the foam that appears when Prajāpati heats the waters is the source of matter for creation.

8. These are Yatis, who may be a class of sages or ascetics; more

likely, however, they are magicians, among whose traditional bag of tricks in ancient India was the ability to make plants suddenly grow. They may be linked with the dancers in verse 6, another aspect of creative shamanism.

9. The verb (*pinv*) implies swelling up as with milk from the breast.

10. Mārtāṇḍa's name originally meant 'born of an egg', i.e. a bird, and is an epithet of the sun-bird or fire-bird of Indo-European mythology. The verb describing what his mother did to him may mean either to throw aside or to miscarry, and a later etymology of Mārtāṇḍa is 'dead in the egg', i.e. a miscarriage. The story of Mārtāṇḍa's still-birth is well known in Hindu mythology: Aditi bore eight sons, but only seven were the Ādityas; the eighth was unformed, unshaped; the Ādityas shaped him and made him into the sun. On another level, Mārtāṇḍa is an epithet of man, born from the 'dead egg' that is the embryo; he is thus the ancestor of man, like Yama or Manu (both regarded as his sons), born to die.

# DEATH

EVEN as the *Rig Veda* speculates in various contrasting, even conflicting ways about the process of creation, so too there is much variation in the speculations about death, and in the questions asked about death. There is evidence of different rituals – cremation (10.16) or burial (10.18), the latter also underlying the image of the 'house of clay' in a hymn to Varuṇa (see 7.89). Several fates are suggested for the dead man: heaven (10.14), a new body (10.16), revival (10.58), reincarnation (10.16), and dispersal among various elements (10.16.3, 10.58). It is also evident that there is a wide range of people that the dead man may hope to join, wherever he goes (10.154), and so it is not surprising that different groups of people are addressed, even within a single hymn: the fathers or dead ancestors in heaven (10.14), the gods (10.16), particularly Yama (10.14, 10.135), the dead man (10.14, 10.135), the mourners (10.14.12 and 10.14.14, 10.18), mother earth and Death himself (10.18). Together, these hymns reveal a world in which death is regarded with great sadness but without terror, and life on earth is preciously clung to, but heaven is regarded as a gentle place, rich in friends and ritual nourishment, a world of light and renewal.

## 10.14 *Yama and the Fathers*

This funeral hymn centres upon Yama, king of the dead, the first mortal to have reached the other world and the path-maker for all who came after him. Verses 1 and 2 address the mourners and describe this ancient path; 4 and 5 invoke Yama to come to the funeral in order that he may lead the dead man to heaven. Verses 3 and 6 invoke famous ancestors already in the world beyond; 7, 8 and 10 speed the dead man on his way, and 9 speeds the evil spirits on *their* way. Yama and his two dogs are addressed in 11 and 12; these dogs are regarded (like many Vedic gods) as dangerous because they kill you (verses 10 and 12) but also as potentially benevolent, because they lead you to heaven (verse 11). Verses 13–15 call upon the priests to offer Soma[1] to Yama, and the final verse recapitulates the two main themes: the farewell to the dead man on the path of Yama, and the offerings of Soma and praise to Yama.

*1* The one who has passed beyond along the great, steep straits,[2] spying out the path for many, the son of Vivasvan,[3] the gatherer of men, King Yama – honour him with the oblation.

*2* Yama was the first to find the way for us, this pasture that shall not be taken away.[4] Where our ancient fathers passed beyond, there everyone who is born follows, each on his own path.

*3* Mātalī[5] made strong by the Kavyas, and Yama by the Angirases, and Bṛhaspati by the Ṛkvans – both those whom the gods made strong and those who strengthen the gods:[6] some rejoice in the sacrificial call, others in the sacrificial drink.

*4* Sit upon this strewn grass, O Yama, together with the Angirases, the fathers. Let the verses chanted by the poets carry you here. O King, rejoice in this oblation.

*5* Come, Yama, with the Angirases worthy of sacrifice:

rejoice here with the Vairūpas,[7] sitting on the sacred grass at this sacrifice. I will invoke Vivasvan, who is your father.

6 Our fathers, the Angirases, and the Navagvas, Atharvans, and Bṛhgus,[7] all worthy of Soma – let us remain in favour with them, as they are worthy of sacrifice, and let them be helpful and kind.

7 [*To the dead man:*] Go forth, go forth on those ancient paths on which our ancient fathers passed beyond. There you shall see the two kings, Yama and Varuṇa, rejoicing in the sacrificial drink.[6]

8 Unite with the fathers, with Yama, with the rewards of your sacrifices and good deeds,[8] in the highest heaven. Leaving behind all imperfections, go back home again;[9] merge with a glorious body.

9 [*To demons:*] Go away, get away, crawl away from here. The fathers have prepared this place for *him*.[10] Yama gives him a resting-place adorned by days, and waters, and nights.[11]

10 [*To the dead man:*] Run on the right path, past the two brindled, four-eyed dogs, the sons of Saramā,[12] and then approach the fathers, who are easy to reach and who rejoice at the same feast as Yama.

11 Yama, give him over to your two guardian dogs, the four-eyed keepers of the path, who watch over men. O king, grant him happiness and health.

12 The two dark messengers of Yama with flaring nostrils wander among men, thirsting for the breath of life. Let them give back to us[13] a life of happiness here and today, so that we may see the sun.

13 For Yama press the Soma; to Yama offer the oblation; to Yama goes the well-prepared sacrifice, with Agni as its messenger.

14 Offer to Yama the oblation rich in butter, and go forth.[14] So may he intercede for us among the gods, so that we may live out a long life-span.[15]

15 Offer to Yama, to the king, the oblation most rich in

honey. We bow down before the sages born in the ancient times, the ancient path-makers.

16 All through the three Soma days,[16] he[17] flies to the six broad spaces[18] and the one great one. Triṣṭubh, Gāyatrī, the metres – all these are placed in Yama.

## NOTES

1. Soma is the sacrificial drink pressed from the Soma plant; it is the ambrosial food offered to the gods to make them immortal.

2. These are the paths leading to the highest heaven, where Yama dwells; they may be the watercourses at the end of the world.

3. A name of the sun, father of Yama.

4. The meaning is either that everyone gets to heaven or that, once there, you never leave (i.e. that there is no rebirth).

5. A name of a god or demi-god who appears only here in the *Rig Veda*.

6. This verse contrasts two groups of individuals to be encountered in the world beyond (an expansion of the 'ancient fathers' mentioned in the previous verse). Mātalī, Yama, and Bṛhaspati are here regarded as semi-divine figures, who are made strong by other gods and by the sacrificial drink, the Svadhā, here – and elsewhere – a name for Soma. The Kavyas, Angirases, and Ṛkvans are families of ancient poets, priests, and singers who make the gods strong and who rejoice in the sacrificial call, the sound 'Svāhā' that they make to call the gods and the fathers to receive the offering.

7. Other priestly clans related to the Angirases.

8. Not merely the dead man's own good deeds but those which are done on his behalf in the funeral ceremonies.

9. The dead man takes on a new, perfect body in place of the old one burnt in the fire (see 10.16); he 'goes back home' to heaven or to earth.

10. The flesh-eating ghouls who live in the burning-ground may contest the dead man's right to enter the world of heaven, or perhaps, as in later Hinduism, they merely wish to eat the corpse.

11. The waters may be the rains (that fall from heaven) or the cool, refreshing waters that are so often described as a feature of heaven, where the days and nights rotate as on earth. Yet another

possible interpretation of the 'resting-place' would be a burning-place on earth, purified by water.

12. Yama's two dogs are the descendants of Saramā, the bitch of Indra (cf. 10.108), who guard the doorway to the other world, like Cerberus in Greece. They may be four-eyed in the sense of sharp-sighted or in reference to the round spots situated above their eyes.

13. The dogs are asked to give back to the mourners the life that was endangered while they were in the shadow of death.

14. That is, back into the world of the living.

15. Here Yama is asked to give life back to the mourners who are not yet ready to die, to keep them among the living who worship the gods, and not to lead them to the dead fathers.

16. The fire that burns during the three days of the Soma ceremony is directly connected with and follows immediately upon the cremation fire.

17. The dead man wanders for three days after death before arriving in heaven.

18. Either the three earths and three heavens (cf. 1.164.6, and 1.164.9) or two of each of the three worlds (earth, air, and sky; cf. 1.154.4). The one great space is the top of the sky, where Yama lives.

## 10.16 *The Funeral Fire*

Agni appears here in various roles: he is the cremation fire, who carries the oblation as well as the dead man to the fathers. In the first part (vv. 1–8), Agni is asked to burn the corpse gently but not too much, to temper it to perfection (*à point*, as Renou puts it) and to send it to the fathers, but not to destroy it. In the second part (vv. 9–12), a new fire is lit to carry the oblation to the gods and to lead the dead man to Yama. Thus the first fire is associated with the corpse and the fathers, and the second fire is associated with the oblation and the gods. In the third part (vv. 13–14), the funeral fire is extinguished.

The recurrent epithet 'Knower of creatures' (Jātavedas) is usually said to apply only to the auspicious, oblation-bearing form of Agni; but here it is also used to invoke, perhaps euphemistically, the corpse-eating Agni as well (vv. 1, 2, 4, and 5). The two fires interact in other ways, too: in verse 9, when the corpse is sufficiently 'cooked' and has undergone purification after its funeral pollution, the first, corpse-burning fire is dismissed to serve the gods and to carry the body to the fathers; at this time, a new, pure fire is summoned (kindled) to carry the oblation to the fathers and to carry to the gods whatever is laid upon it. But the first fire, now purified, is also sent to the sacrifice of the fathers, thus taking on a function similar to that of the second, pristine fire (participation in sacrifice) while retaining its original association with the fathers (in contrast with the gods, the masters of the second fire). This is a transformation, rather than a confusion, for in verse 9 the one fire becomes the other; as both are forms of Agni, he is merely asked to stop burning the corpse and to start carrying the oblation (a role prefigured by the reference to the 'gentle forms' in verse 4). In verse 11, both forms of Agni unite, and in verse 5 the corpse itself becomes the oblation.

The ambiguous nature of Agni in this hymn finds a parallel in the ambiguities surrounding the body of the dead man. Verse 3 states that the body will disperse into sky, earth, and water, while the eye, breath, and limbs go to their cosmic equivalences: sun, wind, and plants. The waters are often identified with the air, the middle realm of space between sky and earth; this would mean that the body disintegrates into the three worlds. But it is not clear whether the body is dispersed into all three places or whether one may choose one or the other; parts of the body (eye, breath, limbs) are specifically distributed, while the dead man himself is said to go into the three worlds.

This might imply that the soul of the dead man goes to these worlds, while his physical parts are distributed elsewhere. But the verse says that the limbs go to the plants, the place to which the soul is consigned in the *Upanisads*, where the doctrine of transmigration is first expounded. Moreover, the breath (often identified with the soul in the *Upanisads*, and here called the *ātman*, the word that came to designate the transmigrating soul) is here said to disperse separately into the wind. Indeed, it seems to be the body, not the soul, of the dead man that Agni is asked to lead to heaven, to Yama, to the fathers, and to the gods, the body that is the focus of the entire hymn. It would thus appear that here, as in several of the more speculative creation hymns, the poet has tried out various, perhaps conflicting, views of the afterlife. These views overlap in the liminal figures of the hymn, for Yama and the fathers are both mortals and immortals, both pure and impure, the ones who receive the corpse but also the ones who receive the oblation and the Soma; moreover, the dead man himself begins as an impure corpse but becomes, by the end of the hymn, himself one of the fathers to whom the oblation is sent.

These problems are compounded by verse 5, which states that the dead man will get a new body (cf. 10.14.8) in order to reach his descendants. This latter word, literally 'remaining' (*śeṣa*), has provoked several interpretations that attempt to circumvent the paradox. Sāyaṇa suggests that it refers to the body that remains after cremation (i.e. the bones); or it may refer to the survivors of the dead man, i.e. the mourners, or to those who have been buried before, i.e. the ancestors whom the dead man will join. But it more likely means the posterity of the dead man, i.e. the people that he has begotten or will beget with his new life and his new body. Is this body to exist in heaven or on earth? A few verses of the *Rig Veda* (and more detailed passages in the Brāhmaṇas) give ample evidence for the concept of the new body in heaven, depicting the afterlife as an improved replica of life on earth, a place where one raises children and watches them grow up. But the idea of a new body on earth is supported by the Brāhmaṇa funeral ceremonies, the *śraddha* offerings in which a man's descendants create for him, ritually, a new body in which he is reborn on earth. If this is the meaning of the verse, it is an early prefiguration of the doctrine of reincarnation.

Finally, if the dead man is to have a new body anyway, what

is the motivation for the desire to keep the old body from being burnt too much (a concept that conflicts paradoxically with the idea of cremating the body in the first place) and to keep it from being destroyed by unclean animals (in verse 6, which may in fact refer to damage done to the live body in the past as well as to the corpse; cf. 10.14.8, where apparently natural 'imperfections' of the body are to be removed)? It would appear that Agni cooks the corpse, a function regarded as the opposite of eating it (as he usually does); cooking raises it to a higher state (fit for heaven), while eating reduces it to a lower state (fit for animals). The wild beasts who would eat the corpse are kept away, as is the omnivorous Agni; instead, the corpse is to be cooked to prepare it for the gods, like the prepared Soma. And Soma, the healer, is asked to assist Agni in cleansing and healing the body (v. 6).

*1* Do not burn him entirely, Agni, or engulf him in your flames. Do not consume his skin or his flesh. When you have cooked him perfectly, O knower of creatures, only then send him forth to the fathers.

*2* When you cook him perfectly, O knower of creatures, then give him over to the fathers. When he goes on the path that leads away the breath of life, then he will be led by the will of the gods.

*3* [*To the dead man:*] May your eye go to the sun, your life's breath to the wind. Go to the sky or to earth, as is your nature;[1] or go to the waters, if that is your fate. Take root in the plants with your limbs.

*4* [*To Agni:*] The goat is your share; burn him with your heat.[2] Let your brilliant light and flame burn him. With your gentle forms, O knower of creatures, carry this man to the world of those who have done good deeds.[3]

*5* Set him free again to go to the fathers, Agni, when he has been offered as an oblation in you and wanders with the sacrificial drink.[4] Let him reach his own descendants, dressing himself in a life-span. O knower of creatures, let him join with a body.

6 [*To the dead man:*] Whatever the black bird has pecked out of you, or the ant, the snake, or even a beast of prey, may Agni who eats all things make it whole, and Soma who has entered the Brahmins.[5]

7 Gird yourself with the limbs of the cow as an armour against Agni,[6] and cover yourself with fat and suet, so that he will not embrace you with his impetuous heat in his passionate desire to burn you up.

8 [*To Agni:*] O Agni, do not overturn this cup[7] that is dear to the gods and to those who love Soma, fit for the gods to drink from, a cup in which the immortal gods carouse.

9 I send the flesh-eating fire far away. Let him go to those whose king is Yama,[8] carrying away all impurities. But let that other, the knower of creatures, come here and carry the oblation to the gods, since he knows the way in advance.

10 The flesh-eating fire has entered your house, though he sees there the other, the knower of creatures; I take that god away to the sacrifice of the fathers.[9] Let him carry the heated drink[10] to the farthest dwelling-place.

11 Agni who carries away the corpse, who gives sacrifice to the fathers who are strengthened by truth – let him proclaim the oblation to the gods and to the fathers.

12 [*To the new fire:*] Joyously would we put you in place, joyously would we kindle you. Joyously carry the joyous fathers here to eat the oblation.

13 Now, Agni, quench and revive the very one you have burnt up. Let Kiyāmba,[11] Pākadūrvā, and Vyalkaśa plants grow in this place.

14 O cool one,[11] bringer of coolness; O fresh one, bringer of freshness; unite with the female frog. Delight and inspire this Agni.

## NOTES

1. Literally, your *dharma*. Sāyaṇa links this with *karma*, interpreting it to mean that the dead man will be reborn according to his good works, to enjoy their fruits in heaven; it may have a more general meaning, according to the way the worlds are arranged in general. But the simplest idea would be 'according to your natural affinities'.

2. This refers to the practice of placing the limbs of a scapegoat over the dead man, so that Agni would consume them and not the corpse with his violent flames.

3. Cf. 10.14.8 and 10.154 for joining with good deeds and the doers of good deeds in heaven.

4. The Svadhā offered to the gods at the funeral. Cf. 10.14.3.

5. Soma appears here in his capacity of god or plant (cf. the cooling plants in the final verses), or simply as the Soma juice inside the priests.

6. This refers to the limbs and caul (inner membrane of the embryo) or skin of a dead cow which would be used in addition to or in place of the scapegoat, while the corpse would be anointed with fat and suet.

7. A wooden cup that the dead man had used in life to make Soma offerings to the gods and to 'those who love Soma' (i.e. the fathers) was placed at the corpse's head, filled with melted butter.

8. The fathers.

9. This could be a sacrifice by the fathers to the gods, or, more likely, a sacrifice to the fathers.

10. The hot oblation for the fathers, who either come to the sacrifice (brought by the non-flesh-eating Agni) or have Agni bring them the drink.

11. The plants in verses 13 and 14, some called by obscure names, others by descriptive epithets ('cool one'), are water plants. These verses accompany the ritual of dousing the fire with water so thoroughly that it produces a marsh where water-plants and frogs may thrive. In later rituals, these items were actually used; here they are merely metaphorically invoked. The female frog, in particular, is a symbol of rain and fertility (cf. 7.103). Thus new life sprouts at the end of the funeral.

## 10.18 *Burial Hymn*

This evocative hymn contains several references to symbolic gestures that may well have been accompanied by rituals similar to those known to us from later Vedic literature. But the human concerns of the hymn are vividly accessible to us, whatever the ritual may have been.

*1* Go away, death, by another path that is your own, different from the road of the gods. I say to you who have eyes, who have ears: do not injure our children or our men.

*2* When you[1] have gone, wiping away the footprint of death,[2] stretching farther your own lengthening span of life, become pure and clean and worthy of sacrifice, swollen with offspring and wealth.

*3* These who are alive have now parted from those who are dead. Our invitation to the gods has become auspicious today. We have gone forward to dance and laugh, stretching farther our own lengthening span of life.

*4* I set up this wall[3] for the living, so that no one else among them will reach this point. Let them live a hundred full autumns and bury death in this hill.[4]

*5* As days follow days in regular succession, as seasons come after seasons in proper order, in the same way order their life-spans, O Arranger, so that the young do not abandon the old.

*6* Climb on to old age, choosing a long life-span, and follow in regular succession, as many as you are. May Tvaṣṭṛ who presides over good births be persuaded to give you a long life-span to live.

*7* These women who are not widows, who have good husbands – let them take their places, using butter to anoint their eyes.[5] Without tears, without sickness, well dressed let them first[6] climb into the marriage bed.

*8* Rise up, woman,[7] into the world of the living. Come here; you are lying beside a man whose life's breath has gone.

You were the wife of this man who took your hand and desired to have you.

9 I take the bow from the hand of the dead man,[8] to be our supremacy and glory and power, and I say, 'You are there; we are here. Let us as great heroes conquer all envious attacks.'

10 Creep away to this broad, vast earth, the mother that is kind and gentle. She is a young girl, soft as wool to anyone who makes offerings;[9] let her guard you from the lap of Destruction.[10]

11 Open up, earth; do not crush him. Be easy for him to enter and to burrow in. Earth, wrap him up as a mother wraps a son in the edge of her skirt.

12 Let the earth as she opens up stay firm, for a thousand pillars must be set up.[11] Let them be houses dripping with butter for him, and let them be a refuge for him here for all his days.

13 I shore up the earth all around you;[12] let me not injure you as I lay down this clod of earth. Let the fathers hold up this pillar for you; let Yama build a house for you here.

14 On a day that will come, they will lay me in the earth, like the feather of an arrow.[13] I hold back speech that goes against the grain,[14] as one would restrain a horse with a bridle.

## NOTES

1. The hymn, that began by addressing death directly, now addresses the company of the mourners.

2. There may have been a ritual to erase the footprints of the mourners, or it may be a simple and straightforward metaphor for the end of mourning.

3. Perhaps a stone to mark the boundary of the world of death.

4. The mound over the grave.

5. Ritually purified butter would be used instead of mascara or eye-shadow to protect the women among the mourners.

6. That is, long before they climb into old age or the grave.

7. The wife of the dead man, who lay down beside him (perhaps

miming copulation, as the queen later did with the dead stallion), until called back with this verse.

8. Probably only done when the dead man was a warrior.

9. That is, to any generous sacrificer, not merely to someone who makes offerings to the earth.

10. Destruction (Nirṛti) is the female personification of disorder and disintegration, in contrast with the orderly and peaceful aspects of death.

11. The metaphorical house built by Yama for the dead man, perhaps symbolized by the urn containing his bones (or his cremated ashes) placed in the earth.

12. The dead man is addressed again.

13. An elliptic metaphor, perhaps referring to the way the feather is stuck into the cleft made for it in the arrow, or as a feather floats gently down to earth when it is freed from the arrow.

14. Perhaps a reference to the poet's satisfaction in having made a good hymn, or his pleasure in returning now to more auspicious subjects, or a statement that the rest is silence. Most likely, a command to remain silent lest one say something ill-omened.

## 10.154 *Funeral Hymn*

The hymn begins with a distinction between levels of spiritual attainment and then asks that the dead man be sent to live among those who are distinguished in one way or another.

*1* For some, the Soma is purified; others sit down for butter.[1] Those for whom honey flows[2] – let the dead man go away straight to them.

*2* Those who became invincible through sacred heat,[3] who went to the sun through sacred heat, who made sacred heat their glory – let him go away straight to them.

*3* Those who fight in battles as heroes, who sacrifice their bodies, or those who give thousands to the priests – let him go away straight to them.

*4* Those who first nursed Order, who had Order and made

Order grow great, the fathers full of sacred heat, O Yama – let him go away straight to them.

*5* Those inspired poets who know a thousand ways, who protect the sun, the seers full of sacred heat, O Yama – let him go away to those who are reborn through sacred heat.

NOTES

1. A distinction between the foods of the gods and the dead fathers. Cf. 10.14.3. and 10.135.1. Though both groups eat both foods, Soma is ambrosia for the gods, while butter is human food for the semi-divine fathers.

2. As honey (Soma) is better than butter, the dead man hopes to go to the gods.

3. *Tapas,* the heat generated by religious activity. Cf. 10.190.

## 10.135 *The Boy and the Chariot*

Though this hymn is traditionally dedicated to Yama, Yama appears only in the first and last verses (which are closely related), framing an allegory of the secret of death. The plot, though obscure, seems to be something like this: The father of a young boy has died, and the boy mentally follows the journey of his father to the realm of Yama, grieving and trying to get him to return; the hymn does not necessarily imply that the boy himself dies or even wants to die. The voice of the father answers the boy, saying that the chariot that the boy has built in his imagination to follow his father is already, unknown to the boy, bringing him after the father. This chariot is the funeral sacrifice or the oblation or the funeral fire that 'carries' the corpse to Yama and the fathers.[1] It is, at the same time, a manifestation of the boy's own wish to see his father.[2] The final verse gives a vision of paradise, perhaps to reassure the boy.[3]

*1* [*The son:*] 'Beneath the tree with beautiful leaves where Yama drinks with the gods, there our father, the head of the family, turns with longing to the ancient ones.[4]

2 'Reluctantly I looked upon him as he turned with longing to the ancient ones, as he moved on that evil way.[5] I longed to have him back again.'

3 [*Voice of the father:*] 'In your mind, my son, you made a new chariot without wheels, which had only one shaft but can travel in all directions. And unseeing,[6] you climbed into it.

4 'My son, when you made the chariot roll forth from the priests,[7] there rolled after it a chant that was placed from there upon a ship.'

5 Who gave birth to the boy? Who made the chariot roll out? Who could tell us today how the gift for the journey[8] was made?

6 How was the gift for the journey made? The beginning arose from it: first they made the bottom, and then they made the way out.[9]

7 This is the dwelling-place of Yama, that is called the home of the gods. This is his reed-pipe that is blown, and he is the one adorned with songs.

## NOTES

1. Cf. 1.164 for the mystic symbolism of the chariot that is the sacrifice, with no wheels and one shaft (10.135.3); and cf. 10.16 for the funeral fire.

2. In later Sanskrit, the 'chariot of the mind' (*mănoratha*) is a word for 'wish'. Cf. 10.85.12 for a chariot made of thought.

3. This hymn may be the kernel of the famous myth of Naciketas, in which a boy travels to the realm of death and converses with Death and with his father. But the present hymn cannot be interpreted as if it were already an expression of that complex myth.

4. The dead ancestors in the realm of Yama. Cf. 10.14.

5. The path of death; probably not Hell, but cf. 10.71.9 and 10.85.30.

6. Literally, not seeing the chariot that you are mounting; symbolically, not understanding the power of the sacrifice.

7. The priests compose the funerary hymns which accompany the corpse and which are thus 'carried' by the chariot and by a

ship (both metaphors for the sacrifice and the oblation) that the priests send away from them.

8. Probably equipment with which the deceased was supplied for the journey to Yama's abode (cf. 10.16.8), here identified with the chant placed on the sacrificial chariot. The word here translated 'gift for the journey' (*anudeyī*) occurs only once more in the *Rig Veda*, to describe the woman who accompanies the bride on her journey to the groom's house (10.85.6).

9. This verse is simultaneously a literal description of the chariot and a figurative reference to the chant, with its opening and closing phrases.

## 10.58 *A Spell to Turn Back the Departing Spirit*

This imprecation to the *manas* – heart, mind, and life-spirit – may have been spoken over a dead man or to a man on the brink of death, to keep the spirit within the body. The central verses refer alternately to earth (3, 5, 7, 9) and sky (4, 6, 8).

*1* If your spirit has gone to Yama the son of Vivasvan far away, we turn it back to you here to dwell and to live.
*2* If your spirit has gone to the sky or to the earth far away, we turn it back to you here to dwell and to live.
*3* If your spirit has gone to the four-cornered earth far away, we turn it back to you here to dwell and to live.
*4* If your spirit has gone to the four quarters of the sky far away, we turn it back to you here to dwell and to live.
*5* If your spirit has gone to the billowy ocean far away, we turn it back to you here to dwell and to live.
*6* If your spirit has gone to the flowing streams of light far away, we turn it back to you here to dwell and to live.
*7* If your spirit has gone to the waters, or to the plants, far away, we turn it back to you here to dwell and to live.
*8* If your spirit has gone to the sun, or to the dawns far away, we turn it back to you here to dwell and to live.

9 If your spirit has gone to the high mountains far away, we turn it back to you here to dwell and to live.

10 If your spirit has gone to this whole moving universe far away, we turn it back to you to dwell and to live.

11 If your spirit has gone to distances beyond the beyond, far away, we turn it back to you to dwell and to live.

12 If your spirit has gone to what has been and what is to be, far away, we turn it back to you to dwell and to live.

## THE ELEMENTS OF SACRIFICE

ALL the hymns of the *Rig Veda* are ritual hymns in some sense, since all were sung as part of the Vedic ceremony, but some are self-consciously devoted to the meaning of the ritual.[1] Even here, pride of place is given to the verbal rather than to the physical aspect of the sacrifice, the origins of sacred speech (10.71) and the powers of sacred speech (10.125). The personal concerns of the priests also inspire considerable interest in the authors of the hymns (priests themselves): the priest whose patron is the king (10.173) laments the loss of his royal friend (10.33) and praises faith and generosity (10.151 and 10.117), while other priests, more securely employed, express their happiness in a hymn that is lively to the point of bawdiness (10.101; cf. 7.103 and 9.112). The meaning of the sacrifice is explored in a hymn that unites all of these themes and expresses them in the form of a series of riddles about the meaning of life (1.164).

### NOTE

1. Cf. especially 10.90, 10.130, 9.112, and the hymns to Agni and Soma.

## 10.71 *The Origins of Sacred Speech*

This hymn speaks of the origins of the sacred word, speech or language (*vāc*, f., a goddess), and of its ritual recreation through the verbal contests of the Vedic sacrifice. The social nature of speech is emphasized, the birth of speech in friendship and its use by all of the assembly (v. 10) and by the four priests with their individual functions (v. 11). The enemy of true speech is represented as the rival of the author of this hymn (vv. 4–6, 9).

*1* Bṛhaspati![1] When they[2] set in motion the first beginning of speech, giving names, their most pure and perfectly guarded secret was revealed through love.

*2* When the wise ones[2] fashioned speech with their thought, sifting it as grain is sifted through a sieve,[3] then friends recognized their friendships. A good sign was placed on their speech.

*3* Through the sacrifice they traced the path of speech and found it inside the sages. They held it and portioned it out to many; together the seven singers[2] praised it.

*4* One who looked did not see speech, and another who listens does not hear it. It reveals itself to someone as a loving wife, beautifully dressed, reveals her body to her husband.

*5* One person, they said, has grown awkward and heavy in this friendship; they no longer urge him forward in the contests. He lives with falsehood like a milkless cow, for the speech that he has heard has no fruit no flower.

*6* A man that abandons a friend who has learned with him no longer has a share in speech. What he does hear he hears in vain, for he does not know the path of good action.

*7* Friends have eyes and ears, but their flashes of insight are not equal. Some are like ponds that reach only to the mouth or shoulder; others are like ponds that one could bathe in.

8 When the intuitions of the mind are shaped in the heart, when Brahmins perform sacrifices together as friends, some are left behind for lack of knowledge, while others surpass them with the power to praise.

9 Those who move neither near nor far, who are not real Brahmins nor pressers of the Soma; using speech in a bad way, they weave on a weft of rags, without understanding.

10 All his friends rejoice in the friend who emerges with fame and victory in the contest. He saves them from error and gives them food. He is worthy to be pushed forward to win the prize.

11 One[4] sits bringing to blossom the flower of the verses. Another sings a song in the Śakvarī metre. One, the Brahmin, proclaims the knowledge of the ancient ways. Another lays out the measure of the sacrifice.

NOTES

1. This epithet, that literally means 'lord of sacred speech', is particularly appropriate here as Bṛhaspati is the patron of speakers and inspired poets.

2. The first poets and seers.

3. The Soma juice is purified by being filtered through a sieve.

4. The Hotṛ priest sits motionless and invokes the gods; the Udgātṛ sings; the Brahmin must make sure that no mistakes are committed, and the Adhvaryu is responsible for ritual activities like pressing the Soma (as in v. 9) and measuring the sacrificial area.

## 10.125 *Speech*

A paean of self-praise to and by Speech, in a more personified form than in 10.71 but implicit in various forms of speech: sacrificial (vv. 2–3, 5), agonistic (v. 6), and cosmic (v. 4), the latter enabling Speech to become identified with the creator

(v. 7) and the absolute godhead, encompassing all gods (vv. 1, 8). Speech is never mentioned by name in the hymn, never actually spoken herself.

1 I move with the Rudras, with the Vasus, with the Ādityas and all the gods. I carry both Mitra and Varuṇa, both Indra and Agni, and both of the Aśvins.
2 I carry the swelling Soma, and Tvaṣṭṛ, and Pūṣan and Bhaga. I bestow wealth on the pious sacrificer who presses the Soma and offers the oblation.
3 I am the queen, the confluence of riches, the skilful one who is first among those worthy of sacrifice. The gods divided me up into various parts, for I dwell in many places and enter into many forms.
4 The one who eats food, who truly sees, who breathes, who hears what is said, does so through me. Though they do not realize it, they dwell in me. Listen, you whom they have heard:[1] what I tell you should be heeded.
5 I am the one who says, by myself, what gives joy to gods and men. Whom I love I make awesome; I make him a sage, a wise man, a Brahmin.
6 I stretch the bow for Rudra so that his arrow will strike down the hater of prayer. I incite the contest[2] among the people. I have pervaded sky and earth.
7 I gave birth to the father on the head of this world. My womb is in the waters, within the ocean. From there I spread out over all creatures and touch the very sky with the crown of my head.
8 I am the one who blows like the wind, embracing all creatures. Beyond the sky, beyond this earth, so much have I become in my greatness.

NOTES

1. Literally, one who is heard or who is famous; a triple pun on the root 'hear' in 'listen', 'they have heard', and 'heeded'. Cf. the Greek *kluein*, *akluein*.

2. Perhaps a verbal contest rather than an actual battle, though

the first part of the verse makes the second meaning possible also.

## 10.173 *Royal Consecration*

This hymn establishes the king upon his throne and makes his future reign secure, playing upon the word *dhruvam* ('firm' or 'steadfast'), which recurs like the refrain in a magic spell. The hymn, part of an elaborate royal consecration ritual (*rājasūyā*), would be accompanied by an oblation of Soma and perhaps by certain magic rituals. The same verses in the *Atharva Veda* are used as an imprecation against earthquakes.

*1* I have brought you here; remain among us. Stay steadfast and unwavering. Let all the people want you, and let the kingship never fall away from you.
*2* Stay right here – do not slip away, but stay unwavering, like a mountain. Stand steadfast here, like Indra, and here uphold the kingdom.
*3* Indra has supported him firmly with a firm oblation. Let Soma – and Brahmaṇaspati also – speak up for him.
*4* Firm is the sky and firm the earth, and firm are these mountains. Firm is all this world, and firm is this king of all the people.
*5* Steadfast let King Varuṇa, steadfast the god Bṛhaspati, steadfast let Indra and Agni maintain your steadfast kingship.
*6* With a firm oblation we touch the firm Soma. Thus let Indra make all the people who bring tribute yours alone.

## 10.33 *Lament of the Aged Priest*

A bard has lost his patron, King Kuruśravaṇa, whose son, Upamaśravas, has succeeded to the throne and no longer employs the old man. The bard invokes Indra (the quintessential generous patron), tries to arouse the young king's pity, and even employs veiled threats to avenge the (perhaps untimely?) death of the old king (vv. 1, 8). Finally, he is resigned to his fate (v. 9).

1 The harnessers of the people[1] have harnessed me; I carry Pūṣan along the way.[2] All the gods protected me. Then a cry arose: 'An evil taskmaster is coming!'
2 My ribs encircle me with pain like rival wives; poverty, nakedness, weakness bind me. My mind flutters here and there like a bird.
3 As rats gnaw at their tails, cares gnaw at me, your singer of praises, O lord of a hundred powers.[3] Have mercy on us once more, generous Indra, and be like a father to us.
4 As a sage I chose as my king Kuruśravaṇa the descendant of Trasadasyu, most generous to those who offer prayer,
5 whose three bays carry me in this chariot toward better times.[4] I will praise him who gave a thousand cows to the priests,[5]
6 Upamaśravas's father, whose words were sweet as a field is a delight to the one who lives on it.
7 Upamaśravas, his son, and grandson of Mitrātithi[6] – remember I am the one who sang the praises of your father.
8 If I had power over the immortals or over mortals, my generous patron would be alive.
9 No one lives beyond the decree of the gods, not even if he has a hundred souls.[7] So I am parted from my companion.

### NOTES

1. Perhaps the gods are meant, as they are said to have protected the singer.

2. The singer, who imagines himself as the horse harnessed to the king's chariot, further imagines Pūṣan, the charioteer of the gods, riding in it.

3. An epithet of Indra.

4. Now that the tables are turned (the old king being dead), the singer is himself in the chariot, pulled by the king's horses that are all he has left of his patronage.

5. Perhaps a subtle hint to Upamaśravas to do the same.

6. Perhaps another name for Trasadasyu, the ancestor of Kuruśravaṇa. The name, meaning 'guest of a friend', has significance for the poet.

7. *Ātman* is the soul or the breath of life, as we might say that a cat has nine lives.

## 10.101 *The Sacrificial Priests*

This hymn is a kind of work-song for priests, likening their ritual work to the work of the farmers in the field, as well as to other occupations (such as weaving, v. 2, and chariot racing, v. 7) and pastimes (such as sexual play, vv. 11–12).

*1* Wake up with one mind, my friends, and kindle the fire, you many who share the same nest.[1] I call Dadhikrā and Agni and the goddess Dawn, all joined with Indra, to help you.

*2* Make your thoughts harmonious; stretch them on the loom; make a ship[2] whose oars will carry us across; make the weapons ready and set them in place;[3] drive the sacrifice forward,[4] my friends.

*3* Harness the plough and stretch the yoke on it; sow the seed in the prepared womb. And if the hearing of our song is weighty enough,[5] then the ripe crop will come nearer to the scythes.

*4* The inspired poets who know how harness the plough and stretch the yokes on either side to win favour among the gods.

*5* Make the buckets ready and fasten the straps well. We want to draw water from the fountain that is easy to draw water from, flowing freely, inexhaustible.[6]

*6* I draw water from the fountain whose buckets are in

place, with good straps, easy to draw water from,
freely flowing and inexhaustible.

7 Keep the horses happy and you will win the stake. Make
your chariot into the vehicle of good fortune. Drink at
the fountain that has Soma-vats for buckets, a pressing-
stone for its wheel, a consecrated goblet for its casing;
this is the fountain where men drink.

8 Make an enclosure,[7] for this is a drink for men. Stitch the
breast-plates thick and broad. Make iron forts that cannot
be breached; make your goblet strong so that nothing
will flow out.

9 I turn toward our cause here your sacrificial attention,
gods, your divine thought that is disposed toward
sacrifice and worthy of sacrifice. Let the great cow[8]
give us milk in thousands of streams of milk, as if
she were walking in a meadow.

10 Pour the tawny one[9] into the lap of wood; carve it
with knives made of stone. Embrace it all around with
ten girths; yoke the draught animal to the two shafts.[10]

11 The draught animal is pressed tight between the two
shafts, like a man in bed with two women. Stand the
tree up in the wood; sink the well deep without dig-
ging.[11]

12 The penis, men, take the penis and move it and stick it
in to win the prize.[12] Inspire Indra, Niṣṭigrī's son,[13]
to come here to help us, to come eagerly to drink Soma.

### NOTES

1. This term denotes companions in general, but here may literally indicate a group of priests who live together. Cf. 10.5.2.

2. The ship that carries the worshipper 'to the other shore' is a common metaphor; here there may be a pun between ship and shuttle ('little ship', in Sanskrit), from the first part of the verse.

3. The weapons are the instruments of the ritual; here the priest's work is likened to that of a warrior, as in verse 8.

4. The sacrifice as a chariot, as in verse 7; cf. 1.164, 10.135, etc.

5. That is, if the patrons pay well enough for it, the sacrifice

will yield a harvest as rich as a grain harvest in which the plants bend to the scythe.

6. The fountain of inspiration and the well of Soma.

7. That is, a walled fortress or a cow-pen, to protect Soma the bull. A series of martial metaphors follows in this verse.

8. The cow as a symbol of the inspiration implicit in the thought of the gods.

9. Soma, here imagined as a sacrificial animal. The knives of stone are the pressing stones. Cf. 10.94.3.

10. The two shafts are the two hands that hold the Soma; the ten girths are the ten fingers.

11. A *triple entendre*: the tree in the wood (forest) is the Soma plant in the wooden bowl and the penis in the womb, the latter simile extended in the last quarter of the verse, that further echoes the imagery of verses 3, 5, 6, and the final verse.

12. A sexual metaphor for Soma pressed in the mortar and pestle.

13. Indra is the son of Aditi, who may be called Niṣṭigrī ('swallower of the rival wife') as she overcomes her rival, Diti. Cf. 10.145.

## 10.117 *In Praise of Generosity*

This hymn, which seems constructed at least in part out of aphorisms, exhorts the worshipper to be generous, both to the gods (through sacrifice) and to the poet (through patronage), as well as to mankind in general. There is also a self-serving level to the advice: fortune is fickle, and the man to whom you give now may have given to you in the past, and may do so again.

*1* The gods surely did not ordain hunger alone for slaughter;[1] various deaths reach the man who is well-fed. The riches of the man who gives fully do not run out, but the miser finds no one with sympathy.

*2* The man with food who hardens his heart against the poor man who comes to him suffering and searching for nourishment – though in the past he had made use of him[2] – he surely finds no one with sympathy.

*3* The man who is truly generous gives to the beggar who

approaches him thin and in search of food. He puts himself at the service of the man who calls to him from the road, and makes him a friend for times to come.

4 That man is no friend who does not give of his own nourishment to his friend, the companion at his side. Let the friend turn away from him; this is not his dwelling-place. Let him find another man who gives freely, even if he be a stranger.

5 Let the stronger man give to the man whose need is greater; let him gaze upon the lengthening path.[3] For riches roll like the wheels of a chariot, turning from one to another.

6 The man without foresight gets food in vain; I speak the truth: it will be his death.[4] He cultivates neither a patron nor a friend. The man who eats alone brings troubles upon himself alone.[5]

7 The plough that works the soil makes a man well-fed; the legs that walk put the road behind them. The priest who speaks is better than the one who does not speak. The friend who gives freely surpasses the one who does not.

8 One-foot surpasses Two-foot; and Two-foot leaves Three-foot behind. Four-foot comes at the call of Two-foot, watching over his herds and serving him.[6]

9 The two hands, though the same, do not do the same thing. Two cows from the same mother do not give the same amount of milk. The powers of two twins are not the same. Two kinsmen do not give with the same generosity.

### NOTES

1. The meaning is that hunger does not always kill, and that there are other ways to die; that though the poor are hungry, the rich man should not forget that he too will die, and so he should share his food with the poor and with the gods.

2. The implication is that the man who is now poor was once powerful, and was flattered and used by the man now rich; the

next verse emphasizes the need to foresee future reversals of this kind.

3. The path of life still to come, in which many upsets are possible.

4. A return to the theme of the first verse: by hoarding food one not only does not avoid death, but brings upon oneself the loss of one's future happiness.

5. By committing the sin of greed, he brings upon himself evils such as poverty and hunger.

6. In the Greek riddle of the sphinx, man walks first on four feet (the crawling baby), then on two feet (the mature man), and finally on three feet (the old man with a cane). In this Indian variant of the riddle, One-foot is the sun (an enigmatic but widespread Vedic theme), Two-foot the human, Three-foot the old man with a cane and Four-foot a dog. In later tradition, the four Ages of man are characterized by the fact that Dharma walks on four, three, two feet, and one foot, as time degenerates.

## 10.151 *Faith*

*1* With faith the fire is kindled; with faith the oblation is offered up. With speech I testify to faith upon the head of happiness.

*2* Faith, make this that I have said dear to the man who gives, dear to the man who wishes to give, dear, O faith, among lavish sacrificers.

*3* As the gods established faith among the formidable Asuras,[1] so establish what we have said among lavish sacrificers.

*4* The gods who sacrifice and are guarded by Vāyu honour faith; with heartfelt intent they honour faith. And with faith they find wealth.

*5* We call to faith at morning, to faith near midday, to faith when the sun sinks down. Faith, establish faith in us.[2]

### NOTES

1. The Asuras are the enemies of the gods, the ancient gods, though perhaps not yet the demons they are in later parts of

the Vedas. For the way in which the gods establish faith (in the gods) in the demons, see 10.124.

2. An almost certainly intended ambiguity: make us have faith, and make others (the generous worshippers) have faith in us (in the priests).

## 1.164 *The Riddle of the Sacrifice* (*Asya Vāmasya*)

This long and complex hymn has inspired many elaborate, detailed glosses and still remains largely obscure. The language, however, is not particularly difficult, and certain major themes emerge with sufficient clarity to encourage the translator to present the hymn in a relatively raw state of exegesis, rather than burden the reader with a critical apparatus out of proportion to the poem itself. Those who seek enlightenment on the many points left unglossed are encouraged to pursue the books and articles listed in the bibliography.

One reason for the great scholarly attention paid to this hymn is that it is traditionally regarded as a riddle – a tradition that waves a red flag before the eyes of Vedic exegetes. And there are solid grounds for this tradition, for many questions are asked outright in the hymn, and others are hidden in a symbolism that seems deliberately labyrinthine. Yet it seems that the poet thought he knew the answers to some of his questions and posed others merely rhetorically, as questions no one would dream of trying to answer. The reader is thus encouraged to solve those that can be solved and to leave the others unanswered.

The hymn demonstrates a unity on two distinct but intersecting levels, explicit and implicit. That is, certain tropes emerge repeatedly to express different ideas, and certain ideas emerge repeatedly to be expressed by different tropes. For example, the hymn mentions cows and birds in several verses; the cow may stand for the Dawn (who is not explicitly named) or the goddess of Speech (who is), and the birds for the sun or the mortal (both explicitly named), while the Dawn may also be represented in verses ostensibly about a woman, and the sun in verses about a horse. I will here try to summarize the recurrent tropes and ideas, and devote the notes to particular idiosyncrasies of the individual verses.

A central theme on the explicit level is the poet's uncertainty about his knowledge and his joy in experiencing an enlightening vision (v. 37; cf. 6.9). Several verses are questions, some never explicitly answered (vv. 4, 6, 17, 18, 48) and perhaps regarded as unanswerable, an expression of the ineffability of the mystic vision; others are posed and answered immediately, almost as a catechism (vv. 34–5). The poet speaks often of the contrast between those who know and those who do not know the answers (4–7, 10, 16, 20–23, 39) or those who say one thing and those who say another (12, 16, 19, 38, 46); elsewhere he merely expresses his scepticism or grateful acceptance of what 'they say' (15, 25). The hymn refers often to things that are hidden or secret (3, 5, 7, 14, 32, 37–8, 45).

Another aspect of the riddle content on the explicit level is the use of deliberate circumlocutions, particularly in association with numbers. Many things come in threes: brothers (1), naves of the wheel (2, 48), stages of the journey (9), mothers and fathers (10), metres (23–5), kindling-sticks (25), long-haired ones (44), hidden parts of speech (45). Closely related to these are the pairs of threes, or sixes: realms of space (6), spokes of the wheel (12), sets of twins (15); and these in turn are doubled to produce twelves: spokes of the wheel (11), shapes of the father (12), twins (15), fellies (48). By further multiplication, we obtain 360 (48) and 720 as a doublet of 360 (11). Other things come in fives – feet (12) and spokes (13) – or tens – horses (14). Seven is a great favourite: sons (1), horses and horses' names (2–3), wheels (3, 12), riders, sisters, and names of cows (3), threads (5), half-embryos (36). A few other numbers occur once: eight, nine, and a thousand (41). Four appears only once (as an addition to three, rather than a doublet of two, in verse 45), a remarkably rare occurrence in a hymn about four-footed animals and four-footed verses. Sometimes several different numbers are applied to the same things (spokes being five or six or twelve, horses being seven or ten, and so forth). This should warn us that it is not possible to make a direct connection between a number and what it symbolizes, though a certain amount of speculation along these lines is possible, as we will see when we consider implicit levels of symbolism in the hymn.

Most important of all the numbers are one and two. The One as the Absolute appears several times (6, 10, 15, 46), and both it, explicitly, (46) and other things, implicitly, are said to be many as well as one: the horse (2), the wheel (14, 48), and the foot of the cow (41). Twos form basic oppositions on the explicit level. We have noted the contrast between the wise and the foolish; another, related to this, is the contrast between the mortal and the immortal (30, 38), supported by recurrent references to one or the other side of the pair: that which is ageless or undying or unbreaking (2, 10–11, 13–15) and that which ages and dies (29, 32). Further contrasts between that with bones and that without bones (4), the near and far sides of the sky (12, 17), up and down (17, 43), two bowls (33), male and female (16), and past and future (19) enrich the dialectic structure of the hymn.

The most explicit and developed contrast is between the two birds (20–22), who occur in other forms as well, as an individual bird (7, 46, 52) and a group of birds (21, 47). Related to the birds, as we shall see, are horses (2, 3, 34, 35), which are in turn related to the chariot (2–3, 9, 12–14, 31, 48); the 'naves' of the chariot pun on the 'navel' of the universe (33–5, *nābhi* referring to both terms). By far the most important animal in the hymn is the cow (7, 9, 17, 26–9, 40–44) with her calf (5, 7, 17, 27–8) and bull (43). The cow is closely related to the images of human procreation: father (12, 18, 22), mother and father (8, 10, 33) (referred to as earth and sky explicitly in 33 and implicitly in others such as 51), mother and son (4, 9), father and son (16), brothers (1), sisters (3), and twins (15, 36). Two Vedic myths lie behind several verses: the mother bears her son and then abandons him (9, 17, 32) and the father incestuously procreates with his own daughter (8).

A final explicit image is closely related to the problem of the inspired solution of the riddle; this is the image of the sacrifice. The hymn begins with a priest (1) and poets who are inspired priests (5, 6); it speaks of the priest's cow (9). There are several references to the goddess of sacred speech (10, 37, 45, 49), to hymns (23–5) and syllables (24, 39, 41–2), ritual laws (43) and the Order which underlies them (11, 37, 47), and finally to the sacrifice itself (15, 35, 50).

How do these interwoven images express meaning in the hymn? On one level, it is clear that the hymn is about the things it is talking about – about riddles and numbers and wisdom and immortality and birds and chariots and horses and cows and speech and the sacrifice, all of which are described in vividly naturalistic detail. But they are also described in terms that make no sense on a naturalistic level (what chariot could have a single wheel, or five spokes at the same time as seven spokes?), and it appears that these distortions arise through the identification of several of the images with abstract ideas, particularly the chariot and birds identified with the sun or year or yearly sacrifice or immortal soul, and the cow or the mother identified with Dawn or Speech. Qualities appropriate to these 'signified' concepts are then reflected back upon the 'signifiers' to stretch the naturalistic image into the realm of pure imagination.

That the bird in the hymn is the sun or fire is a conjecture supported by many explicit references to the sun-bird in the *Rig Veda* (cf. 10.123, 10.177) and by references to the sun in this hymn (14, 26). Many of the verses seem to refer to the birth of the sun/year/sacrifice/sacrificial fire as a calf begotten by his father, the sky, in his mother, the earth (in the form of a cow), or by the sky in his daughter the dawn cow. So, too, the verses about the mortal and immortal may refer to the death and rebirth of the sun at the end of each day or year. The dead one who 'wanders with the sacrificial drink' (30, 38; cf. 10.16.5) or 'enters Destruction' when he is within the womb (32) is the soul of the mortal (or of the mortal sun) whose wandering and rebirth are dependent on the enduring qualities of his nature.

Since the cow that represents the earth or Dawn also stands for the priest's fee (9) or for the goddess of Speech, she serves as a pivot for several symbolic layers; moreover, there is an extended pun throughout the hymn based on the 'feet' of the cow (7, 12, 17, 41) and of the sacred verses (23–4), as well as the 'footprints' or sacrificial traces of the gods (5) – all designated by the term *pada*. Similarly, the word *akṣara* which means both 'syllable' and 'undying' serves as a link between the sacrifice and the immortal sun/soul (24, 39, 42).

Working with these implicit and explicit patterns, it is possible to explain more of the hymn. The sun is often identified with Agni, who is mentioned in the hymn at several points: he is explicitly identified with the One (46); he appears in three forms (1); and he has flames that are like long hair (44). Agni lurks behind other images: he is, like the sun, the first-born child of Order (11, 37, 47) or Truth (cf. 10.5.7) and is born of the waters (52). The interaction of the sun and the waters makes sense of a number of obscure references to a Vedic theory of the rain cycle: the rays of the sun (cows) drink up earthly waters with the lowest point of the ray (the foot) and then give back rain (milk) from their top (head) after they carry the moisture back up to the sun (7, 47, 51, 52). The sun is thus clothed in the waters (7, 31). The relationship between the sun and the sacrifice (through the concept of the yearly solar renewal and yearly sacrifice) is present in the number symbolism linking the chariot (of the sun) with the sacrifice (as in the extended metaphor of 10.135, the opening verse of which is echoed in verse 22 of the present hymn). The seven horses or sons or embryos are seven priests or offerings, the three or six or five naves or spokes are seasons (variously enumerated in different sacrificial reckonings), the twelve are the months, the 360 the days of the years (the 720 the days and nights in pairs), and so forth.

Many particular obscurities remain, of course, and many verses mean several things at once, but when viewed in this overarching framework the hymn reveals a number of consistent questions and answers expressed through a careful network of highly charged symbols.

*1* This beloved grey priest has a middle brother who is hungry and a third brother with butter on his back.[1] In him I saw the Lord of All Tribes with his seven sons.

*2* Seven yoke the one-wheeled chariot drawn by one horse with seven names. All these creatures rest on the ageless and unstoppable wheel with three naves.[2]

*3* Seven horses draw the seven who ride on this seven-wheeled chariot. Seven sisters call out to the place where the seven names of the cows are hidden.

*4* Who saw the newborn one, the one with bones who was brought forth by the boneless one?[3] Where was the breath and blood and soul of the earth? Who can go to ask this from someone who knows?

*5* An ignorant fool, I ask in my mind about the hidden footprints[4] of the gods. Over the young calf the poets stretched out seven threads to weave.

*6* Unknowing, ignorant, I ask for knowledge about it from the poets who know: What is the One who in the form of the unborn propped apart these six realms of space?

*7* Let him who really knows proclaim here the hidden place of that beloved bird. The cows give milk from his head; wearing a cloak, they drank water with their feet.

*8* The mother[5] gave the father a share in accordance with the Order, for at the beginning she embraced him with mind and heart. Recoiling, she was pierced and flowed with the seed of the embryo. The reverent came to praise.

9 The mother was harnessed to the chariot pole of the priest's cow; the embryo remained within the cow-pens. The calf lowed and looked for the many-coloured cow on the three stages of the journey.[6]

10 The One has risen up, holding up three mothers[7] and three fathers, who never wear him down. On the back of the distant sky they speak of Speech, who knows all but does not move all.

11 The twelve-spoked wheel of Order rolls around and around the sky and never ages. Seven hundred and twenty sons in pairs rest on it, O Agni.

12 Some say that the father with his five feet and twelve shapes dwells in his fullness in the farther half of the sky. But others here say that the far-seeing one in the seven-wheeled, six-spoked chariot moves in the near half.[8]

13 All the worlds rest on this five-spoked wheel that rolls around and around. Though heavy-laden, its axle does not get hot, nor has it ever broken in its naves.

14 The unageing wheel rolls out on its rim; the ten yoked horses draw it up the outstretched path. All the worlds are kept in motion on the eye of the sun, that moves on though shrouded in dark space.

15 They say that besides those born in pairs there is a seventh born alone,[9] while the six sets of twins are the sages born from the gods. The sacrifices for them are firmly set, but they change their forms and waver as he stands firm.

16 They are female, but people tell me they are male.[10] He who has eyes sees this, but the blind one does not understand. The poet who is his son has understood this well; the one who knows it would be his father's father.

17 Beneath what is above, and above what is beneath, the cow went upward, holding her calf by the foot.[11] In what direction and to what half of the sky has she gone away? Where did she give birth? Not within the herd.

18 Whoever here knows his father[12] beneath what is above

and above what is beneath – who with such mystical insight can here proclaim the source from which the mind of god was born?

19 Those that are in the future they say are in the past; those that are in the past they say are in the future.[13] The things that you and Indra did, Soma, still pull the axle pole of space as though yoked to it.

20 Two birds, friends joined together, clutch the same tree. One of them eats the sweet fruit; the other looks on without eating.[14]

21 Where the birds sing unblinkingly about their share of immortality among the wise, there the mighty herdsman[15] of the whole world, the wise one, entered me, the fool.

22 The birds that eat honey nest and brood on that tree on whose tip, they say, is the sweet fruit. No one who does not know the father[12] eats that.

23 Only those gain immortality who know that the Gāyatrī foot is based on the Gāyatrī hymn, or that the Triṣṭubh foot is made from the Triṣṭubh hymn, or that the Jagat foot is based on the Jagat hymn.

24 With the Gāyatrī foot they fashion a hymn; with the hymn, a chant; with the Triṣṭubh foot a strophe; with the strophe of two feet or four feet they fashion a speech. With the syllable they fashion the seven tones.

25 With the Jagat he fixed the stream in the sky.[16] In the Rathantara chant he discovered the sun. They say the Gāyatrī has three kindling-sticks, and so its power and magnificence excels.

26 I call to the cow who is easy to milk, so that the milker with clever hands may milk her. Let Savitṛ[17] inspire us with the finest vigour. The pot of milk is set on the fire – this is what I would happily proclaim.

27 The mistress of riches has come, snuffling and longing in her heart for her calf. Let this cow give milk for the Aśvins and grow greater for good fortune.

28 The cow has lowed at her blinking calf, snuffling at his

head to make him low. Longing for his warm mouth, she lows and swells with milk.

29 The one that encloses the cow hums; she that is set over the spluttering flame lows. With her hissing she has put down the mortal; becoming lightning, she has thrown off the cloak.

30 Life that breathes now lies still and yet moves fast, rushing but firmly fixed in the midst of the resting places.[18] The life of the dead one wanders as his nature wills. The immortal comes from the same womb as the mortal.

31 I have seen the cowherd who never tires, moving to and fro along the paths. Clothing himself in those that move toward the same centre but spread apart, he rolls on and on inside the worlds.

32 He who made him knows nothing of him.[19] He who saw him – he vanishes from him. Enclosed within the mother's womb, yet full of progeny, he entered Destruction.

33 The sky is my father; here is the navel that gave me birth. This great earth is my mother, my close kin. The womb for me was between the two bowls[20] stretched apart; here the father placed the embryo in the daughter.

34 I ask you about the farthest end of the earth; I ask you about the navel of the universe. I ask you about the semen of the stallion bursting with seed; I ask you about the final abode of Speech.

35 This altar is the farthest end of the earth; this sacrifice is the navel of the universe. This Soma is the semen of the stallion bursting with seed; this Brahmin priest is the final abode of Speech.

36 The seven half-embryos portion out the semen of the world at Viṣṇu's command. Wise in their thoughts and their heart, themselves surrounded, they surround it on all sides.[21]

37 I do not know just what it is that I am like. I wander about concealed and wrapped in thought. When the first born of Order came to me, I won a share of this Speech.

38 The one who is compelled as his own nature wills goes away and comes back; the immortal came from the same womb as the mortal.[22] The two constantly move in opposite directions; when people perceive the one, they do not perceive the other.

39 The undying syllable of the song is the final abode where all the gods have taken their seat. What can one who does not know this do with the song? Only those who know it sit together here.

40 Be happy eating good fodder, and then we will be happy too.[23] O inviolable cow, eat grass and drink pure water as you graze for ever.

41 The buffalo-cow lowed as she fashioned the flowing waters; she who has a thousand syllables in the final abode became one-footed, two-footed, eight-footed, nine-footed.

42 The quarters of the sky live on the oceans that flow out of her in all directions. The whole universe exists through the undying syllable that flows from her.

43 In the distance I saw the cowdung smoke midway between what is above and what is below. The heroes roasted the dappled bull.[24] These were the first ritual laws.

44 The three long-haired ones[25] reveal themselves at the right moment. During the year, one of them shaves; one looks upon everything with his powers; of one the onrush is visible, but the form is not.

45 Speech was divided into four parts that the inspired priests know. Three parts, hidden in deep secret, humans do not stir into action; the fourth part of Speech is what men speak.[26]

46 They call it Indra, Mitra, Varuṇa, Agni, and it is the heavenly bird that flies. The wise speak of what is One in many ways; they call it Agni, Yama, Mātariśvan.

47 The yellow birds clothed in waters fly up to the sky on the dark path. They have now returned from the home of Order, and at once the earth was drenched with butter.

48 Twelve fellies, one wheel, three naves – who has understood this? Three hundred and sixty are set on it like poles that do not loosen.

49 Your inexhaustible breast, Sarasvatī,[27] that flows with the food of life, that you use to nourish all that one could wish for, freely giving treasure and wealth and beautiful gifts – bring that here for us to suck.

50 The gods sacrificed to the sacrifice with the sacrifice. These became the first ritual laws. These great powers went to the dome of heaven where dwell the Sādhyas, the ancient gods.[28]

51 The same water travels up and down day after day. While the rain-clouds enliven the earth, the flames enliven the sky.[29]

52 The great heavenly bird with wonderful wings, the beautiful embryo of the waters and the plants, that delights us with rains overflowing – I call to him for help.

## NOTES

1. The first brother is the oblation fire with his grey beard of smoke; the second is the southern fire, hungry because it seldom receives the oblation; the third is the domestic fire that is 'fed' the butter oblation. Agni is the Lord of All Tribes, and his sons are the priests.

2. For the magic powers of the three naves, cf. the curing of Apālā (8.91.7).

3. The newborn sun or fire has bones (the male element) though it is born from the boneless one (the female, who gives soft things – blood, breath, spirit), the earth.

4. The footprints of the gods may be the sacrificial laws, which are 'woven' when the gods as poet-priests perform the sacrifice, by weaving their words.

5. The mother of the sun is Dawn, who is pierced by *her* father as well as the sun's father, the Sky; recoiling from incest, she nevertheless does what must be done (the 'Order') and is praised for this.

6. The calf searches for the mother who has abandoned him,

as the mothers of Indra and Vivasvan (another form of the sun) abandon them in Vedic mythology. The three stages of the journey are one-tenth of the thirty-stage journey that the sun traverses every twenty-four hours; or they are the three-day journey of the dead man (cf. 10.14.16).

7. The three mothers and fathers are the three earths and three skies as parents of the sun, here identified with the Absolute. Speech does not inspire every priest, though she is present in them all.

8. The sun is imagined either as supreme in heaven, or as ruling only the lower half, the upper being the abode of Speech.

9. In Vedic mythology, Aditi gives birth to the immortal Ādityas in pairs, while she rejects the sun, Vivasvan, born alone (cf. 10.72.8–9). In the ritual, there are twelve paired months and one odd one, the intercalary month which interrupts the sequence and causes the others to 'change and waver'.

10. The androgyny of the creators appears, on the ritual level, in the fact that the months (a masculine term in Sanskrit) are procreative. The second half of the verse puns upon the father of the sun (the sky) and the father of the poet who competes with and surpasses his own father. Cf. 6.9.2.

11. The dawn cow, between sky (above) and earth (below), has her calf at her heels as she kicks him away; she is alone because she has abandoned him.

12. 'His' father refers both to the poet who knows his own father and the one who knows the sun's father.

13. The rituals of the past become the rituals of the future; the deeds of the gods still remain effective for us now.

14. On the tree of knowledge and immortality, some eat and some cannot.

15. Agni is the herdsman or the cowherd.

16. These deeds are attributed to Indra or the creator in other hymns. The Gāyatrī has three feet, here identified with the kindling-sticks of fire.

17. Savitṛ, the divine obstetrician and embodiment of twilight (cf. 2.38, 1.35), is called to assist the Pravargya ritual in giving birth to the sun. The milk hissing in the pot is the dawn cow snuffling at her calf, the sun; the milk that swells in her udder is the milk that boils; the pot sings a chant, and the cow (the milk) throws off her cover (the lid), as the milk boils over.

18. The death and rebirth of the mortal, or of the mortal sun.

The resting-places of the sun or fire are sky, earth, and the waters, or just the waters.

19. The sun who disappears from the sky (his father), or the breath of life that disappears from the dead body (of the mortal or the mortal sun).

20. The two bowls, literally wooden bowls for Soma, are sky and earth. Cf. 1.160.1.

21. The seven creators or priests fashion the sun from the seed split by the father when he incestuously embraces his daughter. Or the Ādityas fashion the sun from the misformed embryo; while they themselves are still embryos 'surrounded' in the womb, they 'surround', i.e. form into a ball, the semen.

22. The soul that is reborn according to its nature, or the sun. The immortal soul/sun and the mortal body/dead sun or night are on opposite sides of the earth/mind at any given time.

23. Here and in the next two verses the cow is Speech.

24. Soma (explicitly mentioned in verse 35) is the bull. The final phrase also appears as 10.90.16.

25. Three forms of Agni with flames for hair, or three ecstatic sages (cf. 10.136.1). The former interpretation is supported by the second half of the verse: Fire shaves the earth; the sun watches; the wind's path is perceived, but the wind itself is invisible. Cf. 10.168.4.

26. This verse closely resembles 10.90.4.

27. Sarasvatī as goddess of Speech and as the river in the sky (cf. v. 25) and on earth.

28. This verse appears also as 10.90.16.

29. Rain falls from the sun in the sky in return for flame from the sacrifice on earth.

# THE HORSE SACRIFICE

As the supreme symbol of the victorious Indo-Europeans, the horse looms large in the *Rig Veda*, and many gods are called horses – Indra, Dadhikrā, Sūrya, Agni, Soma, the Dawn, and others. In addition to its role as signifier, however, the horse also appears as signified in a group of hymns about the sacrifice of the consecrated stallion, a ceremony that was to become the subject of far more detailed and lengthy discussion in the texts of the Brāhmaṇas a few centuries later.

The horse in the *Rig Veda* is at least three things at once: a real, material creature whose domestication enabled the Indo-Aryans to conquer the Indo-European world; a race-horse that ran in profane and sacred contests; and a precious sacrificial victim. In these three hymns, the horse – in all three of these aspects – is praised, killed, and lamented.

## 1.163 *Hymn to the Horse*

The sacrificial horse is identified with the sun and fire; here he is also identified with several other gods, as well as with the earthly racehorse (who is himself a figure with whom many gods are identified).

1 When you whinnied for the first time, as you were born coming forth from the ocean or from the celestial source,[1] with the wings of an eagle and the forelegs of an antelope – that, Swift Runner, was your great and awesome birth.

2 Yama gave him and Trita harnessed him; Indra was the first to mount him, and the Gandharva grasped his reins. You gods[2] fashioned the horse out of the sun.

3 Swift Runner, you are Yama; you are Āditya; you are Trita, through the hidden design.[3] You are like and not like Soma.[4] They say you have three bonds in the sky.[5]

4 They say you have three bonds in the sky, three in the waters, and three within the ocean.[6] And to me you appear, Swift Runner, like Varuṇa, that is said to be your highest birth.

5 These are the places where they rubbed you down when you were victorious; here are the marks where you put down your hooves. Here I saw your lucky reins, which the Guardians of the Order keep safely.

6 From afar, in my heart I recognized your soul, the bird[7] flying below the sky. I saw your winged head snorting on the dustless paths easy to travel.[8]

7 Here I saw your highest form eager for nourishment in the place of the cow.[9] As soon as a mortal gets the food that you enjoy, the great devourer of plants awakens him.[10]

8 The chariot follows you, Swift Runner; the young man follows, the cow follows, the love of young girls follows. The troops follow your friendship.[11] The gods entrusted virile power to you.

9 His mane is golden;[12] his feet are bronze. He is swift

as thought, faster than Indra. The gods have come to eat the oblation of the one who was the first to mount the swift runner.[13]

*10* The celestial coursers, revelling in their strength, fly in a line like wild geese, the ends held back while the middle surges forward, when the horses reach the racecourse of the sky.

*11* Your body flies, Swift Runner; your spirit rushes like wind. Your mane,[12] spread in many directions, flickers and jumps about in the forests.[14]

*12* The racehorse has come to the slaughter, pondering with his heart turned to the gods. The goat, his kin,[15] is led in front; behind come the poets, the singers.

*13* The swift runner has come to the highest dwelling-place, to his father and mother. May he go to the gods today and be most welcome, and then ask for the things that the worshipper wishes for.

## NOTES

1. A possible reference to the sun born in the ocean and also born from the waters in the sky.

2. The Vasus are a group of gods associated with the sun.

3. Perhaps the magic power of the sacrifice, or the secret power associated with the mysterious Trita, or simply the Vedic power of secret equivalences.

4. As Agni, he is both likened to and contrasted with Soma through the mechanism of parallel oppositions and the Vedic concept of liquid fire or the fiery liquid; as a sacrificial animal, he is joined with Soma in the ritual dimension.

5. The bonds are the three gods named in the first sentence of this verse.

6. The three bonds are multiples of the bond in each of three places named: the sky (v. 3, and the 'highest birth' in Varuṇa), the waters (v. 1, and perhaps also v. 5, where the gods bathed the celestial horse), and the ocean (v. 1, and also implicit in the birth from Varuṇa, god of the ocean).

7. The sun as a bird.

8. The paths that lead to the sun.

9. The cow on three levels: as a symbol of the sun in the sky; as

the cows won by the victorious racehorse; and as the cattle won in raids on horseback.

10. A mysterious sentence. Agni, who devours plants (in forest fires), awakens man every morning (as the sun); the herbivorous horse also devours plants, and is awakened every morning to be fed. The worshipper who 'feeds' the sacrificial fire (or offers oblations to the sun) is 'awakened' when he arrives in heaven. All of these are possible (as the final 'him' must be supplied and has no clear referent).

11. A martial procession behind the war-horse; a sacrificial procession behind the consecrated stallion; a triumphant procession behind the racehorse.

12. The mane (literally, the 'horns') of the horse as a metaphor for the rays of the sun.

13. 'The one' would be Indra, rider of the solar horse according to verse 2, but here it would seem to designate the earthly king, the owner of the earthly horse.

14. Here the rays are scattered by the foliage.

15. Either a scapegoat for the sacrificial horse (cf. 1.162.2–3), or just a companion for the racehorse (as racehorses often have goats, to this day).

## 1.162 *The Sacrifice of the Horse*

Strikingly concrete in its detail, this hymn describes the ancient Indian horse sacrifice, beginning with the ceremonial procession of the horse with the scapegoat, leading to the actual slaughter (vv. 1–7). It then dwells upon the material instruments of the sacrifice which are to accompany the horse to heaven.

*1* Mitra, Varuṇa, Aryaman the Active,[1] Indra the ruler of the Ṛbhus,[2] and the Maruts[3] – let them not fail to heed us when we proclaim in the assembly the heroic deeds of the racehorse who was born of the gods.[4]

*2* When they lead the firmly grasped offering[5] in front of the horse that is covered with cloths and heirlooms, the dappled goat goes bleating straight to the dear dwelling of Indra and Pūṣan.

*3* This goat for all the gods is led forward with the race-

horse as the share for Pūṣan. When they lead forth the
welcome offering[5] with the charger, Tvaṣṭṛ urges him
on to great fame.
4 When, as the ritual law ordains, the men circle three
times, leading the horse that is to be the oblation on the
path to the gods, the goat who is the share for Pūṣan
goes first, announcing the sacrifice to the gods.
5 The Invoker,[6] the officiating priest, the atoner,[7] the
fire-kindler, the holder of the pressing-stones, the
reciter, the priest who prays – fill your bellies with this
well-prepared, well-sacrificed sacrifice.
6 The hewers of the sacrificial stake and those who carry it,
and those who carve the knob[8] for the horse's sacrificial
stake, and those who gather together the things[9] to
cook the charger – let their approval encourage us.
7 The horse with his smooth back went forth into the
fields of the gods, just when I made my prayer. The
inspired sages exult in him. We have made him a welcome
companion at the banquet of the gods.
8 The charger's rope and halter, the reins and bridle on
his head, and even the grass that has been brought up
to his mouth – let all of that stay with you[10] even among
the gods.
9 Whatever of the horse's flesh the fly has eaten, or what-
ever stays stuck to the stake or the axe, or to the hands or
nails of the slaughterer[11] – let all of that stay with you[10]
even among the gods.
10 Whatever food remains in his stomach, sending forth
gas, or whatever smell there is from his raw flesh[11] –
let the slaughterers make that well done; let them
cook the sacrificial animal until he is perfectly cooked.
11 Whatever runs off your body when it has been placed on
the spit and roasted by the fire, let it not lie there in the
earth or on the grass, but let it be given to the gods
who long for it.
12 Those[12] who see that the racehorse is cooked, who say,
'It smells good! Take it away!', and who wait for the

doling out of the flesh of the charger – let their approval encourage us.

13 The testing fork for the cauldron that cooks the flesh, the pots for pouring the broth, the cover of the bowls to keep it warm, the hooks, the dishes – all these attend the horse.

14 The place where he walks, where he rests, where he rolls, and the fetters on the horse's feet, and what he has drunk and the fodder he has eaten – let all of that stay with you[10] even among the gods.

15 Let not the fire that reeks of smoke darken you, nor the red-hot cauldron split into pieces. The gods receive the horse who has been sacrificed, worshipped, consecrated, and sanctified with the cry of 'Vaṣat!'[13]

16 The cloth that they spread beneath the horse, the upper covering, the golden trappings on him, the halter and the fetters on his feet – let these things that are his own bind the horse among the gods.

17 If someone riding you has struck you too hard with heel or whip when you shied, I make all these things well again for you with prayer,[11] as they do[14] with the oblation's ladle in sacrifices.

18 The axe cuts through the thirty-four ribs[15] of the racehorse who is the companion of the gods. Keep the limbs undamaged and place them in the proper pattern. Cut them apart, calling out piece by piece.[16]

19 One is the slaughterer of the horse of Tvaṣṭṛ; two restrain him. This is the rule. As many of your limbs as I set out, according to the rules, so many balls I offer into the fire.[17]

20 Let not your dear soul burn you[18] as you go away. Let not the axe do lasting harm to your body. Let no greedy, clumsy slaughterer hack in the wrong place and damage your limbs with his knife.

21 You do not really die through this, nor are you harmed. You go to the gods on paths pleasant to go on. The two bay stallions, the two roan mares[19] are now your

chariot mates. The racehorse has been set in the donkey's yoke.

22 Let this racehorse bring us good cattle and good horses, male children and all-nourishing wealth. Let Aditi make us free from sin.[20] Let the horse with our offerings achieve sovereign power for us.

NOTES

1. This may be an epithet of Vāyu or Agni, or the name of a distinct god, or an epithet of Aryaman.

2. The Ṛbhus are the craftsmen of the gods.

3. This may be a list of five gods or of seven, depending upon whether one takes the adjectival terms as epithets or separate names.

4. Sāyaṇa says the horse was born from the essential forms of many gods, a common form of mythological creation.

5. This almost certainly refers to the goat, though the commentary suggests that it might be the remains of the burnt offering made the night before.

6. The Invoker is the Hotṛ priest, often identified with Agni. Cf. 1.1.1.

7. This term may designate the priest who portions out the offerings or the one who performs expiations for ritual errors or personal misdeeds (cf. v. 17). Here, as in verse 1, there may be five or seven terms, depending upon whether one takes the adjectival terms (here the third and seventh) as descriptions or separate titles.

8. A piece of wood attached crosswise at the top of the stake.

9. These utensils would be the pot, the wood, etc.

10. Here the horse is directly addressed.

11. Cf. the hope that the human corpse will be made whole (10.16.6) and properly cooked (10.16.1–2).

12. These are the priests who eat the horse (cf. v. 5).

13. The cry that is made when the offering is presented to the gods. Cf. 10.14.3 for the use of Svāhā!, a similar call.

14. The Brahmins who repair the errors committed in the course of the sacrifice.

15. Thirty-four of the horse's ribs (he has thirty-six) are distributed, one to the sun, one to the moon, five to the planets, and twenty-seven to the constellations.

16. The priest names each part as he cuts it, and declares the divinity to whom it is dedicated.

17. These are probably balls of rice that the wives of the king give to the stallion; they may also be balls of meat.

18. That is, do not be sad.

19. The two bay stallions are the horses of Indra, the two roan mares the horses of the Maruts, and the donkey belongs to the Aśvins.

20. This is both a general wish for expiation and a specific wish to be cleansed of the sin of killing the horse.

## 10.56 *Requiem for a Horse*

This hymn is a funerary farewell to a beloved horse. Against this interpretation, later Indian commentarial tradition suggested that the subject of the hymn was the poet's dead son, called 'Victorious Racehorse' (Vājin); and it is worthy of note that the horse is said to travel to heaven, put on a new body, and dwell happily there afterwards, just as the dead man does in another hymn (10.14). But the equine character of the verses is unmistakable. The hymn may refer to a particular ritual, possibly even to the immolation of a sacred horse; verse 3 opens with the exact phrase used at the beginning of the horse sacrifice. It may also be based upon the deification of a great racehorse, as is suggested by the hymn's recurring use of the metaphor of winning heaven as one wins a race (though here it must be noted that the *Rig Veda* often refers to other goals – wealth, sons, long life – won as one wins a race).[1] The idea of a hymn to a horse is not in itself un-Vedic; the *Rig Veda* knows other divine horses, such as Dadhikrā, Tārkṣya, and Etaśa. The horses of heaven are obliquely alluded to in verse 4, where they are said to have more powers than the Fathers and to have been given special mental power by the gods before taking on their heavenly bodies; verse 5 may even imply that all living creatures are somehow bound to or encompassed by the powers of these celestial equines, who gallop around a racecourse made of the space between sky and earth.

Verses 1–5a describe the horse's translation to heaven,

where he is given a new body, gathering into it the qualities that it had on earth (verse 4). He changes into this body as the sun changes its form (verse 2); the sun is also alluded to as the 'light beyond' (verse 1), mediating between the light here (fire, probably the funeral pyre) and the third light (the light in the world of the dead). The 'god who finds the light' (verse 6) may also be the sun; it may, however, be the spirit who leads the horse to the world of the dead, the third light; in general, the term often refers to Agni, Soma, or the Fathers, any of whom would be appropriate here. The final verses speak of the body in more general terms, contrasting the body put on in heaven with the body left on earth in the form of offspring.

*1* This is your one light, and there beyond is your other; merge with the third light. By merging with a body, grow lovely, dear to the gods in the highest birthplace.

*2* Victorious racehorse, let your body, carrying a body,[2] bring blessings to us and safety to you. Staying straight,[3] so that you may carry the great gods, change your own light as one does in heaven.

*3* You are a victorious racehorse with the power to win victory; go happily to the mares who long for you. Go happily to fame and heaven; go happily to the first orders and truths, go happily to the gods, go happily to your flight.

*4* Even the Fathers have no control over their[4] majesty; the gods have placed the power of understanding in the gods.[5] They[4] have gathered together all things that shine, and these have entered their[4] bodies again.

*5* With their great powers they have circled all the middle realm of space, measuring out ancient domains never measured before. All creatures are bound to their bodies.[6] They shower down their offspring in many ways.

*6* By the third action, and in two ways,[7] the sons have set in place the god[8] who finds the light. The fathers have established their own offspring as paternal power, like a thread stretched out among those who are to follow.

7 As if on a ship sailing through high water to all horizons of the earth, crossing over all dangers with ease, Bṛhaduktha[9] has through his great power established his own offspring among those who are to follow and those who have come before.

## NOTES

1. Cf. especially the racehorses of Dawn, 1.92.7.

2. The image of the horse carrying a rider (a body carrying a body) suggests the fire carrying the dead body to heaven and going on (v. 3) to carry the oblation to the gods. Cf. Agni, the horse, as the conveyer, in 1.26.1, 5.2.1 and 10.51.6.

3. Both straight on the path and with a straight (i.e. uncollapsed) back under the weight.

4. 'They' are the horses; the shining things enter the horses' bodies, as the god-inspired powers enter their minds.

5. The gods in heaven give inspiration to the 'gods' newly made, the horses who succeed in reaching heaven.

6. This may refer to the heavenly horses of verses 4–5 or imply that each creature is bound to his own body.

7. The third action is the begetting of children, the 'debt' each Hindu must pay to the Fathers (the first two debts being Vedic study, paid to the sages, and sacrifice, paid to the gods). The 'two ways' may refer to sons and fathers, achieving their ends on earth (by children) and in heaven (by ritual).

8. The sun is here called an Asura, an ancient god.

9. Name of the sage to whom the hymn is attributed.

# GODS OF THE SACRIFICE: AGNI AND SOMA

AGNI and Soma are linked in many ways. As fire and liquid, they are complementary oppositions that unite in the Indo-European concept of the fiery liquid, the elixir of immortality (the ambrosia). As ritual elements, they are invoked more often than any other gods of the *Rig Veda*, as the embodiments of the sacrificial fire and the sacrificial drink. As metaphorical symbols, they are the centre of a complex set of speculations about the nature of the cosmos, taking the form of riddles about something that is lost and then found. The mythologies differ in that the mystery of Agni is the mystery of his birth as well as of his rebirth when he leaves the gods and must be brought back, while the mystery of Soma is the mystery of his descent from heaven. These mythologies join in the image of the sun-bird, a form of Agni (the Indo-European fire-bird), who brings the Soma to earth (cf. 10.123 and 10.177).

The mysteries are questions posed and answered, for Agni and Soma are the two sources of the inspiration that enables the Vedic poet to find and understand the meaning of the sacrifice and of his life. They are different sorts of inspiration: Agni is Apollonian, explaining the sacrifice; he represents the cultivated, cooked, cultured aspects of ritual. Soma is Dionysian, explaining the vision of life; he represents the wild, raw, disruptive aspects of ritual. The Vedic sacrifice embraces them both.

### *Agni*

Agni is the subject of many straightforward hymns about the kindling of and offering into the fire; he is invoked to bring all the gods to the sacrifice (1.1) and to mediate between gods and men (1.26). But several of the hymns to Agni are more enigmatic than paradigmatic. His birth (5.2) is described in purposely elliptic references similar to those used to refer to Agni in the Riddle of the Sacrifice (1.164; cf. also 3.31.1–3). This first appearance of Agni is then linked to subsequent appearances after he has been lost, occasions when he hides (10.5), usually in the waters (10.51), the place of his birth (2.35), or in the body of the arch-enemy of the gods (10.124). The birth and recovery of Agni are two aspects of a great mystery (4.5) that Agni himself inspires the poet to solve (6.9).

## 1.1 *I Pray to Agni*

Appropriately placed at the very beginning of the *Rig Veda*, this hymn invites Agni, the divine priest, to come to the sacrifice.

*1* I pray to Agni, the household priest who is the god of the sacrifice, the one who chants and invokes and brings most treasure.
*2* Agni earned the prayers of the ancient sages, and of those of the present, too; he will bring the gods here.
*3* Through Agni one may win wealth, and growth from day to day, glorious and most abounding in heroic sons.
*4* Agni, the sacrificial ritual that you encompass on all sides – only that one goes to the gods.
*5* Agni, the priest with the sharp sight of a poet, the true and most brilliant, the god will come with the gods.
*6* Whatever good you wish to do for the one who worships you, Agni, through you, O Angiras,[1] that comes true.
*7* To you, Agni, who shine upon darkness, we come day after day, bringing our thoughts and homage
*8* to you, the king over sacrifices, the shining guardian of the Order, growing in your own house.
*9* Be easy for us to reach, like a father to his son. Abide with us, Agni, for our happiness.

NOTES

1. The Angirases were an ancient family of priests, often identified with Vedic gods such as Agni and Indra.

## 1.26 *Agni and the Gods*

This hymn emphasizes the close symbiosis between the sacrificer and Agni, on the one hand, and the sacrificer and the gods, on the other. Agni is asked to intercede as a father would sacrifice for his son, implying a cooperation among worshippers as well as between worshippers and gods. When Agni is pleased, the sacrificer has a 'good fire', and when the sacrificer has a good fire, the gods have a good fire (i.e. they rejoice in a good sacrifice), and so they become generous. The mortal praises Agni and hopes that he will praise (i.e. speak on behalf of) the mortal in turn, even as the mortal praises the gods and hopes that they will praise (i.e. approve of) him (v. 9).

*1* Now get dressed in your robes,[1] lord of powers and master of the sacrificial food, and offer this sacrifice for us.

*2* Young Agni, take your place as our favourite priest with inspirations and shining speech.

*3* The father sacrifices for his son, the comrade for his comrade, the favourite friend for his friend.[2]

*4* May Varuṇa, Mitra and Aryaman, proud of their powers, sit upon our sacred grass, as upon Manu's.[3]

*5* You who were the first to invoke, rejoice in our friendship and hear only these songs.

*6* When we offer sacrifice to this god or that god, in the full line of order, it is to you alone that the oblation is offered.

*7* Let him be a beloved lord of tribes for us, a favourite, kindly invoker; let us have a good fire and be beloved.

*8* For when the gods have a good fire, they bring us what we wish for. Let us pray with a good fire.

*9* So let praises flow back and forth between the two, between us who are mortals and you, the immortal.[4]

*10* Agni, young spawn of strength, with all the fires take pleasure in this sacrifice and in this speech.

## NOTES

1. When Agni becomes the priest, his robes are both the flames and the prayers.

2. Many gods are asked to behave like friends or fathers; here, it is also suggested that one person might sacrifice on behalf of another, and Agni is asked to do this on behalf of the worshipper.

3. A reference to the primeval sacrifice offered by Manu, ancestor of mankind.

4. The verse, which is elliptic, implies both that Agni and the worshipper should enjoy a mutuality of praise and that, through that link, the other gods and the worshippers should enjoy such a mutuality.

## 5.2 *The Birth of Agni*

The hymn begins with obscure references to unknown myths, the gist of which seems to be that Agni has vanished. The sacrificial fire or the domestic fire has suddenly been extinguished. This crisis is then generalized into a vague danger from which Agni is implored to rescue the worshipper, as well as specific dangers such as emotional conflict between parents and children (centring upon the vanishing mother) and the theological problem of the vanishing or otiose god (identified with Varuṇa in v. 8). The appearance of Agni in the first place is the occasion for speculation on the mystery of creation *ex nihilo*, the kindling of the spark of fire out of thin air (cf. 1.164), and the 'setting fire' of Agni (vv. 5–6) becomes a metaphor for the release of the worshipper from constricting anguish.

Indian tradition supplies a specific story to account for the vanishing of Agni in the early verses of this hymn.[1] The priest (who also served as a charioteer – even as Agni is the 'conveyor' of the oblation) of a certain king quarrelled with him over the murder of a male child. Feeling himself falsely accused, the priest left the kingdom in anger, and with him the heat of all the fires in the kingdom went out.[2] The priest was finally called back, and on his return he declared that the king's wife had concealed the heat of the fire. When the priest swore an oath of truth, the fire reappeared and burnt the queen. This story, as obscure in its own way as the hymn it purports to gloss, and most probably a late afterthought, does at least indicate some ways in which the imagery of the birth of a concealed child and the kindling of an extinguished sacrificial fire are intertwined in the hymn.

*1* The young mother secretly keeps the boy tightly swathed and does not give him to the father.[3] The people no longer see before them his altered face, hidden by the charioteer.[4]

*2* Who is the boy that you are carrying, young woman? The chief queen, not the stepmother, gave him birth, for the embryo grew for many autumns. I saw him born when his mother bore him.[5]

*3* I saw him with his golden teeth and pure colour, testing his weapons far from his field, and I gave him the ambrosia that sets one free. What can those who have no Indra, no hymns, do to me?[6]

*4* I saw him moving far away from his field, and his fine herd no longer shining brightly.[7] They could not grasp him, for he had been born; the young women became grey with age.[8]

*5* Who are they[9] who separate my young man from the cows? They have never had a cowherd, not even a stranger.[10] Let those who have seized him set him free. The man of foresight should drive the cattle back to us.

*6* The enemy powers[11] have hidden among mortals[12] the one who is the king of dwellings,[13] himself the dwelling-place of men. Let the magic formulas of Atri[14] set him free; let those who revile be themselves reviled.

*7* When Śunaḥśepha was bound for a thousand,[15] you set him free from the stake, for he sacrificed with fervour. In the same way, Agni, set us free from our bonds when you have settled down here, O wise priest of the oblation.

*8* For when you grew angry you went away from me; the guardian of the laws[16] told me this. Indra discovered you, for he knows; he taught me, and so I have come, Agni.

*9* Agni shines forth with a high light; by his power he makes all things manifest. He overpowers the godless forces of evil magic; he sharpens his two horns to gore[17] the demons.

*10* Let Agni's bellowings reach to heaven as piercing weapons to destroy the demons. His angry glare breaks forth in ecstasy of Soma. The obstacles of the godless cannot hold him back.

*11* Inspired with poetry I have fashioned this hymn of praise for you whose very nature is power, as the skilled artist fashions a chariot. If you receive it with pleasure, Agni, let us win waters and sunlight with it.

*12* 'The bull with the powerful neck, increasing in size and strength, will drive together the possessions of the enemy without opposition.' This is what the immortals said to Agni. Let him grant shelter to the man who spreads the sacred grass; let him grant shelter to the man who offers oblation.

## NOTES

1. Cf. 10.51 and 10.124.

2. In the same way, all fires die out when Śiva is wrongly accused and departs from the Pine Forests.

3. In the sacrificial simile, the lower fire-stick is the mother, that holds back the fire (the child) from the father (the upper stick, or the sacrificer). On the human or anthropomorphic level, the verse describes a common familial conflict.

4. In terms of the traditional gloss (the tale of the king and the priest), the charioteer who hides the fire is the priest; as a cosmic metaphor, the charioteer is the sun's charioteer, or the god Agni himself, and the meaning is that the sacrificial fire is reabsorbed into its celestial form.

5. This verse plays upon the concept of the two mothers of Agni, who is elsewhere explicitly referred to as 'having two mothers' (3.31.2). The first is the official queen who bore him; the second is the despised queen or stepmother, the young woman

mentioned in v. 1, who carries the child away; she is the one whom the priest accuses of concealing the fire.

6. The poet argues that since he has performed the pious act of offering the oblation, and has had a vision of Agni, he is protected. Cf. 8.48.3.

7. The herd is the mass of flames, and the priest is the herder who has left them. Cf. the cow who has left her calf and the herd, 1.164.17.

8. The most likely interpretation of this verse is that 'they' are the flames that cannot hold on to the vanishing Agni and therefore become grey ashes.

9. 'They' in the first phrase seems to refer to men who take the young man (Agni) away from the cows (the flames, his mothers); in the second phrase, 'they' are the flames that lack even a foreign priest (the priest in exile).

10. The departed priest.

11. The men who stole the fire, or the demons who threaten the worshipper.

12. Priests, who are the mortal guardians of Agni.

13. Agni, the domestic hearth.

14. A Vedic priest.

15. A reference to the myth in which Śunaḥśepha was to be sacrificed in place of a thousand cattle but was rescued by a priest (a form of Agni). Cf. the scapegoat for the corpse (10.16.4) and for the horse (1.162.2–4).

16. Varuṇa, when angered, abandons his devotee (7.86); he is the otiose god, who betrays Agni (10.124).

17. Agni appears as a bull, in this and the next verse, as well as in v. 12. The demons, human enemies of the Āryans, rival priests, and godless people are all lumped together as suitable victims for the wrath of Agni in vv. 6–10.

## 2.35 *The Child of the Waters (Apām Napāt)*

The Child of the Waters is often identified with Agni, as the form of fire that appears as the lightning born of the clouds. But he is a deity in his own right, who appears in the Avesta as a spirit who lives deep in the waters, surrounded by females, driving swift horses. As the embodiment of the dialectic conjunction of fire and water, the child of the waters is a symbol central to Vedic and later Hindu cosmology. Sāyaṇa remarks that his name designates the grandson rather than the son of the waters (cf. Greek *nepos*): the herbs and trees are born from the waters, and Agni is born from the herbs and trees (cf. v. 8). This hymn, the only one dedicated entirely to him, plays upon the simultaneous unity and non-unity of the earthly and celestial forms of Agni and the Child of the Waters.

*1* Striving for the victory prize, I have set free my eloquence; let the god of rivers gladly accept my songs. Surely the child of the waters, urging on his swift horses, will adorn my songs,[1] for he enjoys them.

*2* We would sing to him this prayer well-fashioned from the heart; surely he will recognize it. With his divine[2] energy, the child of the waters has created all noble creatures.

*3* Some flow together, while others flow toward the sea, but the rivers fill the same hollow cavern.[3] The pure waters surrounded this pure, radiant child of the waters.

*4* The young women, the waters, flow around the young god, making him shine and gazing solemnly upon him. With his clear, strong flames he shines riches upon us, wearing his garment of butter, blazing without fuel in the waters.

*5* Three women, goddesses,[4] wish to give food[5] to the god so that he will not weaken. He has stretched forth in the waters; he sucks the new milk of those who have given birth for the first time.[6]

*6* The birth of the horse is here[7] and in the sun. Guard our patrons from falling prey to malice or injury. When far away in fortresses of unbaked bricks,[8] hatred and falsehoods shall not reach him.

*7* In his own house he keeps the cow who yields good milk; he makes his vital force swell as he eats the nourishing food. Gathering strength in the waters, the child of the waters shines forth to give riches to his worshipper.

8 True and inexhaustible, he shines forth in the waters with pure divinity.[9] Other creatures and plants, his branches, are reborn with their progeny.[10]

9 Clothed in lightning, the upright child of the waters has climbed into the lap of the waters as they lie down. The golden-hued young women[11] flow around him, bearing with them his supreme energy.

10 Golden is his form, like gold to look upon; and gold in colour is this child of the waters. Seated away from his golden womb,[12] the givers of gold give him food.

11 His face and the lovely secret name of the child of the waters grow when the young women[13] kindle him thus. Golden-hued butter is his food.

12 To him, the closest friend among many,[14] we would offer worship with sacrifices, obeisance, and oblations. I rub his back;[15] I bring him shavings; I give him food; I praise him with verses.

13 Being a bull, he engendered that embryo in the females;[16] being a child, he sucks them, and they lick him. The child of the waters, whose colour never fades, seems to enter the body of another here.[17]

14 He shines for ever, with undarkened flames, remaining in this highest place. The young waters, bringing butter as food to their child, themselves enfold him with robes.

15 O Agni, I have given a good dwelling-place to the people; I have given a good hymn to the generous patron. All this is blessed, that the gods love. Let us speak great words as men of power in the sacrificial gathering.

NOTES

1. Either he will make them beautiful, or he will reward them.
2. As a form of Agni, the child of the waters is an Asura, a high divinity.
3. That is, the ocean.
4. The three mothers of Agni, the waters of the three worlds.
5. Soma or butter.

6. The waters are *primaparas* or *primagravitas*, as the child of the waters is their first child; they themselves are first-born from Brahmā, says Sāyaṇa.

7. Agni is often depicted as a horse, who is in turn identified with the sun; the micro-macrocosmic parallel is enriched by Agni's simultaneous terrestrial and celestial forms, and those of the waters ('here'). Moreover, the sun, like the child of the waters, is born in the waters.

8. The sacrificer asks to be protected by Agni, who is safe even when among enemies who do not control fire and so do not fire their bricks, or who (as the sun) is safe from his enemies when he is in his own 'natural' citadels not made of baked bricks, i.e. the clouds.

9. Here the Child of the Waters is a god (*deva*), not an Asura.

10. Other fires on earth are regarded as branches of Agni, who also appears in plants; on another level, Agni causes all creatures and plants to be reborn.

11. The waters of heaven or earth.

12. The construction is loose, and may imply either that it is Agni who is seated away from his golden womb (cf. 10.121.1) or that the sacrificers are seated around him.

13. Here the young women are the ten fingers, not the waters. The fingers kindle the earthly fire, that grows in the waters (the clouds) secretly and then is fed with butter at the sacrifice.

14. Literally, the lowest, that is the most intimate friend of men among the many gods, and therefore enjoying intimate services as described in the rest of this verse.

15. That is, the fire-altar. Cf. 1.164.1 for the fire-altar as the back of fire.

16. The child of the waters engenders himself. He is father and son, pervading a body that belongs to someone who merely *seems* to be other. For the use of bull/calf imagery to express this paradox, cf. 7.101, the hymn to Parjanya. The father becomes an embryo, the middle form of Agni, the lightning that sucks the waters in the clouds as if they were cows; then they lick him as a cow licks a calf.

17. That is, on earth. This is an explicit statement of the identity of the Child of the Waters with Agni as the sacrificial fire: the former enters the body of the latter.

## 10.51 *The Gods Coax Agni out of the Waters*

This hymn is based upon the myth of the finding of the lost Agni. In this particular episode, it appears that Agni's three brothers have perished in the service of the gods (mediating, serving as priests, carrying the oblation to the gods, as is the task of the sacred fire); in fear of being destroyed in the same way, Agni fled and hid in the waters, the place of his birth,[1] but the gods found him there again. The myth is thus both a conversation between the gods, asking him to return to them, and a dialogue on the dangers of being born at all, since life involves old age and death. The myth of the finding of the lost Agni is an analogue to the myth of the finding of the stolen Soma,[2] and is, in fact, a variant of it, for it is the golden liquid of fire that is the basis of the Indo-European myth of Agni and Soma together.

*1* [*A god:*] 'Great was that membrane,[3] and firm, which enveloped you when you entered the waters. One god, O Agni, knower of creatures, saw all your various bodies.'

*2* [*Agni:*] 'Who saw me? Who among the gods perceived my various bodies?[4] O Mitra and Varuṇa, where are all the fuel-sticks of Agni that lead to the gods?'[5]

*3* [*Varuṇa:*] 'We searched for you in various places, O Agni, knower of creatures, when you had entered into the waters and the plants. It was Yama[6] who discovered you with your many-coloured light which shines beyond the distance of ten days' journey.'

*4* [*Agni:*] 'I fled because I feared the role of oblation-giver, so that the gods would not harness me to it, O Varuṇa. My bodies entered various places; I, Agni, have ceased to consider this task.'[7]

*5* [*Varuṇa:*] 'Come here. Man,[8] who loves the gods, wishes to sacrifice. When you have completed the ritual, Agni, you dwell in darkness.[9] Make smooth the paths which lead to the gods; carry the offerings with a good heart.'

6 [*Agni:*] 'The brothers of Agni long ago ran back and forth on this task like a chariot-horse[10] upon a road. Fearing this, Varuṇa, I went far away. I fled like a buffalo before the bowstring of a hunter.'

7 [*The gods:*] 'We will make your life-span free of old age, O Agni, knower of creatures, so that you will not be harmed when you have been harnessed. Then you will carry the portion of the offering to the gods with a willing heart, O well-born one.'

8 [*Agni:*] 'Give me alone the pre-sacrifices and the post-sacrifices, the nourishing part of the offering; and the clarified butter out of the waters and the Man out of the plants.[11] And let the life-span of Agni be long, O gods.'

9 [*The gods:*] 'The pre-sacrifices and the post-sacrifices will be for you alone, the nourishing parts of the offering. This whole sacrifice will be for you, Agni; the four quarters of the sky will bow to you.'

## NOTES

1. For Agni as child of the waters, see 2.35.

2. Cf. notes on 4.26–7.

3. The word denotes the covering of the embryo in the womb. Agni is the embryo of the waters and so returns to the womb when he hides. The gods point out that even there he was not safe from them.

4. Agni has many forms in different places (lightning, sacrificial fire, the human body, etc.). Cf. 10.16, 6.9, and 1.164.1.

5. Mitra and Varuṇa lead the gods in the search. Agni argues that he cannot be seen in the water, because there are no fuel-sticks there to kindle him. These are the sticks which bring Agni to the gods through the oblation, and the sticks by which he carries the oblation from man to the gods.

6. In one retelling of the myth the gods bribe Agni by allowing him to change places with Yama, sending Yama to the world of the dead and bringing Agni to the world of the gods.

7. That is, he flatly refuses to become their invoker or priest of the oblation (Hotṛ).

8. Here, as elsewhere, the word (Manu) may designate either mankind in general or Manu the eponymous ancestor of mankind.

I think the former is the primary meaning, but since Manu is the brother of Yama who has just been mentioned, there may be resonances with the latter meaning too.

9. That is, you may rest after serving us. Cf. 6.9.1 and 6.9.7, and 10.124.1.

10. Agni is often called a horse, and the expression 'harnessing' him to the task of priest (vv. 4 and 7) thus takes on more specific relevance.

11. The clarified butter is the essence of the waters, the most precious of fluids, and also something that is placed in the waters (in ritual and in cosmogonies, the golden seed – another form of Agni himself – in the waters). The Man of the plants may be the personified god who is the best of the plants (Soma) or the corpse that is given to Agni in the funeral (cf. 10.16) or that is dispersed among the plants (10.16.3). Finally, Man is the 'best' of the plants (ŚB 7.2.4.26) as butter is the best of the fluids.

## 10.124 *Indra Lures Agni from Vṛtra*

Indra speaks on behalf of the gods to lure Agni back when he has fled (cf. 10.51). Agni is hiding inside a father (perhaps Indra's father; cf. 4.18) who is called an Asura, an enemy of the gods though not yet properly a demon; this Asura is eventually identified with the demon Vṛtra. Thus the hymn combines the myth of finding Agni (10.51) with the myth of killing Vṛtra (1.32). Varuṇa and Soma are also said to have been with the Asura and to abandon him when Agni is persuaded to do so. Indra invites Agni to return (v. 1), and Agni accepts (v. 2); Varuṇa and Soma follow (vv. 3–4), and are further encouraged by Indra's promises (vv. 6–7). The poet then praises Indra for winning these allies (vv. 8–9).

*1* [*Indra:*] 'Agni! Come to this sacrifice of ours, that has five roads, three layers, and seven threads.[1] Be our oblation-bearer and go before us. For far too long you have lain in darkness.'

*2* [*Agni:*] 'Secretly going away from the non-god,[2] being a god and seeing ahead I go to immortality.

Unkindly I desert him who was kind to me, as I go from
my own friends to a foreign tribe.'
3 [*Varuṇa:*] 'When I see the guest of the other branch,[3]
I measure out the many forms of the Law. I give a
friendly warning to the Asura father: I am going from
the place where there is no sacrifice to the portion that
has the sacrifice.'
4 [*Soma:*] 'I have spent many years within him. Now I
choose Indra and desert the father. Agni, Soma, Varuṇa –
they fall away. The power of kingship has turned around;
therefore I have come to help.'[4]
5 [*Indra:*] 'Varuṇa, these Asuras have lost their magic
powers,[5] since you love me. O king who separates
false from true, come and rule my kingdom.
6 'This was the sunlight, this the blessing, this the light
and the broad middle realm of space.[6] Come out, Soma,
and let us two kill Vṛtra. With the oblation we sacrifice to
you who are the oblation.'[7]
7 The poet through his vision fixed his form in the sky;
Varuṇa let the waters flow out without using force.
Like his[8] wives, the shining rivers make him comfortable;
they swirl his colour[9] along their current.
8 They[10] follow his supreme Indra-power;[11] he dwells
in those who rejoice in their own nature. Choosing him
as all the people choose a king, they have deserted
Vṛtra whom they loathe.
9 They say that the yoke-mate of those full of loathing[12]
is a swan who glides in friendship with the divine waters.
The poets through their meditation have seen Indra
dancing to the Anuṣṭubh.

NOTES

1. For the number mysticism of the sacrifice, cf. 1.164.

2. That is the Asura, Vṛtra. Cf. 10.51.7, where Agni demands immortality.

3. That is, when Varuṇa sees that Agni is the guest of the Asuras (his 'own friends'; cf. 2.35.2) rather than the gods (the 'foreign

tribe'), and that therefore the Asuras have the sacrifice, Varuṇa measures out (i.e. formulates and creates) the ritual laws for the gods.

4. That is, realizing that the gods are getting the upper hand again, Soma the king returns to assist at their sacrifice.

5. The power of illusion particularly associated with Asuras such as Vṛtra; cf. 1.32.4.

6. Apparently Indra is telling Varuṇa and Soma that all the powers of light that belong to the gods are once again theirs, now that the dark power of the Asuras has been overcome.

7. Cf. sacrificing the sacrifice to the sacrifice, 10.90.16.

8. Indra's wives, the waters that he frees when he kills Vṛtra.

9. Indra, the poet, places his stamp upon his dominion again, both in form and in colour. His colour (*varṇa*) is both the sign that typifies his species (gods in contrast with Asuras) and, perhaps, the bright colour of the gods and Āryans in contrast with the darkness of the Asuras and Dāsas.

10. The waters.

11. Indra's power consists in the forces of his nature (kingship, fertility, sacrifice, etc.); he rejoices in these and in people who, in their turn, rejoice in their own particular powers and nature.

12. That is, those who loathe Vṛtra have as their helper (yoke-mate) Indra, here visualized by the poet as a swan dancing in the waters. Those who loathe Vṛtra are primarily those who desert him (Agni, Soma, Varuṇa), as well as the waters whom Indra has released and the worshippers who rejoice in Indra's victory.

## 4.5 *The Mystery of Agni*

This obscure hymn may be an indirect description of an oral contest about Agni. The poet or poets tantalize us with oblique references to a secret revealed by Agni and revealing Agni; this secret is alluded to with expressions such as 'the gift' (v. 2), 'the inner meaning' (v. 3), 'this thought so high and deep' (v. 6), 'the vision that illuminates' (v. 7), 'this speech of mine' (v. 8). The opponents of the poet appear in various pejorative forms ('those who break the commandments', 'those without Order or truth', 'those whose speech is empty and contrary', who 'follow a false path', etc.). There is also an extended pun upon the word *padam*, which designates a footprint (v. 3), a 'deep place' (hell? – in v. 5), perhaps with a double meaning of 'this riddle' (i.e. 'this mysterious verse'), the place of the sun-bird (v. 8), the Order (v. 9) and the cow (v. 10), and a path (v. 12). These meanings are linked: to know the verse (*padam*) is to know how to follow the footprint (*padam*) along the path (*padam*) to the sacred place (*padam*) of the sun-bird, who is the symbol of the Order and is in turn symbolized by the cow.

The actual content of the secret concerns the identity of Agni with a bull, with the substance inside the leather-skin of food (a metaphor for an udder or the clouds or the earth or the human stomach, the latter being the site, in later Hinduism, of the digestive fire 'Of-all-men'), with the calf of the dappled cow Pṛśṇi (the earth) or of the cows of dawn, and with the disc of the sun or the sun-bird, the round 'face of the gods'. Agni's parents are sky and earth, or the fire-sticks (v. 10); in the latter case, he hungers for the offering of butter as a calf hungers for milk, the 'precious substance' in the udder of Pṛśṇi; as the sun, the calf of the dawn, Agni is followed by her. Thus the solar, sacrificial, and bovine images intertwine. The gift that Agni gives the poet is the 'clarifying vision' that sees that Agni is always present in all of these forms. To find the secret is to find the cows, or their milk, or to find the hidden sun – to find Agni, the sacred fire.

*1* How shall we with one accord give homage to the benevolent Agni Of-all-men? Great light, by his great and full growth he has propped up the sky as a buttress props a rampart.

*2* Do not reproach the self-ruled god who gave this gift to me, for I am a simple mortal, while he is the clever immortal, the insightful, most manly and impetuous Agni Of-all-men.

*3* The strong bull with sharp horns and seed a thousandfold has a mighty and double tone.[1] As one reveals the

hidden footprint of a cow, Agni has declared to me the
inner meaning.
4 Let the generous Agni, sharp-toothed with white-hot
flame, devour those who break the dear, firm command-
ments of Varuṇa and the watchful Mitra.[2]
5 Wilful as women without brothers, wicked as wives who
deceive their husbands, those who are evil, without
Order or truth, have engendered this deep place.[3]
6 O Agni, who makes things clear, who am I, that upon
me when I have broken no commandments you have
boldly placed like a heavy burden this thought so high
and deep, this fresh question with seven meanings
for the offering?
7 Let our vision that clarifies through sacrificial power
reach him who is the same everywhere; the precious
substance of the dappled cow is in the leather-skin of
food, and the disc of the sun has mounted to the head
of the earth-cow.
8 What of this speech of mine should I proclaim? They
murmur about the secret hidden in the depths: when
they have opened the mystery of the cows of dawn, like
a door upon a flood, he[4] protects the beloved head of
the earth-cow, the place of the bird.
9 This is that great face of the great gods, that the cow of
dawn followed as it went in front. I found it shining
in the place of the Order, moving swiftly, swiftly.
10 As he blazed beside his parents with his open mouth, he
thought of the precious hidden substance of the dappled
cow. In the farthest place of the mother, facing the
cow, the tongue of the bull, of the flame, stretches forth.
11 When questioned I speak reverently of the Order, if
I may, trusting in you who know all creatures. You
rule over all this, over all the riches in heaven and all
the riches on earth.
12 What is ours of this, what riches, what treasure? Tell
us, for you understand, you who know all creatures.[5]
Hiḍden is the farthest end of our road, where we have
gone as those who fail follow a false path.

13 What are the limits? What are the rules? What is the goal? We wish to go there as racehorses speed towards the victory prize. When will the Dawns, goddesses and wives of immortality, spread over us their light with the colour of the sun?

14 Those whose speech is empty and contrary, insipid and petty, who leave one unsatisfied, what can they say here, Agni? Unarmed, let them fall defeated.

15 The face of the bull, of this deity kindled for beauty, shone forth in the house. Clothed in white, beautiful in form and rich in gifts, he glowed like a home full of riches.

NOTES

1. The bellow of the bull is likened to the two tones of the Vedic hymn (the high and middle pitch).

2. Varuṇa and Mitra are the keepers of the moral law. Cf. 5.85.7.

3. A possible reference to Hell (cf. 7.104.3). But here the meaning is more positive (as both 'deep' and 'place' are positive terms in this and in other hymns of the *Rig Veda*), and the phrase more likely refers to the world of light under the earth, where the sun moves from West to East at night.

4. Agni.

5. Jātavedas. Cf. 10.16.

## 6.9 *Agni and the Young Poet*

A young poet, doubting his powers in the ritual competition (v. 2), seeks inspiration from Agni himself in solving the riddle of Agni, as usual a riddle of origins. The first and last verses (and v. 5) speak of the cosmic Agni, the sun that disappears at night (v. 1) or when he flees[1] or is simply not present before light is created (v. 7). He appears among mortals as the ritual fire (v. 4) and as the power of inspiration (5b–d), that teaches the poet how to surpass his own father (vv. 2–3); this inspiration transfigures the poet, but also makes him even more aware of the impossibility of describing Agni (v. 6).

1 The dark day and the bright day, the two realms of space,[2] turn by their own wisdom. As Agni Of-all-men was born, like a king he drove back the darkness with light.

2 I do not know how to stretch the thread, nor weave the cloth, nor what they[3] weave as they enter the contest. Whose son could speak here such words that he would be above and his father below?

3 He[4] is the one who knows how to stretch the thread and weave the cloth; he will speak the right words. He who understands this[5] is the guardian of immortality; though he moves below another, he sees above him.

4 This is the first priest of the oblation;[6] look at him. This is the immortal light among mortals. This is the one who was born and firmly fixed,[7] the immortal growing great in his body.

5 He is light firmly fixed for everyone to see,[8] the thought swiftest among all who fly. All the gods, with one mind and one will, rightly come to the one source of thought.[9]

6 My ears fly open, my eye opens, as does this light that is fixed in my heart. My mind flies up, straining into the distance. What shall I say? What shall I think?

7 All the gods bowed to you in fear, Agni, when you hid yourself in darkness.[10] May Agni Of-all-men save us with his help; may the immortal save us with his help.

## NOTES

1. Cf. 10.51 and 10.124.

2. Night and day, the dark and light sides of the sun, become part of the dark and light halves of the universe.

3. The other sages in the contest. For the image of weaving the sacrifice, cf. 10.130.1–2.

4. Agni himself, or the inspired poet.

5. The thread that stretches from earth to heaven, as well as the thread of inspiration that enables him to weave his poem; a form of the *axis mundi* as well as the spiritual link between gods and men.

6. The Hotṛ of whom Agni is the archetype. The invoker of the gods.

7. The ritual fire established in the tradition; also the sun fixed in the sky.

8. The sun, who sees all, is seen by all, and allows everyone to see.

9. Agni as the source of inspiration, or the man who knows Agni.

10. Cf. 10.51.5 and 10.124.1.

## 10.5 *The Hidden Agni*

Riddles and speculations about the nature of Agni make use of various tropes and metaphors familiar from other hymns, not only the Agni hymns but the cosmological and cosmogonic corpus and the meditations on the sacrifice. The image of the hidden and concealed Agni predominates and links the other images.

*1* The one sea with many births,[1] support of treasures, he sees out of our heart. He clings to the udder in the lap of the two who are concealed;[2] the path of the bird is hidden in the midst of the fountain.

*2* The buffaloes bursting with seed, veiling themselves have united with the mares in the same stable.[3] The poets hide the path of the Truth;[4] they keep secret their highest names.

*3* The two who are made of Truth yet made of magic have come together; they have made a child and given birth to him and made him grow. He is the navel of all that moves and is firm, who with his mind stretches the thread of the poet.

*4* For the waves of truth, the refreshing foods, have always clung to the well-born child for reward.[5] Wearing a cloak, the two world-halves made him grow on butter and food and honey.

*5* Full of desire, the wise one brought the seven red sisters out of the honey to see.[6] Born long ago, he was yoked in mid-air; seeking a robe to hide him, he found Pūṣan's.[7]

6 The poets fashioned seven boundaries; he who was trapped[8] went to only one of them. The pillar of life's vigour, he stands in the nest of the Highest, among the supports at the end of the paths.

7 Non-existence and existence are in the highest heaven, in the lap of Aditi and the birth of Dakṣa.[9] Agni is for us the first-born of Truth in the ancient vigour of life: the bull – and also the cow.[10]

NOTES

1. A double meaning: Agni himself is born many times, and he is responsible for many births.

2. Heaven and earth are the parents of Agni, but so are the two fire-sticks.

3. The flames of Agni are often feminine, but they are also called male buffaloes, bulls, or stallions full of seed; their 'stable' (literally, their nest, as in v. 6) is the wood in which they rest together with the females of the breed, also the flames. Or the male and female animals may be the male and female sticks.

4. *Ṛta*, often translated as 'Order' (cf. 1.164.11, 1.164.37, 1.164.47), in this late hymn, seems better translated as 'truth'.

5. The magic nourishment is part of the realm of Order or truth, embodied in Agni; these powers nurse him for pay, for the reward of maintaining their own prosperity and that of the world.

6. The seven sisters are the mares who are Agni's flames, here said to break out of the sweet butter poured on the fire. They come forth both to see and to be seen, a double meaning often attributed to the sun.

7. Symbolism relating to the birth of the sun, as well as to the concealment of Agni.

8. Literally, suffering from the feeling of being unable to move freely, a word often translated as 'in anguish' but here perhaps more literally hemmed in.

9. For existence and non-existence, cf. 10.129.1; for Dakṣa and Aditi, cf. 10.72.4.

10. The androgyny of Agni, already present in a veiled form in verse 2, here becomes explicit. For Parjanya as the bull and cow, see 5.83 and 7.101.

# SOMA

THE Soma plant is visualized in the *Rig Veda* as a god and as a liquid, pressed by stones in wooden bowls and filtered through a woollen sieve. These processes are described in some detail (9.74, 10.94) and are the inspiration for a rich cloth of imagery woven by the Vedic poet, an imagery also applied to the flowing of the sacrificial butter (4.58): women uniting with lovers, wild animals attacking, rivers flowing to the sea. Soma can be dangerous (8.79.7–8; 8.48.10) but the effects of drinking Soma are usually admired, or at least sought after: a sense of immense personal power (10.119, particularly valuable in the god Indra), intimations of immortality (9.113), the assurance of immortality (8.48), and the hallucinations of trance (10.136). Soma's form and activities are referred to in several other hymns in this collection: 8.91, 9.112, 10.85, 10.94, 10.109; the story of his descent from heaven (4.26–7) is the only episode in his mythology narrated in any detail.

## 8.79 *This Restless Soma*

*1* This restless Soma – you try to grab him but he breaks away and overpowers everything. He is a sage and a seer inspired by poetry.

*2* He covers the naked and heals all who are sick. The blind man sees; the lame man steps forth.

*3* Soma, you are a broad defence against those who hate us, both enemies we have made ourselves and those made by others.

*4* Through your knowledge and skills, rushing forward you drive out of the sky and the earth the evil deed of the enemy.

*5* Let those who seek find what they seek: let them receive the treasure given by the generous and stop the greedy from getting what they want.

*6* Let him[1] find what was lost before; let him push forward the man of truth. Let him stretch out the life-span that has not yet crossed its span.

*7* Be kind and merciful to us, Soma; be good to our heart, without confusing our powers in your whirlwind.

*8* King Soma, do not enrage us; do not terrify us; do not wound our heart with dazzling light.

*9* Give help, when you see the evil plans of the gods in your own house.[2] Generous king, keep away hatreds, keep away failures.

NOTES

1. Soma or the man inspired by Soma.

2. Soma is asked to intercede for the worshipper among the other gods, as Agni often does.

## 9.74 *Soma Pressed in the Bowls*

This hymn describes in metaphors the pressing of Soma in the Soma-bowls and the pouring of the juices through a filter made of wool. The processes are likened to the milking of rain out of the clouds and the downpouring of the torrents upon the earth; to the pouring of seed into a womb to produce children; and to the winning of a race. In addition to their function as metaphors, these images serve also to express the goals of life that the poet hopes will be achieved by the Soma sacrifice: rain, fertility, and wealth. Cows appear in all of these metaphors: as symbols of the milk or water with which the Soma is mixed; as clouds from which rain is milked; as women who bear children; and as the prize to be won by the racehorse. Soma appears sometimes as a male animal (calf, horse, bull), sometimes as a female (identified with the cows), like Parjanya and Agni in other hymns; he is further identified with more abstract and general forms such as the navel of Order, the pillar of the sky (here identified with the stalk of the Soma plant), and the pasture or lap of Aditi – the highest heaven (here identified with the Soma bowl). The metaphors intertwine in many ways, as when rain is called the seed of the sky or the water in the bowl is called a wave of the cosmic ocean.

*1* Like a new-born child he bellows in the wood,[1] the tawny racehorse straining to win the sun. He unites with the sky's seed that grows great with milk.[2] With kind thoughts we pray to him for far-reaching shelter.

*2* He who is the pillar of the sky, the well-adorned support, the full stalk that encircles all around, he is the one who by tradition sacrifices to these two great world-halves. The poet[3] holds together the conjoined pair, and the refreshing foods.

*3* The honey of Soma is a great feast; the wide pasture of Aditi is for the man who follows the right way. Child of dawn, the bull who rules over the rain here, leader of the waters, worthy of hymns, he is the one who brings help here.

*4* Butter and milk are milked from the living cloud; the navel of Order, the ambrosia is born. Together those who

bring fine gifts satisfy him; the swollen men[4] piss down
the fluid set in motion.
5 The stalk roared as it united with the wave;[5] for man he
swells the skin that attracts the gods. He places in the
lap of Aditi the seed by which we win sons and grand-
sons.
6 Relentlessly they[6] flow down into the filter of a thousand
streams; let them have offspring in the third realm of
the world. Four hidden springs pouring forth butter
carry down from the sky the ambrosia that is the oblation.
7 He takes on a white colour when he strains to win; Soma,
the generous Asura, knows the whole world. He clings
to inspired thought and ritual action as he goes forth;
let him hurl down from the sky the cask full of water.
8 Now he has gone to the white pot coated by cows; the
racehorse has reached the winning line and has won
a hundred cows for Kakṣīvat, the man of a hundred
winters.[7] Longing for the gods in their heart, they[8]
hasten forth.
9 Clarifying Soma, when you are sated with waters your
juice runs through the sieve made of wool. Polished by
the poets, Soma who brings supreme ecstasy, be sweet
for Indra to drink.

## NOTES

1. Soma as a new-born calf or horse wanders in the 'forest' of the wooden pressing-bowls.

2. The seed of heaven is the rain that mixes with the milk of the clouds, as Soma mixes with the milk in the bowls.

3. Soma is identified with the sun, who is called a poet, propping apart and holding together the pair of sky and earth, his parents.

4. The Maruts are the swollen men (clouds) who urinate the Soma (a male image) after it has been milked from the clouds (a female image). Soma is the living, androgynous cloud from which milk and rain are pressed.

5. Soma is the stalk; the wave is the water that mixes with it. The skin of the plant swells like the leather water-skin likened to the

rain-clouds (cf. 1.85.5, 5.83.7) or the overturned cask (v. 7), both attributes of Parjanya.

6. The streams of Soma likened to rains are to have their 'offspring' in the third realm, for the floods of rain renew themselves in heaven. Cf. 1.164.

7. Kakṣīvat, said to have been saved by the Aśvins (1.116.7), may have regained his youth, as did many others helped by the Aśvins.

8. The Soma juices, or the priests.

## 10.94 *The Pressing-Stones*

A hymn to the stones that press the Soma juice. The noise that they make while grinding the stalks of the plant, and their action in devouring (i.e. destroying) the fibres while releasing the juices, suggest the actions of animals (cows, bulls, horses) that growl or bellow and swallow the liquid.

*1* Let them[1] raise their voices, and let us raise our voices. Speak your speech[2] to the stones that speak, when you stones, you mountains full of Soma, rush to bring the rhythmic sound to Indra.

*2* They speak in a hundred ways, a thousand ways, howling with their green jaws.[3] Working busily and well to do the good work, the stones have succeeded in eating the oblation even before the priest of the oblation.

*3* They speak: they have found the honey. They growl and gnaw on the cooked meat.[4] As they snap at the branch of the red tree,[5] the bulls who have grazed well begin to bellow.

*4* They speak loudly, excited by the exhilarating drink. They shout to Indra: they have found the honey. Artfully they danced with the sisters that embrace them,[6] making the earth echo with their stampings.

*5* The eagles have sent their cry up to the sky. Ardently the dark hinds danced in the meadow. They plunge deep to the rendezvous with the lower stone; they infuse it with floods of the seed of the sun-bright one.[7]

*6* Like brawny draught animals yoked together, these

bulls bear the shaft and pull as a team. When they bellow, panting and chewing the cud, they sound like race-horses whinnying.

7 Sing to them that have ten girths,[8] ten yoke-straps, ten harnesses, ten reins that never wear out, to them that are yoked ten times to bear ten shafts.

8 The stones are swift horses; their bridle with ten thongs fits them comfortably. They have tasted the filtered juice of the first pressing of the Soma juice milked from the stalk.

9 These Soma-eaters kiss Indra's pair of bays. As they milk the stalk they sit upon the ox.[9] When Indra has drunk the honey they have milked he grows great and acts like a bull.

10 Your stalk is a bull; surely you will not be harmed. You are always overflowing with nourishment, sated with food. You are lovely in your splendour like the daughter of a rich man at whose sacrifice you stones rejoice.

11 Porous or not porous, the stones never tire, never rest, never die; they are never sick or old or shaken by passion; nicely fat, they are free from thirst and desire.

12 Your fathers[10] are entirely firm in age after age; peace-loving, they do not budge from their spot. Untouched by age, the companions of the tawny one[11] are like the saffron tree;[12] they have made the sky and the earth listen to their uproar.

13 The stones speak the same when they are unyoked and when they are on their journey, with their stampings like the noises of men who drink deeply. Like those who sow seed and grow grain, they gobble up the Soma without diminishing it as they lap it up.

14 They have raised their voices for the sacrificial juice, like playful children jostling a mother. Set free the inspiration of the one who presses Soma, and let the stones that we hold in awe return to being stones.[13]

## NOTES

1. The stones are first referred to, and then are addressed after the priests, at the end of the verse.

2. Here the poet addresses the priests, whose chants of invocation to Indra are equated with the noise of the stones that Indra hears.

3. Their jaws are green with the juice of the Soma plant, also called yellow, red (as in v. 3), or tawny.

4. Soma is here imagined as a sacrificial animal eaten by the stones.

5. Soma.

6. The ten fingers that hold the stones.

7. Soma.

8. The ten fingers again, here imagined as draught animals as in the previous verse.

9. The Soma stalks are placed upon an oxhide.

10. The mountains, as in verse 1, are the fathers of the stones.

11. Soma is the tawny one; as he grows in the mountains, they are his companions.

12. The stones (or the mountains) become yellow through contact with Soma.

13. That is, lose those awesome qualities that they took on during the ritual and return to being mere stones. The ritual objects must be desanctified after the ritual.

## 4.58 *Butter*

The clarified butter is visualized in three forms (v. 3): as the actual butter used as the oblation, as the Soma juice, and as perfected speech in the heart of the poet.

*1* The wave of honey arose out of the ocean; mingling with the stalk,[1] it became the elixir of immortality, that is the secret name of butter: 'tongue of the gods', 'navel of immortality'.

*2* We will proclaim the name of butter; we will sustain it in this sacrifice by bowing low. When it has been pronounced, let the Brahmin priest hear it. This four-horned buffalo[2] has let it slip out.[3]

*3* Four horns, three feet has he; two heads and seven

hands has he. Bound threefold, the bull bellows. The great god has entered mortals.

4 In the cow the gods found the butter that had been divided into three parts and hidden by the Paṇis.[4] Indra brought forth one form, Sūrya one, and from the very substance of Vena[5] they fashioned one.

5 These streams of butter flow from the ocean of the heart,[6] enclosed by a hundred fences so that the enemy cannot see them. I gaze upon them; the golden reed[7] is in their midst.

6 Our words flow together like rivers, made clear by understanding deep within the heart.[8] These waves of butter flow like gazelles fleeing before a hunter.

7 Like whirlpools in the current of a river, the young streams of butter surge forth and swell with the waves, overtaking the wind like a chestnut racehorse that breaks through the sides of the track.[9]

8 Smiling, the streams of butter rush to Agni like beautiful women to a festival. They touch the fuel-sticks, and Agni joyously woos them.

9 I gaze upon them. They are like girls anointing themselves with perfumed oil to go to a wedding. Where Soma is pressed, where there is a sacrifice, there the streams of butter are made clear.

10 Let a fine song of praise flow forth, and a race that wins cows. Bring us auspicious riches. Lead this sacrifice of ours to the gods. The honeyed streams of butter become clear.

11 The whole universe is set in your essence within the ocean, within the heart, in the life-span.[10] Let us win your honeyed wave that is brought to the face of the waters as they flow together.

## NOTES

1. The Soma stalk mixes with the water to make the juice of immortality.

2. Soma is imagined as a buffalo and, in the next verse, as a bull.

3. He emits the secret, the Soma, and his seed, all as butter.

4. Indra released the cows that had been penned up by the Paṇis (human and demonic enemies of the invading Indo-Aryans), finding the butter (Soma as milk) within them. Cf. 3.31 and 10.108.

5. The seer identified with the sun-bird. Cf. 10.123.

6. The Soma juices, once imbibed, are said to be in the heart, as is the poet's inspiration.

7. The Soma plant full of butter and seed.

8. Soma is clarified in the filter, butter is clarified by boiling, and thought is clarified in the heart.

9. The track is simultaneously the fence around the race-track, the banks of the river, and the normal channels of thought.

10. The life-span belongs both to butter (that gives immortality, as Soma) and to the poet (whose inspiration, in the ocean that is his heart, gives him immortality).

## 4.26–7 *Soma and Indra and the Eagle*

These two closely related hymns centre upon the myth of the theft of the elixir of immortality. This Indo-European theme appears in Russia as the fire-bird and in Greece as the myth of Prometheus – for Soma is the 'fiery juice', simultaneously fire and water (Agni-Ṣomau), that gives immortality. Soma is born in heaven (or in the mountains) and closely guarded by demonic powers; an eagle carries Indra to heaven to bring the Soma to men and gods (or an eagle brings the Soma to Indra – cf. 4.18.13), escaping with merely the loss of a single feather from the one shot loosed by the guardian archer.

The first hymn begins with a song of drunken self-praise by Indra (vv. 1–4; cf. 10.119) and then tells the story of the eagle (vv. 5–7). The second hymn begins with the self-praise of the eagle (v. 1), then a verse spoken by Soma, and a return to the narration of the myth.

### 4.26

*1* [*Indra:*] 'I was Manu and I was the Sun;[1] I am Kakṣīvat, the wise sage.[2] I surpassed Kutsa the son of Arjuna;[3] I am the inspired Uśanas[4] – look at me!

2 'I gave the earth to the Āryan; I gave rain to the mortal
who made an offering. I led forth the roaring water;[5]
the gods followed after my wish.
3 'Ecstatic with Soma I shattered the nine and ninety
fortresses of Śambara[6] all at once, finishing off the
inhabitant as the hundredth, as I gave aid to Divodāsa
Atithigva.
4 'O Maruts, the bird shall be supreme above all birds, the
swift-flying eagle above all eagles, since by his own
driving power that needs no chariot wheels, with his
powerful wings he brought to man the oblation loved by
the gods.'
5 Fluttering[7] as he brought it[8] down, the bird swift as
thought shot forth on the wide path; swiftly the eagle
came with the honey of Soma and won fame for that.
6 Stretching out in flight, holding the stem, the eagle
brought the exhilarating and intoxicating drink from
the distance. Accompanied by the gods,[9] the bird
clutched the Soma tightly after he took it from that
highest heaven.
7 When the eagle had taken the Soma, he brought it
for a thousand and ten thousand pressings at once.
The bringer of abundance[10] left his enemies behind
there; ecstatic with Soma, the wise one left the fools.

4.27

1 [*The eagle:*] 'While still in the womb, I knew all the
generations of these gods. A hundred iron fortresses
guarded me,[11] but I, the eagle,[12] swiftly flew away.'
2 [*Soma:*] 'He[13] did not drag me out against my will, for
I surpassed him in energy and manly strength. In a
flash, the bringer of abundance left his enemies behind as
he outran the winds, swelling with power.'
3 As the eagle came shrieking down from heaven, and as
they[14] led the bringer of abundance down from there
like the wind, as the archer Kṛśānu,[15] reacting quickly,
aimed down at him and let loose his bowstring,

4 the eagle bearing Indra brought him down like Bhujyu[16] from the summits of heaven, stretching out in swift flight. Then a wing feather[17] fell in mid-air[18] from the bird as he swooped on the path of flight.

5 The white goblet overflowing with cows' milk, the finest honey, the clear juice offered by the priests[19] – now let the generous Indra raise it to drink until ecstatic with Soma; let the hero raise it to drink until ecstatic with Soma.

## NOTES

1. In his ecstatic sense of self-importance and omnipotence, Indra identifies himself with various mythic personages; the sun is another form of the prize won by the celestial fire-bird (or, in other variants, the sun is the fire-bird himself), and Manu, the eponymous ancestor of mankind, is the one to whom the Soma is brought (v. 4).

2. Indra identifies himself with the sage whom he inspires. Cf. Kakṣīvat in 9.74.8.

3. Indra and Kutsa are sometimes enemies in the *Rig Veda*, sometimes allies in feats such as fighting with the serpent Śuṣṇa and stealing the solar disc.

4. Uśanas is an inspired sage and priest.

5. By destroying the fortresses of the demons, Indra releases the waters; cf. 1.32.

6. A demon, the enemy of Indra and of Divodāsa; with Indra's help, Divodāsa destroys the demon's fortresses that imprison the eagle with the Soma.

7. In fear of the archer shooting at him (4.27.3).

8. The Soma.

9. The gods as the attendants of Indra.

10. Indra, perhaps riding on the eagle. Elsewhere (cf. 1.116.13), the bringer of abundance (Purandhi) is a female divinity.

11. Again an allusion to the demon's fortresses (cf. 4.26.3), in which the eagle is kept; perhaps the Soma was guarded there and the eagle was kept there after the theft, though Soma may have been imprisoned alone earlier in order to forestall the theft.

12. The eagle boasts in response to Indra's praise of him (4.26.4).

13. The eagle, or Indra riding on the eagle.

14. Probably the gods, or perhaps the winds mentioned in the previous verse.

15. A demon placed as guardian over the Soma.

16. The Aśvins rescued Bhujyu from the ocean. Cf. 1.116.3–4.

17. The feather turned into a plant used as a substitute for the Soma plant.

18. Half-way between sky and earth.

19. The Adhvaryus, responsible for the performance of the Soma ritual.

## 10.119 *The Soma-Drinker Praises Himself*

Under the influence of the drug Soma, a sage or god praises himself.[1] The god may be Indra or Agni, though the former is more likely and is supported by the Indian commentarial tradition; either god may be incarnate in the worshipper speaking the hymn. As he drinks, his boasts become progressively more Gargantuan.

*1* This, yes, this is my thought: I will win[2] a cow and a horse. Have I not drunk Soma?

*2* Like impetuous winds, the drinks have lifted me up. Have I not drunk Soma?

*3* The drinks have lifted me up, like swift horses bolting with a chariot. Have I not drunk Soma?

*4* The prayer has come to me[3] as a lowing cow comes to her beloved son. Have I not drunk Soma?

*5* I turn the prayer around in my[3] heart, as a wheelwright turns a chariot seat. Have I not drunk Soma?

*6* The five tribes[4] are no more to me than a mote in the eye.[5] Have I not drunk Soma?

*7* The two world halves[6] cannot be set against[7] a single wing of mine.[8] Have I not drunk Soma?

*8* In my vastness, I surpassed the sky and this vast earth. Have I not drunk Soma?

*9* Yes! I will place the earth here, or perhaps there. Have I not drunk Soma?

*10* I will thrash the earth soundly, here, or perhaps there. Have I not drunk Soma?

*11* One of my wings is in the sky; I have trailed the other below.[9] Have I not drunk Soma?

*12* I am huge, huge! flying to the cloud. Have I not drunk Soma?

*13* I am going[10] – a well-stocked house, carrying the oblation to the gods.[11] Have I not drunk Soma?

NOTES

1. Cf. 4.26.1–3, 4.27.1.

2. The verb can mean to win for oneself or for someone else. If Indra is speaking, he wants them for himself; if Agni, to transmit to the other gods or to give to the poet; if the poet, to give to the gods. Since the poet imagines that he has become a god, all of these meanings are simultaneously present.

3. As a god, he receives the prayer and 'turns it around' to decide whether or not to accept it; as a poet, he receives the inspiration of the prayer and 'turns it around' to perfect it.

4. The whole of the Vedic tribal world.

5. Alternatively, worth no more than a glance.

6. Sky and earth.

7. 'Set against' both in the sense of set in opposition to and set up as equal to.

8. Agni takes the form of a bird or a winged horse, but the poet may simply feel that he is flying, a frequent symptom of drug-induced ecstasy. Cf. 10.136.2–4.

9. He imagines himself to have grown so large that he touches heaven and earth at the same time.

10. A salutation of farewell, as he heads for heaven and the gods.

11. A compound image, of a house full of Soma (his stomach being the larder), a flying palace (common in later Indian mythology), and the god Agni carrying the oblation – the Soma – to the gods.

## 9.113 *The Ecstasy of Soma*

The poet begins by inviting Indra to drink Soma with him and then invokes Soma for himself, praising him. He then asks Soma to make him immortal, as he becomes inspired under the hallucinogenic influence of the drug (v. 6).

*1* Let Indra the killer of Vṛtra drink Soma in Śaryaṇāvat,[1] gathering his strength within himself, to do a great heroic deed. O drop of Soma, flow for Indra.

*2* Purify yourself, generous Soma from Ārjīka,[1] master of the quarters of the sky. Pressed with sacred words, with truth and faith and ardour,[2] O drop of Soma, flow for Indra.

*3* The daughter of the sun has brought the buffalo raised by Parjanya.[3] The divine youths have received him and placed the juice in Soma. O drop of Soma, flow for Indra.

*4* You speak of the sacred, as your brightness is sacred; you speak the truth, as your deeds are true.[4] You speak of faith, King Soma, as you are carefully prepared by the sacrificial priest. O drop of Soma, flow for Indra.

*5* The floods of the high one, the truly awesome one, flow together. The juices of him so full of juice mingle together as you, the tawny one, purify yourself with prayer. O drop of Soma, flow for Indra.

*6* Where the high priest speaks rhythmic words, O Purifier, holding the pressing-stone, feeling that he has become great with the Soma, giving birth to joy through the Soma, O drop of Soma, flow for Indra.

*7* Where the inextinguishable light shines, the world where the sun was placed, in that immortal, unfading world, O Purifier, place me. O drop of Soma, flow for Indra.

*8* Where Vivasvan's son is king,[5] where heaven is enclosed, where those young waters are[6] – there make me immortal. O drop of Soma, flow for Indra.

*9* Where they move as they will, in the triple dome, in the third heaven of heaven, where the worlds are made of light, there make me immortal. O drop of Soma, flow for Indra.

*10* Where there are desires and longings, at the sun's zenith,

where the dead are fed and satisfied,[5] there make me
immortal. O drop of Soma, flow for Indra.

11 Where there are joys and pleasures, gladness and delight,
where the desires of desire are fulfilled, there make me
immortal. O drop of Soma, flow for Indra.

NOTES

1. The mountains where Soma is found.

2. *Tapas*, the heat generated by sacrificial activity (and, later, by asceticism).

3. The daughter of the sun is the wife of Soma; Soma is sometimes called a buffalo (or a bull or stallion); Parjanya, god of fructifying rain, makes Soma and other plants grow (cf. 5.83.1, 5.83.5, 5.83.10; 7.101.2, 7.101.6).

4. That is, the deeds done under the influence of Soma are true (cf. *in vino veritas*).

5. Yama, the son of Vivasvan, is king in the world of the dead, here (and elsewhere in the *Rig Veda*) thought of as being in heaven, where the dead are nourished by the offerings made to them by their descendants.

6. The cosmic waters born in heaven.

## 8.48 *We Have Drunk the Soma*

This hymn celebrates the effects of Soma, particularly the feeling of being set free and released into boundless open space, and the belief that the drinker is immortal.

1 I have tasted the sweet drink of life, knowing that it
inspires good thoughts and joyous expansiveness to the
extreme, that all the gods and mortals seek it together,
calling it honey.[1]

2 When you penetrate inside, you will know no limits,[2]
and you will avert the wrath of the gods. Enjoying
Indra's friendship, O drop of Soma, bring riches as a
docile cow[3] brings the yoke.

3 We have drunk the Soma; we have become immortal;[4]
we have gone to the light; we have found the gods. What

can hatred and the malice of a mortal do to us now, O immortal one?

4 When we have drunk you, O drop of Soma, be good to our heart, kind as a father to his son, thoughtful as a friend to a friend. Far-famed Soma, stretch out[5] our life-span so that we may live.

5 The glorious drops that I have drunk set me free in wide space. You have bound me together in my limbs as thongs bind a chariot. Let the drops protect me from the foot that stumbles[6] and keep lameness away from me.

6 Inflame me like a fire kindled by friction; make us see far; make us richer, better. For when I am intoxicated with you, Soma, I think myself rich. Draw near and make us thrive.

7 We would enjoy you, pressed with a fervent heart, like riches from a father. King Soma, stretch out our life-spans as the sun stretches the spring days.

8 King Soma, have mercy on us for our well-being. Know that we are devoted to your laws. Passion and fury are stirred up.[7] O drop of Soma, do not hand us over to the pleasure of the enemy.

9 For you, Soma, are the guardian of our body; watching over men, you have settled down in every limb. If we break your laws, O god, have mercy on us like a good friend, to make us better.

10 Let me join closely with my compassionate friend[8] so that he will not injure me when I have drunk him. O lord of bay horses,[9] for the Soma that is lodged in us I approach Indra to stretch out our life-span.

11 Weaknesses and diseases have gone; the forces of darkness[10] have fled in terror. Soma has climbed up in us, expanding. We have come to the place where they stretch out life-spans.

12 The drop that we have drunk has entered our hearts, an immortal inside mortals. O fathers,[11] let us serve that Soma with the oblations and abide in his mercy and kindness.

13 Uniting in agreement with the fathers, O drop of Soma, you have extended yourself through sky and earth. Let us serve him with an oblation; let us be masters of riches.
14 You protecting gods, speak out for us. Do not let sleep or harmful speech[12] seize us. Let us, always dear to Soma, speak as men of power in the sacrificial gathering.
15 Soma, you give us the force of life on every side. Enter into us, finding the sunlight, watching over men. O drop of Soma, summon your helpers and protect us before and after.[13]

## NOTES

1. Here, as elsewhere in the hymns to Soma, honey is not a reference to the product of bees or the Indo-European mead made from it, but refers to the essence and sweetness of the ambrosia.

2. Inside the human body, the Soma becomes 'boundless' in the sense of producing a feeling of infinite expansion, a sensation characteristic of psychedelic drugs. But the word (*aditi*) may also be taken as the proper name of the goddess Aditi, for Soma is called the youngest son of Aditi and Aditi's function of liberating from sin might be relevant here: Soma, Aditi's son, purifies from within and pacifies the angry gods.

3. The term denotes an obedient female animal, probably a draught animal; it could be a mare or a cow. Cf. Dawn harnessing docile cows to her chariot in order to bring treasure to the singer (1.92.2). These animals, though naturally fierce in the Indo-European world, were also capable of being tamed.

4. The poet has a vision of what life in heaven would be like, a kind of vague, temporary immortality, lasting 'a long time'.

5. The verb means to cross in a forward direction, as one would cross a river, to push the farther bank of the life-span farther away. Cf. ŚB 11.1.6.6, in which Prajāpati sees the end of his life as one would see the farther bank of a river. The metaphor is repeated in vv. 7 and 10–11, and the idea of prolonging life (or of obtaining the limited immortality which consists in a full life-span) is central to the hymn. Cf. also the recurrent Vedic themes of 'stretching the thread' of the sacrifice and expanding in space.

6. The releasing effect of the drug described in the first part of this verse is immediately contrasted with a binding, perhaps by

Soma, perhaps by someone else, and then with some sort of stumbling; this stumbling may involve actual injury, prefigured in the 'binding with thongs' and followed by the 'lameness' of the next phrase. The verse may also imply more metaphysical mistakes, but the literal meaning might refer to stumbling and falling in physical clumsiness as a result of the ecstasy induced by Soma.

7. Soma stirs not only the emotions of the drinkers but also the unpredictable emotions of the enemy mentioned in the next phrase.

8. Soma.

9. Indra, here as elsewhere identified with Soma. The singer approaches Indra to come 'for' Soma in the sense of 'in order to enjoy' Soma or 'in return for being given' Soma, but in any case to act, like Soma, to prolong life, or even to allow Soma to remain in the belly for a long time.

10. Personified as females.

11. The fathers, as drinkers of Soma, are called to witness.

12. 'Harmful speech' may mean injurious slander or may refer to the violation of the vows of remaining awake and silent in the rite of initiation into the Soma sacrifice. Cf. 10.18.14.

13. The worshipper asks to be surrounded and protected now and forever in his drug-induced vulnerability.

## 10.136 *The Long-haired Ascetic*

The long-haired ascetic (Keśin), an early precursor of the Upaniṣadic yogi, drinks a drug (probably some hallucinogen other than Soma) in the company of Rudra, the master of poison and a god who is excluded from the Soma sacrifice. The hallucinations described in the hymn are related to but not the same as those attributed to Soma-drinkers in 9.112, 10.119, etc.

*1* Long-hair holds fire, holds the drug, holds sky and earth. Long-hair reveals everything, so that everyone can see the sun.[1] Long-hair declares the light.

*2* These ascetics, swathed in wind,[2] put dirty red rags on.[3] When gods enter them, they ride with the rush of the wind.

3 'Crazy with asceticism, we have mounted the wind.[4] Our bodies are all you mere mortals can see.'

4 He sails through the air, looking down on all shapes below.[5] The ascetic is friend to this god and that god, devoted to what is well done.

5 The stallion of the wind, friend of gales, lashed on by gods – the ascetic lives in the two seas, on the east and on the west.

6 He moves with the motion of heavenly girls[6] and youths, of wild beasts. Long-hair, reading their minds, is their sweet, their most exciting friend.

7 The wind has churned it[7] up; Kunaṃnamā[8] prepared it for him. Long-hair drinks from the cup, sharing the drug[9] with Rudra.

## NOTES

1. This act is attributed to other Vedic gods, too. Cf. 1.50.5.

2. That is, they are naked; but the connection with the wind is also literally important, as in verses 3, 5, and 7.

3. Some are naked, some wear red (later saffron) rags.

4. The ascetic rides the wind as if it were a horse; cf. v. 5. The ascetic controls the wind by controlling his own breath.

5. This act is often attributed to the sun. The ecstatic ascetic takes on the characteristics of several gods. The verse also describes the sensation of flying outside of one's own body, observed below (cf. v. 3).

6. The Apsarases or nymphs of heaven, with their companions the Gandharvas.

7. The drug.

8. A female deity who appears only here; her name may indicate a witch or a hunchback.

9. *Viṣa*, a drug or poison.

# INDRA

INDRA, the king of the gods, is frequently mentioned in hymns to other gods. As the great Soma-drinker, he appears often in the Soma hymns (cf. 10.119), and it is he who lures Agni away from the waters or the demons (10.51, 10.124). He is central to hymns about the Maruts (1.165, 1.170–71), Atri (5.40), Apālā (8.91), and Vṛṣākapi (10.86), and appears as a very important bit player in many others.

Indra's family life is troubled in ways that remain unclear. His birth, like that of many great warriors and heroes, is unnatural; there are also strong hints that he may have killed his father (4.18). So, too, he is in turn challenged by his own son, whom he apparently overcomes (10.28). The incestuous implications in these relationships may have led the Vedic poet to append to one of the Indra hymns the tale of another incestuous birth and infancy, apparently that of Agni (3.31.1–3; cf. 5.2.1).

But the hymns return again and again to clearer and more straightforward stories: the heroic deeds of Indra. The killing of Vṛtra (1.32) is frequently alluded to in other hymns, as is the freeing of the cows in the cave (3.31, 10.108), which shares much of the symbolism and significance of the battle with Vṛtra. Other deeds, such as the beheading of the sacrifice (10.171), are mentioned without being fully explained in the *Rig Veda*, though later mythological texts often expand upon them.

Indra's famous generosity – particularly when he is exultant from copious draughts of Soma – and his endearing anthropomorphism embolden the poet to imagine himself in Indra's place (8.14). These same qualities, however, may have led worshippers even in Vedic times to devalue Indra, the beginning of a process that culminates in his total loss of worship in the Hindu period; in answer to these implicit expressions of doubt, the poet reaffirms his faith in Indra as the greatest of the Vedic warrior gods (2.12).

## 4.18 *The Birth and Childhood Deeds of Indra*

This obscure dialogue is partially illuminated by the recognition of its place in Indo-European mythology: it refers, in purposely mysterious tones, to the story of a male god concealed by his mother from a father who threatens to kill him, a father whom he himself then kills. The hymn alternates between narrative and direct discourse, the latter spoken by Indra and his mother, the former by the poet who questions them and elicits answers that attempt to vindicate and justify the actions of the two protagonists. None of the principals in the drama is named except Indra; later commentary identifies the mother with Aditi and the father with Tvaṣṭṛ (who appears in the hymn, though not explicitly as the father).

The hymn begins with the story of Indra's birth: his mother kept him in the womb for many years (v. 4), not, she insists, in absence of maternal feeling but for Indra's sake – i.e. to protect him; the hymn does not tell us why this was necessary, but it may well be because his father was jealous of Indra's great powers (v. 5), a suspicion ultimately proved valid when Indra kills his father (v. 12). As the dialogue begins, Indra is still inside the womb and wishes to break out through her side; she attempts to dissuade him (v. 1), but he insists on being born (v. 2). She then hides him (v. 3), presumably still in fear of his father. Again Indra refuses to be protected, but follows her to Tvaṣṭṛ's house, where he drinks the Soma (v. 3). In response to the narrator's accusations (vv. 4–5), she calls upon the waters to witness her good motives in treating Indra as she did (vv. 6–7), and speaks of being guiltless of the wounds Indra incurred in fighting the demon Vṛtra (vv. 8–9), who is analogized with Indra's father. The narrator then recapitulates the story of Indra's birth (v. 10) and the slaying of Vṛtra, in which Viṣṇu came to Indra's aid (v. 11). Upon being questioned about killing his father (v. 12), Indra protests that he had no choice, being in terrible danger until the eagle brought him the Soma (v. 13).

1 [*Indra's mother:*] 'This[1] is the ancient, proven path by
which all the gods were born and moved upward. By this
very path he should be born when he has grown great.
He should not make his mother perish in that way.'[2]
2 [*Indra:*] 'I cannot come out by that path; these are bad
places to go through. I will come out cross-wise, through
the side. Many things yet undone must I do; one[3] I will
fight, and one[4] I will question.'
3 [*Narrator:*] He watched his mother as she went away:[5]
'I cannot help following: I will follow.' In Tvaṣṭṛ's house
Indra drank the Soma[6] worth a hundred cows, pressed
in the two bowls.
4 Why has she pushed him far away, whom she carried for
a thousand months and many autumns? For there is no
one his equal among those who are born and those who
will be born.[7]
5 As if she thought he was flawed,[8] his mother hid Indra
though he abounded in manly strength. Then he stood
up and put his garment on by himself; as he was born he
filled the two world-halves.
6 [*Indra's mother:*] 'These waters[9] flow happily, shouting
"Alalā!", waters that were screaming together like right-
eous women.[10] Ask them what they are saying, what en-
circling mountain[11] the waters burst apart.
7 'Are they speaking words of praise and invitation[12] to
him? Do the waters wish to take on themselves the flaw
of Indra?[13] With his great weapon my son killed Vṛtra
and set these rivers free.
8 'Still a young woman, I did not throw you away for my
sake; nor did Evil-childbirth[14] swallow you up for my
sake. But for my sake the waters were kind to the child,[15]
and for my sake Indra stood up at once.
9 'Not for my sake did the shoulderless one[16] wound you,
generous Indra, and strike away your two jaws;[17]
though wounded, you overpowered him, and with your
weapon you crushed the head of the Dāsa.'[18]
10 [*Narrator:*] The heifer[19] gave birth to the firm, strong,

unassailable bull, the stout Indra. The mother let her calf
wander unlicked,[20] to seek his own ways by himself.
11 And the mother turned to the buffalo:[21] 'My son, the
gods here are deserting you.'[22] Then Indra, wanting to
kill Vṛtra, said, 'Viṣṇu, my friend, stride as far as you
can.'[23]
12 Who made your mother a widow?[24] Who wished to kill
you when you were lying still or moving?[25] What god
helped you when you grabbed your father by the foot and
crushed him?[26]
13 [*Indra:*] 'Because I was in desperate straits, I cooked the
entrails of a dog,[27] and I found no one among the gods
to help me. I saw my woman[28] dishonoured. Then the
eagle brought the honey to me.'[29]

## NOTES

1. The conventional birth passage through the womb; Indra, like so many folk heroes, refuses to be born in this way. Cf. Soma talking in the womb, 4.27.1.

2. She argues that he will kill her if he bursts out through her side. In fact, several Indian mythological heroes (including the Buddha) are conceived and/or born through the side without injury to the parent (as is about to be the case with Indra now), but some do indeed kill their mothers (or androgynous fathers) in this way.

3. Vṛtra, who is alluded to several times in this hymn.

4. The verb 'to question' here contrasts with the verb 'to fight', and indicates that Indra will either speak to make a treaty (with Viṣṇu) or speak before killing (Tvaṣṭṛ). The former seems more likely; the question that he asks of Viṣṇu is the request to have him stride forward (v. 11).

5. The commentator says that she died, but the hymn makes this unlikely; she merely abandons him, as the true mother of the Indo-European hero usually does. Cf. 5.2.1–2, where Agni's mother hides him from his father for many years in her womb.

6. According to later tradition, Indra killed Tvaṣṭṛ in order to get the Soma away from him.

7. The argument is either, Why did she try to kill him when she

knew he was so powerful that he couldn't be killed, or, Why did she try to kill him when she knew he was destined to be a great hero? In fact, she merely pushed him away in order to preserve him, but one is reminded of the mother of Mārtāṇḍa, Aditi (who is traditionally identified as the mother of Indra as well), who pushed her son away to kill him (10.72.8).

8. The flaw may be a physical birth flaw such as Mārtāṇḍa had, the cause of Aditi's rejection of him. Again, this suspicion is invalid: Indra is *not* physically flawed. But the phrase may also foreshadow the moral flaw which is to be a problem to Indra, the guilt of the slaughter of Vṛtra, alluded to in verse 7.

9. The waters set free when Vṛtra was killed (1.32.1, 1.32.8, 1.32.11–12, etc.). Also, perhaps, the waters in which Indra was placed to hide him from danger (cf. 1.32.10 and 10.51).

10. At first the waters scream for help when Vṛtra assaults them; then they chortle onomatopoetically when they are set free.

11. The cavern where Vṛtra kept the waters penned up. Cf. 1.32.11 and 3.31.5.

12. A technical term for a formula of praise and laudatory epithets, used to call a god.

13. The flaw or stain is the sin incurred in killing Vṛtra. Later myths narrate at great length the way in which Indra asked the waters (and other creatures) to take upon themselves a portion of this stain.

14. This may be the name of a demonness who swallows children, whose name indicates that she brings evil to those in childbirth (i.e. causes the death of the child or the mother or both) or brings forth evil. More likely, however, it is the name of the river who 'swallows up' Indra – not for the sake of his mother (i.e. not because she was a rejecting mother), but for *his* sake – to save him from danger.

15. The mercy of the waters may be their kindness in adopting him when his mother was forced to abandon him, or their willingness to forgive him for the sin of killing the demon (for their benefit) and to take part of the sin upon them. Indra's mother takes credit for persuading them to do this, and for letting Indra stand up at once, though earlier (v. 5) the poet emphasizes that Indra did this despite her efforts to hide him.

16. Vṛtra. Cf. 1.32.5.

17. Elsewhere it is said that Vṛtra wounded Indra in this way, shattering his jaws (1.32.12). Indra's mother seems to be saying that

it wasn't *her* fault that Indra got into such trouble; *she* had tried to keep him safe in her womb.

18. The serpent is identified with the native enemy, or slave, of the conquering Āryan. See 1.32.11.

19. Indra's mother is here called a cow who has not yet given birth to a calf. Indra is her first-born. Cf. the mothers of Agni as *primaparas*, 2.35.5.

20. That is, she did not hold him close to her after he was born, but pushed him away uncared for, like a cow who fails to eat the afterbirth and lick the calf. Moreover, as Indra was not born through the womb, there would be no afterbirth.

21. Indra.

22. A possible reference to the episode in which the Maruts left Indra to fight Vṛtra all alone. This point is debated (by the Maruts) in 1.165.6–7.

23. Indra asks Viṣṇu to stride forward to help him, but he also refers to Viṣṇu's famous talent for creating space (as Indra does by killing Vṛtra) by striding. Cf. 1.154.

24. This might be a question put by Viṣṇu to Indra, but is more likely asked by the narrator.

25. That is, while he was still lying in the womb or coming out of it. Indra himself tries to kill the Maruts when they are in the womb of their mother.

26. The same language is used to describe the killing of Vṛtra and the killing of Indra's father. This is not to imply that these are one and the same, but they are strangely linked: Tvaṣṭṛ is Vṛtra's father in later Indian tradition. In any case, the two deeds are closely parallel in this hymn: Indra's father must be killed, just as the dragon must be killed, and Indra's mother tries to prevent both slaughters at first (as Vṛtra's mother is said to participate in the battle with Indra, in 1.32.9) and finally acquiesces and takes Indra's side, at least in the fight with Vṛtra and perhaps, by implication, in the parricide. Cf. the way in which the mother of Agni holds Agni by the foot when she abandons him, 1.164.17.

27. This comes to be the quintessential polluting act in later Hinduism, an act that is particularly used in mythology as an example of what one is *allowed* to do in dire straits: one may even eat a dog. Indra seems to be arguing that, if this is so, one can surely kill one's father under similar circumstances.

28. Indra's wife has not yet been mentioned in this hymn, nor is it clear why she would be dishonoured; elsewhere (1.86.1, 1.86.4–5,

1.86.9) she is dishonoured when Indra loses power, and the gambler's wife is dishonoured when he is ruined (10.34.11). It is possible that the 'woman' is Indra's mother, whom he regards as dishonoured by the actions of her husband, Indra's father, and therefore avenges by committing parricide.

29. This seems to contradict the statement that Indra took the Soma from Tvaṣṭṛ's house (v. 3), as well as the implication that Indra accompanied the eagle on the journey to get the Soma (4.26.7, 4.27.3–4). Evidently what is meant is that once Indra had killed his father (Tvaṣṭṛ?), he had access to the Soma in all of its forms.

## 10.28 *Indra Chastises His Son*

This dialogue begins *in medias res*, but the situation can be sketchily reconstructed from what follows: A son of Indra gave a sacrifice and invited the gods; all but Indra came to it, for Indra was angry with the son's pretensions to be another Indra. The son's wife worried about Indra's absence, and Indra then appeared, responding to his son's hasty offerings with a series of riddles intended to humble him. The son at first pretends to be too naïve to understand, but when Indra speaks more directly about the consequences of challenging the gods, the son asserts himself, and finally, overcome by the violence of Indra's increasingly patent fables, praises the god his father.

*1* [*Sacrificer's wife:*] 'All the rest of the band of my friends has come, but my husband's father has not come. He would have eaten barley meal and drunk Soma and gone back home well fed.'

*2* [*Indra:*] 'The sharp-horned bull bellowed as he stood over the height and breadth of the earth. In all combats I protect the man who presses Soma and fills my two bellies.'[1]

*3* [*Sacrificer:*] 'They are pressing out the impetuous, exhilarating Soma juices with the pressing-stone, for you, Indra. Drink them! They are cooking bulls for you; you will eat them, generous Indra, when they summon you with food.'

4 [*Indra:*] 'Singer, understand this that I say: The rivers carry their currents upstream. The fox crept up to the lion from behind. The jackal fell upon the wild boar out of an ambush.'[2]

5 [*Sacrificer:*] 'How can I, a simpleton, understand what is said by you who are wise and powerful?[3] You who know should tell us truly: towards which side is your peaceful chariot shaft going, generous one?'[4]

6 [*Indra:*] 'They truly praise me as the powerful one; my chariot shaft is going straight up to the lofty sky. I crush down many thousands at once, for my begetter begot me to have no enemy to conquer me.'

7 [*Sacrificer:*] 'The gods truly know *me* as the powerful one, a fierce bull in one action after another, Indra. Exhilarated by Soma, I killed Vṛtra with my thunderbolt, and I opened up the cow-pen by force for the devout worshipper.'[5]

8 [*Indra:*] 'The gods went out and took their axes; they cut down trees and came there with their servants. They laid the good wood in the boxes but burnt the scrub wood right there.'[6]

9 [*Sacrificer:*] 'The rabbit swallowed up the knife as it came towards him; with a clod I split the mountain far away.[7] I will put the great in the power of the small; the calf becomes strong and attacks the bull.'

10 [*Indra:*] 'That is the way the eagle caught his talon and was trapped, like a lion caught in a foot-snare. Even the buffalo was caught when he got thirsty: a crocodile dragged him away by the foot.[8]

11 'In the same way let a crocodile drag away by the foot all those who oppose the feeding of priests. As they all eat the bulls that have been set free, they themselves destroy the powers of their body.[9]

12 [*Sacrificer:*] 'Those who hastened in person to Soma with hymns of praise have become supreme in their sacrificial

acts and devout rituals. Speaking like a man, measure out prizes for us. In heaven you have earned fame and the name of hero.'

NOTES

1. The imagery of the first two verses, including the references to Indra's two bellies and the role of the sacrificer's wife, is similar to that of the Vṛṣākapi hymn, 10.86.14–15.

2. Indra implies that the son, like a fox or jackal, by trying to be Indra, who is like a lion or wild boar, is both creating a topsy-turvy world (in which the rivers flow the wrong way and the cowardly animals attack the fierce) and foolishly taking on more than he can handle.

3. Cf. the young man who challenges his father in 4.5.2 and 6.9.2.

4. That is, are you on the side of simple mortals or wise immortals? The answer in the next verse seems to be that Indra is on his own side, or the side of the gods.

5. The son here explicitly claims credit for the deeds of Indra (1.32, 3.31), as other gods do from time to time; in offering the Soma that enables Indra to perform these deeds, the sacrificer to a certain extent participates in them.

6. Indra implies that the gods are able to distinguish the good (wood or Indras) from the worthless; the former they take home in boxes on wagons, the latter they destroy – a thinly veiled threat to the pretender.

7. Another allusion to Indra's splitting of the mountain in which the cows were trapped. Cf. 3.31.

8. Indra's warning to anyone who takes on too great an opponent or becomes careless.

9. Indra threatens those who take to themselves praise due to the gods, Soma due to the gods, or food due to the gods or priests.

## 1.32 *The Killing of Vṛtra*

The greatest of Indra's heroic deeds was the slaying of the dragon Vṛtra, an act which also symbolizes the releasing of the waters or rains which Vṛtra had held back, the conquest of the enemies of the Āryans, and the creation of the world out of the body of the dragon. The thunderbolt of Indra is a club which, as a phallic symbol, is also a symbol of fertility, the source of seed as well as rain; sexual imagery also underlies the contrast between the castrated steer and the bull bursting with seed. Rain imagery is also prominent; Vṛtra is a cloud pierced in his loins or in his bellies, for elsewhere he is said to have swallowed all the universe, which Indra must free from him; the cows to which the waters are compared are also rain-clouds. Vṛtra may be imagined as a shoulderless serpent or as a dragon whose arms and legs Indra has just cut off; he is primarily a symbol of danger, constriction, and loss. The battle is waged with magic as well as with weapons; Indra uses magic to make himself as thin as a horse's hair, and Vṛtra uses magic to create lightning and fog. Indra wins, of course, and verse 14 refers to a similar feat of rescue performed by the eagle,[1] but only as a simile in the context of another myth: Indra is said to have fled after killing Vṛtra and to have been punished for the crime of murder. This hymn, however, ends on a note of affirmation for Indra's victory.

*1* Let me now sing the heroic deeds of Indra, the first that the thunderbolt-wielder performed. He killed the dragon and pierced an opening for the waters; he split open the bellies of mountains.

*2* He killed the dragon who lay upon the mountain; Tvaṣṭṛ[2] fashioned the roaring thunderbolt for him. Like lowing cows, the flowing waters rushed straight down to the sea.

*3* Wildly excited like a bull, he took the Soma for himself and drank the extract from the three bowls in the three-day Soma ceremony.[3] Indra the Generous seized his thunderbolt to hurl it as a weapon; he killed the first-born of dragons.

*4* Indra, when you killed the first-born of dragons and overcame by your own magic the magic of the magicians, at that very moment you brought forth the sun, the sky, and dawn. Since then you have found no enemy to conquer you.

*5* With his great weapon, the thunderbolt, Indra killed the

shoulderless Vṛtra, his greatest enemy. Like the trunk of
a tree whose branches have been lopped off by an axe, the
dragon lies flat upon the ground.
6 For, muddled by drunkenness like one who is no soldier,
Vṛtra challenged the great hero who had overcome the
mighty and who drank Soma to the dregs. Unable to
withstand the onslaught of his weapons, he found Indra
an enemy to conquer him and was shattered, his nose
crushed.
7 Without feet or hands he fought against Indra, who
struck him on the nape of the neck with his thunderbolt.
The steer who wished to become the equal of the bull
bursting with seed, Vṛtra lay broken in many places.
8 Over him as he lay there like a broken reed the swelling
waters flowed for man.[4] Those waters that Vṛtra had
enclosed with his power – the dragon now lay at their
feet.
9 The vital energy of Vṛtra's mother ebbed away, for Indra
had hurled his deadly weapon at her. Above was the
mother, below was the son; Dānu[5] lay down like a cow
with her calf.
10 In the midst of the channels of the waters which never
stood still or rested, the body was hidden. The waters
flow over Vṛtra's secret place; he who found Indra an
enemy to conquer him sank into long darkness.
11 The waters who had the Dāsa[5] for their husband, the
dragon for their protector, were imprisoned like the cows
imprisoned by the Paṇis.[5] When he killed Vṛtra he split
open the outlet of the waters that had been closed.
12 Indra, you became a hair of a horse's tail when Vṛtra struck
you on the corner of the mouth. You, the one god, the
brave one, you won the cows; you won the Soma; you
released the seven streams so that they could flow.
13 No use was the lightning and thunder, fog and hail that
he[6] had scattered about, when the dragon and Indra
fought. Indra the Generous remained victorious for all
time to come.

14 What avenger of the dragon did you see, Indra, that fear entered your heart when you had killed him? Then you crossed the ninety-nine streams like the frightened eagle[7] crossing the realms of earth and air.

15 Indra, who wields the thunderbolt in his hand, is the king of that which moves and that which rests, of the tame and of the horned.[8] He rules the people as their king, encircling all this as a rim encircles spokes.

NOTES

1. Cf. 4.26–7.

2. Tvaṣṭṛ is the artisan of the gods, sometimes an enemy of Indra (cf. 4.18) but here his ally.

3. Cf. 10.14.16.

4. Manu was the eponymous ancestor of mankind; the verse may refer to the waters that flowed at the time of the great flood, when Manu alone was saved, or to the waters that flowed for the sake of mankind at the time of the piercing of Vṛtra (cf. 1.165.8). The latter seems more likely – or both at once.

5. Dānu is the mother of Vṛtra and of other demons called Dānavas; Dāsa is another name for Vṛtra and also, in the sense of 'slave', for other human and demonic enemies of Indra; the Paṇis are a group of such enemies, said to have stolen and penned up the cows until Indra released them (see 3.31 and 10.108).

6. 'He' is Vṛtra, trying his magic in vain against Indra's (cf. v. 4).

7. Possibly the eagle (Indra in disguise) that stole the Soma (4.26–7).

8. According to Sāyaṇa, the 'tame' are animals that do not attack, such as horses and donkeys, while the 'horned' are fierce animals like buffaloes and bulls.

## 3.31 *The Cows in the Cave*

Indra split open the cave where the cows were pent up, releasing them and winning them. This myth expresses simultaneously the successful cattle raids of the Indo-Aryans against the people they conquered, the process of birth out of the womb, the releasing of the waters (symbolized by cows) pent up by the demons of drought, the finding (and hence creating) of the dawn rays of the sun (also symbolized by cows), and the poet's discovery and release of his own inspirations. The martial level of the myth is fleshed out by references to Indra's assistants, simultaneously the Angiras priests (who thus tie the myth to the fourth level, the poet's inspiration) and the Maruts or storm-clouds (tying it to the second level, the end of the drought). The theme of finding and creating the sun is expanded in the first three verses of the hymn, which describe the birth of fire in an obscure allegory of incest that also alludes to the winning of treasure (the wealth of cattle again).

*1* The driver[1] wise in the Law came, speaking devoutly as he chastened his daughter's daughter.[2] When the father strove to pour[3] into his daughter, his heart eagerly consented.

*2* The son of the body did not leave the inheritance to the sister; he made her womb a treasure-house for the winner.[4] When the mothers[5] give birth to the driver,[1] one of the two who do good deeds is the maker, and the other derives the gain.

*3* Trembling with his tongue, Agni was born to honour the sons of the great rosy one.[6] Great was the embryo, great was their birth, and great the growth, through sacrifice, of the lord of bay horses.[7]

*4* The conquerors surrounded the challenger;[8] they brought forth great light out of darkness. The dawns recognized him and came to meet him; Indra became the only lord of cows.

*5* The wise ones[9] struck a path for those[10] who were in the cave; the seven priests drove them on with thoughts pressing forward. They found all the paths of the right way; the one who knew was the one who entered them, bowing low.

*6* If Saramā[11] finds the breach in the mountain, she will complete her earlier great pathfinding. The swift-footed

one led out the head of the undying syllables;[12] knowing
the way, she was the first to go towards the cry.
7 The most inspired one came, behaving like a friend.[13]
The mountain made ripe the fruit of its womb for the one
who performed great deeds.[14] The young hero, proving
his generosity, won success with the youths; then Angiras
right away became a singer of praise.[15]
8 The image of this creature and that creature, he knows all
who are born. Standing in the forefront, he killed
Śuṣṇa.[16] Knowing the path of the sky, longing for cows,
he went before us, singing. The friend freed his friends
from dishonour.
9 With a heart longing for cows they sat down while with
their songs they made the road to immortality. This is
their very seat, still often used now, the lawful way by
which they wished to win the months.[17]
10 Glancing about, they rejoiced in their own possessions
as they milked out the milk of the ancient seed.[18] Their
shout heated the two worlds. They arranged the off-
spring, dividing the cows among the men.[19]
11 He himself, Indra the killer of Vṛtra, with songs released
the rosy cows together with the offspring and the obla-
tions. Stretching far, the cow was milked of the sweet
honey-like butter that she had held for him.
12 They made a seat for him as for a father,[20] for these great
deeds revealed a great, shining seat. They propped their
two parents apart with a pillar; sitting down, they raised
the wild one[21] high up.
13 When the abundant female[22] determined to crush down
the one who had grown great in a single day[23] and had
pervaded the two world-halves, all irresistible powers
came to Indra, in whom flawless praises come together.
14 I long for your great friendship, for your powerful help.[24]
Many gifts go to the killer of Vṛtra. Great is praise; we
have come to the kindness of the lord. Generous Indra,
be good to us as our shepherd.
15 He won great land and much wealth, and he sent the

booty to his friends. Radiant with his men, Indra gave birth to the sun, the dawn, motion,[25] and fire.

*16* This house-friend has loosed into a single channel even the wide dispersed waters that shine with many colours, the honeyed waters made clear by the inspired filters. Rushing along by day and night, they drive forward.[26]

*17* The two dark bearers of treasure, worthy of sacrifice,[27] follow the sun with his consent, when your beloved, impetuous friends[28] embrace your splendour to draw it to them.

*18* Killer of Vṛtra, be the lord of lovely gifts, the bull who gives life to songs of praise for a whole life-span. Come to us with kind and friendly favours, with great help, quickly, O great one.

*19* Like Angiras I honour him and bow to him, making new for the ancient one a song that was born long ago.[29] Thwart the many godless lies, and let us win the sun, generous Indra.

*20* The mists that were spread about have become transparent;[30] guide us safely across them. You, our charioteer, must protect us from injury. Soon, Indra, soon, make us winners of cows.

*21* The killer of Vṛtra as lord of cows has shown us cows; he went among the dark ones with his rosy forms.[31] Revealing lovely gifts in the right way, he has opened up all his own gates.

*22* For success in this battle where there are prizes to be won, we will invoke the generous Indra, most manly and brawny, who listens and gives help in combat, who kills enemies and wins riches.

## NOTES

1. Agni is here and in verse 2 referred to as the driver or transporter, the one who carries the oblation to the gods in his chariot.

2. The extended metaphor of the first three verses may represent the priest as the father, his daughter as the sacrificial butter held in the spoon, and the son as the fire 'begotten' (kindled) by the priest.

3. The priest pours butter into the spoon, and the father pours seed into his daughter.

4. The winner is the son or brother, who apparently marries his sister so that her inheritance (the treasure) passes back through him to his heirs. For incest with brother and father, cf. Pūṣan with his mother and sister (6.55). In the ritual metaphor, the inheritance is the butter which falls from the spoon (her 'womb') into the fire.

5. The mothers of Agni are the kindling-sticks or the hands that hold them; the two who do good deeds, also regarded as the mothers of Agni, are the priest who 'makes' the fire and the sacrificer who derives the gain from it.

6. The Angiras priests, who tend Agni and own cows, are born of the rosy sky.

7. Indra is the lord of bay horses, 'grown' and aided in battle by the priests (Angirases) who feed him Soma in their sacrifices.

8. The Maruts and Angirases are the conquerors who closely surround Indra, the challenger not of them but of the cattle-thieves.

9. The priests again.

10. The noun is feminine, referring to the cows.

11. The bitch of Indra, the swift-footed one who finds the way to the cave. Cf. 10.108. The first part of this verse may be spoken by Indra.

12. Here the cows are explicitly identified with sacred speech. Cf. 1.164.

13. Indra or the leader of the Angirases (called Angiras) may be the inspired one, exalted by drinking Soma. Cf. 10.108.8. He feigns friendship as Saramā is tempted to do; cf. 10.108.9–10.

14. That is, the mountain yielded its contents, the cows, to Indra.

15. Angiras praises Indra in order to strengthen him. The song may be directly quoted in the next verse.

16. Śuṣṇa is the demon of drought.

17. The Angirases sit down to perform the sacrifice that will give Indra the strength to win the cows who give the milk of immortality, and to acquire the power of the monthly sacrifices or the list of months in which the sacrifice was offered.

18. The milk of the cows is equated with seed and with rain.

19. They distributed the booty of calves and cows, the calves (as milk) being gifts for the priests.

20. Indra is like a father to the Angirases. The seat is both his

resting-place and a term for the special sacrifice (*sattra*) performed by the Angirases on Indra's behalf. The priests separate the worlds, making a place for the sacrifice to Indra by revealing the space of the realm between sky and earth.

21. The sun, created here, as usual, by the propping apart of sky and earth, as well as by being 'discovered' in the cave.

22. An obscure term (Dhiṣaṇā) designating the bowl of Soma, the bowl of sky or of earth, or a goddess of abundance. Here she inspires Indra.

23. Indra's deed of freeing the cows from the cave is assimilated to his deed of killing Vṛtra (who grew great in one day) and releasing the waters.

24. The worshipper addresses Indra directly.

25. Perhaps the orbit of the sun, or the passing of time, or the course of the sacrifice.

26. That is, they drive (transitively) the horses who pull the chariots of the waters that mix with the Soma.

27. The dark ones are night and twilight.

28. The Maruts.

29. Cf. 1.1.2.

30. Cf. the dispersed mists of Vṛtra, 1.32.13.

31. The dark ones are the aboriginal enemies of the Āryans, or the dark forces of evil, illuminated by the rosy lights of the dawns/Maruts/priests, as in verse 17.

## 10.108 *Saramā and the Paṇis*

This conversation takes place in the midst of a myth told in later texts at some length. The Paṇis are demons who live in the sky on the other side of the river Rasā that separates the world of gods and men from the world of demons; the name also refers to tribal people who are the enemies of the Vedic people on earth. These Paṇis stole the cows of the Angirases and hid them in mountain caves; the sages joined with the gods – Indra, Soma, Agni, and Bṛhaspati – to get the cattle back.[1] They sent Saramā, the bitch of Indra, to follow the trail of the cows, which she succeeded in doing. Reaching the hiding-place, she engaged in the conversation recorded in this hymn, one in which the Paṇis appear at first secure and sarcastic but soon become worried and attempt, unsuccessfully, to bribe Saramā.

1 [*The Paṇis:*] 'With what desire has Saramā come to this place? The road stretches far into distant lands. What is your mission to us? How did you find your way here? And how did you cross the waters of the Rasā?'

2 [*Saramā:*] 'I have journeyed here, sent as the messenger of Indra, and I desire your great treasures, O Paṇis. Because they feared being jumped across, they[2] helped me to do it; thus I crossed the waters of the Rasā.'

3 [*Paṇis:*] 'What is Indra like, Saramā? What is the appearance of him who sent you here as his messenger from afar? If he comes here, we will make friends with him, and he will be the herdsman of our cattle.'

4 [*Saramā:*] 'I know him as one who cannot be tricked; he tricks others, he who sent me here as his messenger from afar. The deep streams do not hide *him*;[3] you Paṇis will lie there slain by Indra.'

5 [*Paṇis:*] 'These are the cows which you desire, lovely Saramā, having flown beyond the ends of the sky. Who would release them to you without a fight? And we have sharp weapons.'

6 [*Saramā:*] 'Your words, O Paṇis, are no armies. Your evil bodies may be proof against arrows, the path that goes to you may be impregnable, but Bṛhaspati will not spare you in either case.'

7 [*Paṇis:*] 'Saramā, this treasure-room full of cows, horses, and riches is set firm in cliffs of rock. Paṇis who are good sentinels guard it. You have come in vain on this empty path.'

8 [*Saramā:*] 'The sages – Ayāsyas, Angirases, and Navagvas[4] – roused by Soma will share this enclosed cave of cattle among them. Then the Paṇis will spit back these words.'

9 [*Paṇis:*] 'Saramā, since you have come here, compelled by the force of the gods, we will make you our sister. Do

not go back, fair one; we will give you a share of the cattle.'

10 [*Saramā:*] 'I know no brotherhood, nor sisterhood; Indra and the Angirases, who inspire terror, know them. When I left them, they seemed to me to be desirous of cattle. Paṇis, run far away from here.

11 'Run far into the distance, Paṇis. Let the cattle come out by the right path and disappear, the cattle which Bṛhaspati, the inspired sages, the pressing-stones and Soma found when they had been hidden.'

### NOTES

1. Cf. 3.31.

2. The waters. At the critical moment of the journey, the river Rasā was worried about losing her reputation as a great river if a dog could jump across her; so she helped Saramā by building a ford.

3. A possible reference to Vṛtra lying under the water, killed by Indra. Cf. 1.32.8, 1.32.10. For tricking the tricky, cf. 1.32.4.

4. Families of Vedic sages.

## 10.171 *Indra Beheads the Sacrifice*

1 You, Indra, helped forward the chariot of Iṭat, who pressed Soma; you heard the call of the man who offered Soma.

2 You severed from his skin the head of the rebellious Sacrifice[1] and went with it to the home of the man who offered Soma.

3 You, Indra, set loose in a moment the mortal Venya for Āstrabudhna when he thought of it.[2]

4 You, Indra, should bring to the East the sun that is now in the West, even against the will of the gods.[3]

NOTES

1. An allusion to the myth, later expanded, that Indra in anger beheaded the sacrifice when it threatened the gods and became incarnate in human form.

2. Venya is known to the *Rig Veda*, but all else in this verse is obscure.

3. The sun was thought to travel from west to east by night, under the earth. Why the gods should oppose this is unclear.

## 8.14 *'If I were Like You, Indra'*

*1* If I were like you, Indra, and all alone ruled over riches, the man who praised me would have the company of cows.

*2* I would do my best for him, I would want to give things to the sage, O Husband of Power, if I were the lord of cattle.

*3* For the one who sacrifices and presses Soma your opulence is a cow milked of the cattle and horses with which she swells to overflowing.

*4* There is no one, neither god nor mortal, who obstructs your generosity, Indra, when you are praised and you wish to give rich gifts.

*5* The sacrifice made Indra grow greater when he rolled back the earth and made the sky his own diadem.

*6* We ask help from you Indra, you who have grown great and have won all treasures.

*7* In the ecstasy of Soma, Indra spread out the middle realm of space and the lights, when he shattered Vala.[1]

*8* He drove out the cows for the Angirases, making visible those that had been hidden, and he hurled Vala down headlong.

*9* The lights of the sky were made firm and fast by Indra, so that they cannot be pushed away from their fixed place.

*10* Like the exhilarating wave of the waters, your praise, Indra, hastens along; your ecstasies have shone forth.

*11* For the hymns of praise and the songs of praise make you grow great, Indra, and you bring happiness to the singer of praises.

*12* Let the two long-maned bay horses bring Indra to drink Soma here at the sacrifice of the giver of rich gifts.

*13* With the foam of the waters, Indra, you tore off the head of the demon who would not let go,[2] when you conquered all challengers.

*14* You whirled down the Dasyus who wanted to climb up to the sky, Indra, when they had crept up by using their magic spells.[3]

*15* You scattered to every side the ones that did not press Soma; as Soma-drinker you are supreme.

NOTES

1. Vala is the demon who pens up the cows, as in 3.31 (though he is not named in that hymn).
2. The demon Namuci.
3. Cf. 2.12.12.

## 2.12 *'Who is Indra?'*

As if to answer the challenges of the atheists, or at least of those who question the divinity of Indra (v. 5), the poet insists that Indra is indeed the god who did what he is said to have done. These concerns, and the verbal patterns used to express them, are repeated in a later hymn about the Creator (10.121).

*1* The god who had insight the moment he was born, the first who protected the gods with his power of thought, before whose hot breath the two world-halves tremble at the greatness of his manly powers – he, my people, is Indra.

*2* He who made fast the tottering earth, who made still the quaking mountains, who measured out and extended the expanse of the air, who propped up the sky – he, my people, is Indra.

3 He who killed the serpent and loosed the seven rivers,
who drove out the cows that had been pent up by Vala,[1]
who gave birth to fire between two stones,[2] the winner of
booty in combats – he, my people, is Indra.
4 He by whom all these changes were rung, who drove the
race of Dāsas[3] down into obscurity, who took away the
flourishing wealth of the enemy as a winning gambler
takes the stake – he, my people, is Indra.
5 He about whom they ask, 'Where is he?', or they say of
him, the terrible one, 'He does not exist', he who dimi-
nishes the flourishing wealth of the enemy as gambling
does – believe in him! He, my people, is Indra.
6 He who encourages the weary and the sick, and the poor
priest who is in need, who helps the man who harnesses
the stones to press Soma, he who has lips fine for drink-
ing – he, my people, is Indra.
7 He under whose command are horses and cows and vil-
lages and all chariots, who gave birth to the sun and the
dawn and led out the waters, he, my people, is Indra.
8 He who is invoked by both of two armies, enemies
locked in combat, on this side and that side, he who is
even invoked separately by each of two men standing on
the very same chariot,[4] he, my people, is Indra.
9 He without whom people do not conquer, he whom they
call on for help when they are fighting, who became the
image of everything, who shakes the unshakeable – he,
my people, is Indra.
10 He who killed with his weapon all those who had com-
mitted a great sin, even when they did not know it, he
who does not pardon the arrogant man for his arrogance,
who is the slayer of the Dasyus, he, my people, is Indra.
11 He who in the fortieth autumn discovered Śambara living
in the mountains,[5] who killed the violent serpent, the
Dānu,[6] as he lay there, he, my people, is Indra.
12 He, the mighty bull who with his seven reins let loose the
seven rivers to flow, who with his thunderbolt in his hand
hurled down Rauhiṇa[7] as he was climbing up to the sky,
he, my people, is Indra.

13 Even the sky and the earth bow low before him, and the mountains are terrified of his hot breath; he who is known as the Soma-drinker, with the thunderbolt in his hand, with the thunderbolt in his palm, he, my people, is Indra.

14 He who helps with his favour the one who presses and the one who cooks,[8] the praiser and the preparer, he for whom prayer is nourishment, for whom Soma is the special gift, he, my people, is Indra.

15 You[9] who furiously grasp the prize for the one who presses and the one who cooks, you are truly real. Let us be dear to you, Indra, all our days, and let us speak as men of power in the sacrificial gathering.

## NOTES

1. Vala is an enemy, human or demonic, who kept the cows from Indra. See 8.14.7–8 and 3.31.

2. The fire kindled by flints, or the sun or lightning between the two worlds. Cf. 3.31.1–3.

3. Dāsas (also called Dasyus, as in v. 10) are the enemies of the Āryans, called 'slaves' and enslaved.

4. The image of the two armies is expanded in the corresponding hymn, 10.121.6. The two men on the same chariot are the charioteer/priest and the warrior/king.

5. Śambara was a demon who kept the Soma from Indra in mountain fortresses; cf. 4.26.3.

6. Vṛtra. Cf. 1.32.9.

7. A more obscure enemy, about whom nothing but this is known. Cf. 8.14.14.

8. The one who presses and the one who cooks the Soma.

9. Here the poet addresses Indra directly, closing with traditional phrases.

## GODS OF THE STORM

CLOSELY associated with Indra in his capacity as god of the thunderstorm, the Maruts are also linked to Rudra (1.85; cf. 2.33 and 1.114). It is precisely the overlapping of their functions with those of Indra that underlies a series of hymns debating their several rights to the sacrificial offering (1.165, 1.170, 1.171); ultimately, Indra is affirmed to be supreme. Indra is also intimately connected with Parjanya the raincloud, who is, like Indra, called a bull (5.83) but is also called a cow (7.101). This androgyny appears elsewhere in the *Rig Veda* associated with sky and earth, and Soma and Agni, but in later mythology it becomes an important characteristic of Prajāpati and Śiva. Vāta, the Gale, a less important but equally vivid aspect of the storm, is said to drive a chariot (10.168), like the sun and the sacrifice (1.164). Parjanya and Vāta differ from the Maruts in being relatively straightforward personifications of natural phenomena; the Maruts, like Indra, are multivalent, symbolizing warriors and acting as aids to mankind as well as bringing fertilizing storms.

## The Maruts

The Maruts are wind-gods portrayed always as a group, as a band of warriors who serve Indra. Since Rudra is their father, they are also called Rudras; their mother is the dappled cow of earth, Pṛśṇi.

*1* The team of horses on the course, the Maruts, the sons of Rudra, workers of marvels, adorned themselves like women and made the two world-halves grow strong. Trembling, the heroes drink to ecstasy in the rites.

*2* They have grown to greatness; the Rudras have made a mansion in heaven. Singing their song and creating the power of Indra,[1] they whose mother is the dappled cow have put on glory.

*3* When the handsome ones whose mother is a cow adorn themselves with their ornaments, they put shining things on their bodies. They drive away every attacker. Butter flows all along their path.[2]

*4* Good warriors who shine forth with their spears, shaking with their formidable power even those who cannot be shaken – when you Maruts have yoked to your chariots the dappled gazelles[3] swift as thought,

*5* when you have yoked the dappled gazelles to your chariots, speeding the stone forward to win the contest,[4] then the streams are let loose from the chestnut stallion.[5] Like a leather skin,[6] they wet the earth with water.

*6* Let your swift-gliding teams bring you here. Flying swiftly with your arms,[7] come forward. Sit down on the sacred grass; a wide seat has been made for you Maruts. Drink in ecstasy from the sweet juice.

*7* They grew great by their own power; they climbed up to the dome of the sky and made for themselves a broad seat. When Viṣṇu helped the bull excited by Soma-drinking, they sat down like birds on the beloved sacred grass.[8]

8 Striding briskly like heroes ready to fight, like men
eager for fame, they array themselves for battles. All
creatures fear the Maruts; these men with terrible faces
are like kings.
9 When the artful Tvaṣṭṛ had turned[9] the well-made golden
thunderbolt with its thousand spikes, Indra took it to do
heroic deeds. He killed Vṛtra and set free the flood of
waters.
10 They[10] forced up the fountain with their power; they
split open even the mountain on its solid base.[11] Blowing
their reed-pipe, the Maruts who give fine gifts per-
formed joyous deeds in the ecstasy of drinking Soma.
11 They forced up the fountain in a stream that shot to
the side; they poured out the spring for the thirsty
Gotama. Shining brilliantly, they came to him with aid.
They fulfilled the desire of the sage in their own ways.
12 The shelters that you have for the devout man – extend
them threefold to the man who believes in you.[12]
Give them to us, O Maruts, bulls. Give us the wealth
of fine heroes.[13]

## NOTES

1. As the poet gives power to Indra by singing the hymn, so the Maruts give themselves Indra's powers by singing their howling storm songs.

2. Butter is here symbolic of rain and the sap of life, as well as the ritual offering and the Soma that the Maruts love.

3. Unspecified female dappled animals pull the Maruts' chariots; they could be mares, but other Rig Vedic evidence makes it more likely that they are gazelles.

4. The winds compete in hurling rocks and crushing boulders, as men compete in bowling or shot-put.

5. The rain is the sperm or urine of the horse of heaven – the cloud or heaven itself.

6. The image is that of a wineskin bag pouring out the rain (cf. this simile in the hymn to Parjanya, 5.83.7); a secondary connotation might be the pouring down of water on to the earth likened to a skin being tanned with fluids.

7. That is, flapping your arms like wings to speed you faster. Cf. 10.81.3.

8. The bull is Indra. When Viṣṇu helped Indra in the fight against Vṛtra, the Maruts came and helped, too. But cf. 1.165.6.

9. Turned on his lathe.

10. The Maruts. A reference to a story told by the commentator: The sage Gotama was afflicted with thirst and prayed to the Maruts for water. They made a fountain in the distance, brought it near him, gave it to him to drink from, and bathed him in it.

11. As Indra pierced the mountain to release the waters in the fight with Vṛtra.

12. That is, the poet singing the present hymn.

13. Literally, the wealth that consists in having fine heroes, but also, by implication, the wealth brought by fine heroes.

## 1.165, 1.170, 1.171

## *Indra, the Maruts, and Agastya*

In this group of hymns, Indra and the Maruts argue over their rights to a sacrificial offering; this sacrifice is attributed by tradition to the sage Agastya, though his name is mentioned only once in the hymns. Several texts offer different versions of the myth underlying this cycle: (a) Agastya had dedicated a hundred dappled cows to the Maruts, but he sacrificed them to Indra. The Maruts became angry and went to Agastya, who sang these hymns to conciliate them. (b) Indra took away the cows intended for the Maruts; the Maruts grabbed his thunderbolt. Then Agastya and Indra conciliated the Maruts with these hymns. (c) Agastya took an offering that had been dedicated to Indra and wanted to give it to the Maruts. Despite the variations, the underlying conflict is consistent and forms a thread through all the hymns in the series, a thread that conforms most closely to the second of the three variant glosses. In the first hymn (1. 165), Indra wishes to go to Agastya's sacrifice and encounters the Maruts in heaven; as their conversation progresses, Indra becomes more and more confident, the Maruts more and more subdued; finally they refer to their former praise of him and allay his anger, and they all go together to the sacrifice. In an intervening hymn not translated here (1.169), the reconciliation is further developed. Then (1.170) Agastya is faced with the problem of choosing between the mighty Indra and the now somewhat chastened Maruts. Finally (1.171), Agastya apologizes to both Indra and the Maruts and prays to all of them.

### 1.165 *Indra and the Maruts*

*1* [*Indra:*] 'With what shared finery have the Maruts, who are of the same youth, from the same nest, mingled together? With what intention, and from what place have they come? These bulls sing their breathless song in their desire to win riches.

*2* 'Whose chants have the young men taken pleasure in? Who has turned the Maruts to his sacrifice? With what great thought will we make them stop here as they swoop through the middle realm of space?'[1]

*3* [*Maruts:*] 'Indra, where are you coming from, all alone though you are so mighty? What is your intention, true lord? Will you make a pact with us, now that you have met us in our finery? Master of bay horses, tell us what your purpose is for us.'

*4* [*Indra:*] 'The chants, the thoughts, the Soma-pressings are good for me. Breathlessness[2] surges in me; the pressing-stone is set out for me. The hymns are longing, waiting for me. These two bay horses are carrying us to them.'

*5* [*Maruts:*] 'Because of this,[3] we have adorned our bodies and harnessed the self-willed horses next to the chariot; and now we have yoked does[4] for greater power. Indra, you have always acknowledged our independent spirit.'

*6* [*Indra:*] 'Where was that independent spirit of yours, Maruts, when you left me all alone in the fight with the dragon?[5] *I* was the one, fierce and strong and mighty, who bent aside the lethal weapons of every enemy with my own weapons.'

7 [*Maruts:*] 'You did much with us as allies, with our manly powers yoked in common, O bull. For we will do much, most valiant Indra, if we set our minds and will to do it, O Maruts.'[6]

8 [*Indra:*] '*I* killed Vṛtra, O Maruts, by my Indra-power, having grown strong through my own glorious rage. With the thunderbolt on my arm I made these all-luminous waters move well for man.'[7]

9 [*Maruts:*] 'No one can overcome your power, generous Indra; no one your equal is known to exist among the gods; no one being born now or already born could get such power. Do the things you will do, as you have grown strong.'

10 [*Indra:*] 'Even when I am alone, my formidable power must be vast; whatever I boldly set out to do, I do. For I am known as terrible, O Maruts; whatever I set in motion, Indra himself is master of that.

11 'Your praise has made me rejoice, lordly Maruts, the sacred chant worthy of hearing that you made here for me – for Indra the bull, the good fighter – that you my friends made in person for me, your friend, in person.

12 'Thus they shine forth facing me, the blameless band who take to themselves fame and the drink of ecstasy. Luminous and golden Maruts, you have pleased me when I looked at you, and you will please me now.'

13 [*The poet:*] Who has celebrated you here,[8] Maruts? Journey as friends to your friends. Shining brightly, inspire thoughts. Be witness to these truths of mine.

14 [*Indra:*][9] 'Since the wisdom of Mānya[10] brought us here, as the hope of gifts brings the singer to one who gives, therefore turn to the inspired seer. Let the singer chant these sacred words for you, Maruts.'

15 [*The poet:*] This praise is for you, Maruts, this song of the poet Māndārya Mānya.[10] Let him obtain vital strength for his body through the nourishing and inspiring drink. Let us find a welcoming circle of sacrificers who shower us with gifts.

## NOTES

1. Indra wishes to conceive an idea so 'arresting' that it will stop the Maruts in their tracks as they fly between sky and earth.

2. Here, as in verse 1, breathlessness indicates the excitement of combat.

3. That is, because the sacrifice is ready and the Maruts want to have it themselves.

4. The gazelles are yoked in front, in addition to the horses right next to the chariot.

5. Indra mocks the Maruts for their 'independence' and accuses them of remaining uncommitted when he fought Vṛtra. Cf. 4.18.11.

6. Here the speaker is addressing the other Maruts, as if to elicit their support in his boast to Indra.

7. A reference to the episode in which, after killing Vṛtra and releasing the waters, Indra led Manu to safety on the flood waters. Cf. 1.32.8.

8. The poet asks what sacrificer here (i.e. on earth, rather than in heaven where the conversation has been taking place) has attracted the Maruts.

9. This verse also makes sense in the mouth of the poet, who has come to the sacrifice in hope of being given gifts, or even in the mouth of the Maruts, one of whom would be addressing the others, as in verse 7.

10. This may be a name of Agastya or of his son.

## 1.170 *Agastya and the Maruts*

Indra is silent during this conversation, but both groups of speakers address most of their remarks to him.

*1* [*Agastya:*] 'Today is nothing and tomorrow is nothing. Who understands the mystery? If one depends on someone else's intention, all that one wished for is ruined.'[1]

*2* [*Maruts:*] 'Why do you want to destroy us, Indra? The Maruts are your brothers; treat them well. Do not kill us in a violent clash.

*3* 'Brother Agastya, why do you dishonour us though

you are our friend? For we know what is in your mind: you do not wish to give us anything.'[2]

4 [*Agastya:*] 'Make ready the altar; kindle the fire in front of it. In it[3] we two[4] will spread a memorable sacrifice for you, the immortal.[5]

5 'Lord of riches, you rule over riches. Lord of friendship, you are the best reconciler of friends. Speak in agreement with the Maruts, Indra, and eat the oblations at the right ritual moment.'

NOTES

1. Agastya seems to be apologizing to the Maruts for making the offering to Indra; he argues that Indra took away what Agastya had intended for the Maruts, and he is helpless to prevent it.

2. This is an indirect answer to Agastya's apology in verse 1; they argue that he did not even *intend* to sacrifice to them, and indeed he then speaks to Indra alone.

3. In the fire, or perhaps in the altar.

4. Perhaps Agastya together with another priest, his son (cf. 1.165.14).

5. Here Agastya speaks only to Indra, though he goes on to ask Indra to conciliate the rejected Maruts.

## 1.171 *Agastya Prays to Indra and the Maruts*

1 I come to you with this homage, and with a hymn I beg for the kindness of the mighty.[1] Willingly and knowingly lay aside your spiteful anger, Maruts; unharness your horses.[2]

2 This praise and homage fashioned in the heart and in the mind was made for you, Maruts, for you who are gods. Come and enjoy it with your mind, for you are the ones who make homage grow.

3 Let the Maruts have mercy on us when they have been praised and the generous and most beneficent one[3] has been praised. Let our smooth woods[4] stand up and ready all our days, O Maruts, through our desire to conquer.

4 I shrank away from this mighty Indra, trembling in fear, O Maruts. It was for you that the oblations were laid out, but we set them aside.[5] Forgive us!

5 The fame by which the Mānas[6] became distinguished for their power in the daybreaks of all the successive dawns – give us that fame, O strong and terrible bull with the terrible Maruts, giver of overpowering strength.[7]

6 Protect your men from those who could overpower them by force, O Indra;[8] make the Maruts give up their spiteful anger, for they bring good omens; you have been made the overpowering conqueror. Let us find a welcoming circle of sacrificers who shower us with gifts.

NOTES

1. In the plural, addressing the Maruts, as the rest of the verse makes clear.

2. That is, stop here and accept our sacrifice.

3. Indra.

4. Perhaps a metaphor for the fire-sticks, the spear, or the phallus.

5. That is, we gave them to Indra, instead, because he frightened us.

6. Perhaps the name of generous patrons, who gave the cows of dawn to the priests. Cf. the patron Mānya in 1.165.14–15.

7. Indra is the terrible, overpowering bull, here asked to overpower the Maruts.

8. Having apologized to the Maruts in 1.170, Agastya now asks Indra (who is supposed to be on Agastya's side, having accepted his sacrifice) to protect his men (i.e. his worshippers) from those who are more powerful (the Maruts).

## 5.83 *Parjanya, the Bull*

Only three hymns are dedicated to Parjanya, who is the personification of the rain-cloud, often represented as a male animal. Closely associated with thunder and lightning, he inspires vegetation and produces fertility in cows, mares, and women. So rich is the abundance with which he responds to the poet's plea that at the end of the hymn he is begged not to send too much rain.

1 Summon the powerful god with these songs; praise Parjanya; win him over with homage. The bellowing bull, freely flowing with luscious drops, places his seed in the plants as an embryo.

2 He shatters the trees and slaughters the demons; he strikes terror into every creature with his enormous deadly weapon.[1] Even the sinless man gives way before the god bursting with seed like a bull, when the thundering Parjanya slaughters those who do evil.

3 Like a charioteer lashing his horses with a whip, he makes his messengers of rain appear.[2] From the distance arise the thunder-peals of a lion, when Parjanya makes the sky full of rain-clouds.

4 The winds blow forth, the lightnings fly, the plants surge up, the sky swells, the sun overflows.[3] The sap of life quickens in every creature when Parjanya refreshes the earth with his seed.

5 By your law, the earth bends low; by your law, all animals with hoofs quiver; by your law, plants of all forms bloom. By these powers, Parjanya, grant us safe shelter.

6 Give us rain from heaven, O Maruts. Make the streams of the seed-bearing stallion overflow as they swell. Come here with your thunder, pouring down waters, for you are our father, the bright sky-god.

7 Bellow and thunder; lay your seed. Fly in circles around the world in your chariot full of water. Drag the leather water-bag upside down, untied. Let the hills and the valleys become level.[4]

8 Draw up the enormous bucket and pour it down. Let the streams flow forth, set free. Drench heaven and earth with butter. Let there be a good drinking-place for the cows.

9 Parjanya, when you bellow loudly and thunder and

slaughter those who do evil, everything that exists upon the earth rejoices.

10 You have sent the rain; now hold it back. You have made the deserts easy to cross over. You have made the plants grow so that there is food, and you have found inspired poetry for living creatures.

### NOTES

1. The thunderbolt.
2. Clouds foretelling rain, or the Maruts. He drives them as the charioteer drives horses.
3. According to Indian theory, during the rainy season the sun flows with the water that it has drawn up during the preceding hot season. Here, at the very brink of the storm, the sun begins to pour back its rain. Cf. 1.164.51–2.
4. The water rises so high that both hills and valleys are covered. Cf. 1.85.5, for the leather bag.

## 7.101 *Parjanya, the Cow*

The poet addresses the rain-cloud, Parjanya, whose three voices are lightning, thunder, and rain. Though he is a bull full of seed, his udder is the cloud milked of rain, and his calf is the fire born of lightning. The three lights may be the lights of the three worlds, or fire, sun, and moon (or wind). The sterile (i.e. milkless) cow is the cloud that does not give rain; the cow that brings forth is the cloud that rains. The mother, earth, receives the milk, rain-water, from the father, the sky; the sky thrives on the rain and the son (the group of creatures on earth) thrives on water.

1 Raise the three voices with light going before them, voices that milk the udder that gives honey.[1] The bull created the calf, the embryo of the plants, and roared as he was born.

2 The god who causes the plants to increase, and the waters, who rules over the entire world, may he grant

us triple refuge and comfort, the triple light that is of good help to us.

3 Now he becomes a barren female, now one who gives birth; he takes whatever body he wishes. The mother receives the milk of the father; with it the father increases and prospers, and with it the son thrives.[2]

4 All worlds rest on him – the triple skies and the triple flowing waters. The three vats that drench pour forth in all directions the overflowing honey.[3]

5 Let this speech reach close to the heart of Parjanya who rules by himself, and let him rejoice in it. Let life-giving rains come to us, and let the plants guarded by the gods bear good berries.

6 He is the bull who places the seed in all plants; in him is the vital breath of what moves and what is still. Let this truth protect me for a hundred autumns; protect us always with blessings.

### NOTES

1. On another level, the subject of the verse may be Soma, the three voices are the chants when the Soma is pressed, and the udder that gives honey is the Soma plant (while, in the cosmic metaphor, it is the rain-cloud, the udder of the heavenly cow).

2. In this verse, the ritual level would make Soma the son: the rain enters the Soma plant and later returns to the cloud (as evaporation), or, more likely, to heaven (the gods) in the form of a Soma oblation.

3. Again, the three vats are clouds full of rain or Soma vessels full of Soma.

## 10.168 *The Gale Wind*

This hymn is to Vāta, a particularly violent and concrete form of the wind.

1 O, the power and glory of the chariot of the gale! It breaks things into pieces as it passes by, making a sound like thunder. Touching the sky as it moves, it

makes red streaks;[1] passing along the earth, it scatters the dust.

2 The tempests[2] race together after the gale; they come to him like women to a rendezvous. Yoked with them to a single chariot, the god who is the king of this whole universe passes by.

3 Moving along his paths in the middle realm of space, he does not rest even for a single day. Friend of the waters, first-born keeper of the Law, where was he born? What was he created from?

4 Breath of the gods, embryo of the universe, this god wanders wherever he pleases. His sounds are heard, but his form is not seen.[3] Let us worship the gale with oblation.

## NOTES

1. The red streaks may be the redness of the sky during rain, or the chestnut horses of the wind; the term is also used of the clouds at dawn, especially when there is thunder, and of the ruddy hue of lightning.

2. These are the 'extensions' or companions of the wind, whirlwinds or downpours, feminine beings.

3. Cf. 1.164.44.

# SOLAR GODS

IN the nineteenth century, Max Müller conceived and popularized the theory that all the gods of the *Rig Veda* were aspects of the sun. Solar mythology has now been eclipsed, but it is certainly true that many of the Vedic gods have some connection with the sun, that many of the creation hymns involve the discovery of the sun, and that many of the closing benedictions include a plea that the worshipper may continue to see the sun. Viṣṇu is a particularly solar god (cf. 1.154), and Agni and Soma have strong solar characteristics; other gods are more vaguely solar, being described as shining or golden and dwelling in the sky.

There is, in addition, a group of gods connected with the sun in various concrete ways. Dawn is incarnate as a goddess closely associated with the Aśvins (1.92), who are themselves the sons of Vivasvan, the sun. The Aśvins are given credit for accomplishing many acts of benefit to mankind, particularly the rescue of people in danger (1.116); many of these remain obscure, but one, the rescue of Atri, is described at length (5.78). Atri, in turn, is said to have found the lost sun (5.40), an act that may be seen as a variant of the original act of creation itself, the making or finding of the sun (usually attributed to Indra), or merely surviving the danger of an eclipse.

The sun is personified primarily as Sūrya (1.50); metaphorically, he is associated with the sun-bird (10.177), who is in turn personified in a mysterious sage named Vena (10.123). Pūṣan is the charioteer of the sun and is therefore associated with journeys and travellers (1.42); he is also the god who presides over the unharnessing of chariots at the end of the day (6.55). Savitṛ is the 'Driver' who inspires and impels men to action; he, too, is invoked not only by day but at sunset (2.38) and at night (1.35). The dark aspect of the sun, which is manifest even in the hymns to Dawn, is balanced by a vision of the light embodied in the benevolent aspect of night (10.127).

## 1.92 *Dawn and the Aśvins*

The central and recurring metaphor in this hymn to Uṣas (personification of dawn) is that of harnessing tawny cows or bay horses to her chariot, in which she is to bring all riches to the men who worship her. The chariot is both a simple instrument of portage, a kind of cosmic Wells Fargo wagon, and symbolic of the victory chariot by which all riches are won. The metaphor is complicated and enriched by the fact that the lights of dawn themselves are regarded as cows or mothers, who come of their own accord to be milked at dawn.

*1* See how the dawns have set up their banner[1] in the eastern half of the sky, adorning and anointing[2] themselves with sunlight for balm. Unleashing themselves like impetuous heroes unsheathing their weapons, the tawny cows, the mothers, return.

*2* The red-gold lights have flown up freely; they have yoked the tawny cows who let themselves be yoked. The dawns have spread their webs in the ancient way; the tawny ones have set forth the glowing light.

*3* They sing like women busy at their tasks, coming from a distant place with a single harnessed team,[3] bringing refreshing food day after day to the man of good actions, the man of generosity, the man who sacrifices and presses the Soma.

*4* Like a dancing girl, she puts on bright ornaments; she uncovers her breast as a cow reveals her swollen udder. Creating light for the whole universe, Dawn has opened up the darkness as cows break out from their enclosed pen.

*5* Her brilliant flame has become visible once more; she spreads herself out, driving back the formless black abyss. As one[4] sets up the stake in the sacrifice, anoint-

ing[2] and adorning it with coloured ornaments, so the
daughter of the sky sets up her many-coloured light.
*6* We have crossed to the farther bank of this darkness;
radiant Dawn spreads her webs. Smiling like a lover
who wishes to win his way, she shines forth and with
her lovely face awakens us to happiness.
*7* The shining daughter of the sky, bringing rich gifts,
is praised by the Gotamas.[5] Measure out offspring and
strong men as the victory prizes, Dawn, the rewards
that begin with cattle and culminate in horses.
*8* Let me obtain great riches of glory and heroic men,
Dawn, riches that begin with slaves and culminate in
heroes. Fortunate in your beauty, incited by the victory
prize you shine forth with the fame of great achieve-
ments.
*9* Gazing out over all creatures, the goddess shines from
the distance facing straight towards every eye. Awaken-
ing into motion everything that lives, she has found the
speech of every inspired poet.[6]
*10* The ancient goddess, born again and again dressed in the
same colour, causes the mortal to age and wears away
his life-span,[7] as a cunning gambler carries off the stakes.
*11* She has awakened, uncovering the very edges of the
sky; she pushes aside her sister.[8] Shrinking human
generations, the young woman shines under her lover's
gaze.[9]
*12* Spreading out her rays like cattle, like a river in full flood
the brightly coloured one shines from the distance.
The fortunate goddess does not break the laws of the
gods but becomes visible, appearing by the rays of the
sun.
*13* Dawn, you who hold the victory prize, bring us that
brightly coloured power by which we establish children
and grandchildren.
*14* Dawn, rich in cows, rich in horses, resplendent giver of
gifts, shine your riches upon us here and now.
*15* Harness your red-gold horses now, O prize-giving
Dawn, and bring all good fortunes to us.

*16* O Aśvins[10] who work wonders, turn your chariot that brings cattle, that brings gold, and with one mind come back to us.
*17* You Aśvins who gave a shout from heaven[11] and made light for mankind, bring us strength.
*18* May those who wake at dawn[12] bring here to drink the Soma the two gods who work wonders and give joy, moving on paths of gold.

## NOTES

1. The banner that the dawns plant in the sky, as if to stake out a territory, may be a streak of dawn light revealing the darkened universe, or it may be the sun; it is also a battle banner, as the verse goes on to liken the dawns to warriors.

2. The verb means both to anoint and to adorn; in verse 1, the dawns adorn themselves with the sun and anoint themselves with light; in verse 5 the priest anoints the stake with clarified butter and adorns it with coloured ornaments, a metaphor which also recalls the setting up of the banner in verse 1.

3. The phrase indicates that the team has travelled a *yojana*, the distance one can traverse with a single 'yoking', without having to change the team.

4. The priest. Here Dawn is likened to a man, as she is in verse 1 (a warrior) and verse 10 (a gambler). She is a potent, sinister figure.

5. The family of sages to whom this hymn is attributed.

6. 'Found' both in the sense that she finds it for him (inspires him) and finds it in him (accepts his praise).

7. Here, and in the next verse, Dawn steals away the life-span (cf. 1.179.1) of mortals, while remaining young herself and acting for the benefit of the gods. She steals our youth as a gambler (perhaps by deception) takes away someone else's stakes (cf. 2.12.5 and 10.34.6).

8. The night.

9. Her lover, as the next verse makes clear, is the sun, whose love is reflected in her.

10. Three verses addressed to the Aśvins are appended to this hymn, attracted by the metaphor of the chariot that brings riches and by the ideas of awakening (vv. 17–18) and dawn (v. 18).

11. They shout to wake people up at sunrise.

12. The priests.

## 1.116 *The Deeds of the Aśvins*

1 For the Nāsatyas[1] I offer praises, as one sets an offering on
sacred grass, driving them forward as the wind drives
rain-clouds; the two of them brought a wife to the young
Vimada on a chariot swift as an arrow,[2]
2 trusting in their horses with strong wings and swift
gaits or in the incitements of the gods. Your donkey,
Nāsatyas, won a thousand in the prize race with Yama.[3]
3 Tugra had left Bhujyu in the cloud of water as a dead
man leaves behind his wealth. You brought him back,
Aśvins, in ships that were alive, that swam through
the realm of air far from the water.
4 With birds that flew on for three nights and three
days you Nāsatyas brought Bhujyu to the far shore of
the ocean, to the edge of the wetness, in three chariots with
six horses and a hundred feet.[4]
5 You did the deeds of heroes in that ocean that has no
beginning, no support, no handhold, when you Aśvins
carried Bhujyu home after he had climbed on board
your ship that has a hundred oars.
6 The white horse that you Aśvins gave to the man who
had poor horses, to be a joy to him for ever, this great
gift of yours has become famous, and the racehorse of
Pedu can still be summoned by his master.[5]
7 You lords of men granted the wish of Pajriya Kakṣīvat
when he praised you: you poured forth from the hoof
of your potent stallion a hundred pots of wine as if
from a sieve.
8 With snow you warded off the red-hot fire; you brought
him[6] sustaining nourishment. When Atri was led down
into the glowing oven, you Aśvins led him and all his
followers back up again safely.
9 You Nāsatyas overturned the well: you made the base on
the top and the rim slanting down.[7] Like water for
drinking, the streams flowed for riches for the thousand
thirsty people of Gotama.

10 You Nāsatyas stripped away the sheath of flesh from Cyavana when he had grown old, as if it were a cloak.[8] You masters stretched out his life-span when he had been abandoned and made him the husband of young girls.

11 Manly Nāsatyas, your helpful protection was worthy of praise and admiration, when, knowing how to do it, you dug out Vandana who was hidden like a treasure.[9]

12 As thunder announces rain, I announce – for reward – your enormous master-deed, lords: that Dadhyañc, the son of the Atharvan priest, told you about the honey through the head of a horse.[10]

13 Nāsatyas who enjoy many things, the bringer of abundance[11] called for your hands to give great help as you came to her. You heard the cry of the wife of the impotent man as if it was a command, and you Aśvins gave her a son with golden hands.

14 You manly Nāsatyas released the quail right out of the mouth of the wolf. You who enjoy many things gave sight to the poet when he lamented.

15 At the turning-point in Khela's race the mare broke a leg, like the wing of a bird; right then you gave Viśpalā[12] an iron leg so that she could run for the rich prize that had been set.

16 When Ṛjrāśva carved up a hundred rams for the she-wolf, his father made him blind.[13] You Nāsatyas, wonder-working healers, gave him two eyes so that he saw with perfect sight.

17 The daughter of the sun mounted your chariot like a woman winning her goal with a racehorse.[14] All the gods agreed to it in their hearts. You Nāsatyas are strongly attracted to beauty.

18 When you Aśvins drove on your journey to Divodāsa and to Bharadvāja, your trusty chariot brought a treasure: a bull and a dolphin were yoked together.[15]

19 Bringing wealth with good kingship, long life blessed with fine children and true heroism, you Nāsatyas with

one mind came with prizes to Jahnāvī,[16] who offered you a sacrificial portion three times a day.

20 You carried Jāhuṣa away in the night on good paths through the realms of space when he was surrounded on all sides, and with your chariot that breaks through barriers you unageing Nāsatyas drove through the mountains.

21 You Aśvins helped Vaśa in the battle when in one morning he won thousands. With Indra at your side you bulls drove disasters and attacks away from Pṛthuśravas.

22 You raised up water from the bottom of the deep well to the top for Śara Ārcatka to drink. You Nāsatyas used your powers to make the barren cow swell with milk for Śayu when he was exhausted.

23 For Viśvaka Kṛṣṇiya, who needed help and praised you and was a righteous man, you Nāsatyas used your powers to bring back Viṣṇāpū for him to see again, he who had been lost like a stray cow.[17]

24 When Rebha lay for ten nights and nine days bound by his enemy and immersed inside the waters, broken into pieces thrown in the water, you drew him out as one draws out Soma with a ladle.[18]

25 I have proclaimed your wondrous deeds, Aśvins. Let me be lord over this world, with good cattle and good sons; let me see and win a long life-span and enter old age as if going home.

## NOTES

1. The Aśvins are said to be 'unfailing' or 'saviours' or 'born of the nose' (from the nostrils of their mother, Saraṇyū) or 'not-untrue', for possible glosses of Nāsatyas.

2. This is the first of numerous references in this hymn to the deeds of the Aśvins, some known from the *Rig Veda* or other ancient texts, some obscure. Vimada was attacked when taking his bride home; the Aśvins brought her to him on their own chariot.

3. The donkey is sometimes said to pull the Aśvins' chariot; here

they employ him in a race, probably on the occasion of the marriage of Sūryā (cf. 10.85.8–9, 10.85.15–16).

4. Bhujyu, mentioned often in the *Rig Veda*, was rescued from drowning. The ship's hundred 'feet' are the oars, mentioned by name in the next verse.

5. Pedu was given a white horse that killed snakes; before this, he had no good horse.

6. Atri was thrown by the Asuras into a fiery pit, whence the Aśvins rescued him.

7. The overturned well is a metaphor for the rain-cloud that saves Gotama from drought, a rescue elsewhere credited to the Maruts (1.85.10–11).

8. Cyavana, often identified with Atri, was kept in a pit or box where he had no access to his wife, until the Aśvins freed him and rejuvenated him. Cf. 5.78.

9. Vandana (perhaps yet another name for Atri?) was similarly trapped and aged, and similarly rescued by the Aśvins.

10. Dadhyañc was given a horse-head with which he told the Aśvins about Soma and the beheading of the sacrifice; Indra then cut off that head, and Dadhyañc's own head was restored by the Aśvins.

11. Purandhi is a divinity connected with abundance and childbirth, sometimes associated or even identified with Indra (cf. 4.26.7, 4.27.2, 2.38.10). Here she is a woman whom the Aśvins assist in giving birth (cf. 5.78.16, which refers to a woman with an impotent husband).

12. Viśpalā is the name of Khela's racing mare restored by the Aśvins.

13. The she-wolf for whom Ṛjrāśva slaughtered the rams is said to have been one of the donkeys of the Aśvins in disguise.

14. The Aśvins, brothers of Sūryā, are also her husbands, winning her in a chariot-race competition. Cf. 10.85.8–9, 10.85.15–16; cf. also 10.102 for a woman charioteer.

15. Bharadvāja was the priest of Divodāsa; the bull and dolphin are yoked both as a proof of the Aśvins' power and to pull the chariot on land and water. For the unusual chariot animals, cf. 10.102.

16. Probably the wife of Jahnu, a great sage.

17. Viṣṇāpū was the son of Viśvaka Kṛṣṇiya.

18. Rebha was dead in the water, killed by several different methods, and the Aśvins brought him back to life.

## 5.78 *The Rescue of Atri*

The first set of three verses invokes the Aśvins; the second triad tells of Atri's rescue; the third prays for the successful birth of a child. These three parts are closely interrelated, for the Aśvins 'delivered' Atri from a pit as the child is delivered from the womb. The tale of Atri is known in several different variants, but the basic plot is that certain enemies kept Atri away from his wife at night, locked in a pit, a box, or a room in his own house; every morning they would take him out. After suffering in this way for a long time, Atri conceived the idea of praising the Aśvins, the physicians – particularly the obstetricians – of the gods (vv. 1–3); they came to him, took him out, and vanished; Atri made love to his wife but then went back into the pit at dawn as before, for he was afraid. In the pit he was inspired with the verses telling of his rescue (vv. 4–6). Whether the child whose birth is to be protected in the final three verses is the result of Atri's stolen visit to his wife seems unlikely; rather, the tale of Atri is told to provide a model for any happy delivery.

*1* Aśvins, unfailing ones,[1] come to us; do not turn away. Fly here like two swans to the Soma-juice.

*2* Aśvins, like two gazelles, like two buffaloes to the grassy meadow, fly here like two swans to the Soma-juice.

*3* Aśvins, rich in prizes, enjoy the sacrifice and grant our wish. Fly here like two swans to the Soma-juice.

*4* As Atri climbed down into the pit[2] and called to you like a woman in need of help,[3] then you Aśvins came with the fresh, welcome speed of an eagle.

*5* 'Open, O tree,[4] like the womb of a woman giving birth.[5] Aśvins, hear my cry and set free the man seven times unmanned.'[6]

*6* When the sage seven times unmanned was frightened and in need, with your magic spells you Aśvins bent the tree together and apart.[7]

7 As the wind stirs up a lotus pond on all sides, so let the child in your womb stir and come out when it is ten months old.

8 As the wind and the wood and the ocean stir, so let the ten-month-old child come down together with the afterbirth.

9 When the boy has lain for ten months in the mother, let him come out alive and unharmed, alive from the living woman.

NOTES

1. The Nāsatyas are 'true' or unfailing in that they do what they say they will do.

2. Elsewhere in the *Rig Veda* Atri is rescued by the Aśvins from a fiery pit. Cf. 1.116.8.

3. The word particularly designates a woman in pangs of labour. This forms a further link with the last three verses.

4. The tree may be the wooden box or the wooden door of the room in which Atri is confined.

5. A further, and this time explicit, link with the last three verses.

6. This may be an epithet of Atri (Saptavadhri) or of another man rescued by the Aśvins. Atri and Saptavadhri appear together on other occasions, where it seems more likely that they are a pair rather than a single character. But Atri himself is 'unmanned' (literally, castrated, the term used to refer to a steer in contrast with a bull – cf. 1.32.7 and 10.102.7, 10.102.12) by those who keep him from his wife. The two men are thus closely parallel, if not identical. Cf. 1.116.13.

7. The image of splitting apart the tree – pressing its sides together and then stretching them apart – to let Atri out is another birth metaphor.

## 5.40 *Atri and the Lost Sun*

This hymn may describe the experience of an eclipse (verse 5 seems best interpreted in this light) or the myth of the finding of the sun at the time of creation – or, in classical mythic fashion, both at once. The first four verses invoke

Indra; verses 1–6 describe the mythic deeds of Indra, overlapping with verses 6–9 describing the role of the high priest Atri both in assisting Indra and in accomplishing the miracle himself.

*1* Come, lord of Soma,[1] come and drink the Soma that has been pressed by the stones, O Indra, bull with bulls,[2] greatest killer of Vṛtra.

*2* The pressing-stone is a bull; the ecstasy is a bull; the pressed-out Soma is a bull, O Indra, bull with bulls, greatest killer of Vṛtra.

*3* As a bull I call to you, the bull with the thunderbolt, with various aids, O Indra, bull with bulls, greatest killer of Vṛtra.

*4* Impetuous bull with the thunderbolt, the king who breathes hard as he overpowers the mighty, Vṛtra-slayer and Soma-drinker – let him yoke his two bay horses and come here to us. Let Indra drink to ecstasy in the midday Soma pressing.

*5* When the demon of sunlight[3] pierced you, Sun,[4] with darkness, then all creatures looked like a confused man who does not know where he is.

*6* As you, Indra, struck down the sunlight-demon's magic spells that were turning beneath the sky,[5] then Atri with the fourth incantation[6] found the sun that had been hidden by the darkness pitted against the sacred order.[7]

*7* [*The sun:*] 'Let not the attacker swallow me up in his jealous spite and terrifying rage, for I am yours, Atri. You are my friend,[8] whose favour is real.[9] I hope that both you and King Varuṇa will help me now.'

*8* The high priest Atri set the pressing-stones to work and honoured the gods with devout obeisance, seeking to win their protection. He set the eye of the sun in heaven and made the magic spells of the demon of sunlight disappear.

*9* The Atris found again the sun that the sunlight demon had pierced with darkness, for no others could do this.

## NOTES

1. Indra is the lord of Soma, the best Soma-drinker.

2. The bulls are the Maruts.

3. Svarbhānu, 'sunlight', is a demon (Asura) who devours the sun, either in the course of its annual waning, or in its daily setting, or in its occasional eclipses. In later mythology he becomes Rāhu, who devours both the sun and the moon. He is a 'sunlight' demon whose name is constructed like the name of the 'cookie-monster': he eats sunlight as the monster eats cookies.

4. Sūrya.

5. The sun could not shine down to earth as the magic placed a barrier beneath it.

6. Later texts tell that the first three spells did not work. Sāyaṇa suggests that this may also be a reference to the first four stanzas of this hymn, that invoke Indra.

7. The sacred law or order (*ṛta*), the way of nature, would not have made the sun dark at that time. This seems to imply an eclipse rather than some natural darkening of the sun in winter or at night.

8. A pun on 'friend' and the name of the god Mitra, ally of Varuṇa.

9. That is, whatever you help me with is sure to come true.

## 1.50 *The Sun, Sūrya*

The Sun in this hymn drives a chariot whose rays (also called banners) are said to be seven mares. In his fiery aspect, he is identified with Agni 'Knower of Creatures' (Jātavedas), and through the recurrent image of seeing and being seen and giving light that allows others to see he is further identified with Varuṇa, the eye of the gods.

*1* His brilliant banners draw upwards the god who knows all creatures, so that everyone may see the sun.

*2* The constellations, along with the nights, steal away like thieves, making way for the sun who gazes on everyone.

*3* The rays that are his banners have become visible from the distance, shining over mankind like blazing fires.

*4* Crossing space, you are the maker of light, seen by

everyone, O sun. You illumine the whole, wide realm of space.

5 You rise up facing all the groups of gods, facing mankind, facing everyone, so that they can see the sunlight.

6 He is the eye with which, O Purifying Varuṇa, you look upon the busy one[1] among men.

7 You cross heaven and the vast realm of space, O sun, measuring days by nights, looking upon the generations.

8 Seven bay mares carry you in the chariot, O sun god with hair of flame, gazing from afar.

9 The sun has yoked the seven splendid daughters of the chariot; he goes with them, who yoke themselves.

10 We have come up out of darkness, seeing the higher light around us, going to the sun, the god among gods, the highest light.

11 As you rise today, O sun, you who are honoured as a friend, climbing to the highest sky, make me free of heartache and yellow pallor.[2]

12 Let us place my yellow pallor among parrots and thrushes, or let us place my yellow pallor among other yellow birds in yellow trees.

13 This Āditya[3] has risen with all his dominating force, hurling my hateful enemy down into my hands. Let me not fall into my enemy's hands!

NOTES

1. A probable reference to the diligent sacrificer.

2. Jaundice (yellow pallor) is analogous to yellow sunlight; hence the sun is invoked to dispense homoeopathic medicine.

3. The sun is one of the children of Aditi (cf. 10.72), a group of solar gods called Ādityas.

## 10.123 *Vena*

A strange, mystical hymn to a sage or god named Vena ('longing'); the imagery plays upon Vena's identification both with Soma and with the sun, more particularly with the sun-bird that is (or wins) Soma (cf. 4.26–7). The pressing of Soma, the rising of the sun, and the birth of speech and inspiration (cf. 1.164) run as parallel themes through the hymn.

*1* This Vena drives forth those who are pregnant with the dappled one.[1] Enveloped in a membrane of light,[2] he measures out the realm of space. In the union of the waters and the sun, the inspired priests lick him with prayers as if he were a calf.[3]

*2* Vena whips the wave high out of the ocean.[4] Born of the clouds, the back of the loved one has appeared,[5] shining on the crest at the highpoint of Order. The women[6] cry out to the common womb.

*3* The calf's many mothers from the same nest stand lowing at their common child. Striding to the crest of Order, the voices lick the honeyed drink of immortality.

*4* Knowing his form, the inspired ones yearn for him, for they have come towards the bellow of the wild animal, the buffalo.[7] Going on the right path, they have climbed to the river. The divine youths have found the immortal names.[8]

*5* The nymph,[9] the woman, smiling at her lover bears him to the highest heaven. The lover moves in the wombs of the lover. Vena sits on the golden wing.[10]

*6* Longing[11] for you in their heart, they saw you flying to the dome of the sky as an eagle, the golden-winged messenger of Varuṇa, the bird hastening into the womb of Yama.

*7* Then the divine youth[12] climbed straight back up into the dome of the sky bearing his many-coloured weapons. Dressing himself in a perfumed robe, looking like sunlight, he gives birth to his own names.[13]

*8* When the drop comes to the ocean,[14] looking upon the wide expanse with the eye of a vulture, then the sun, rejoicing in the clear light, takes on his own names in the third realm.

## NOTES

1. The dappled one (Pṛśṇi) is both the Soma stalk, brightly coloured, and the sun, represented as a dappled bull; the pregnant ones are thus the waters that mix with the Soma and the dawns that hold the sun, and Vena is said to bring them forth simultaneously.

2. As an embryo (the image projected from the first half of the verse), Soma is born in a burst of light (a membrane; cf. 10.51.1), as is the sun, who is the subject of the second sentence in the verse, while the third refers primarily to Soma.

3. Soma is often likened to a new-born calf licked by a cow, as is Agni. Cf. 4.18.10 and 2.35.13.

4. The sage brings the wave of sacred speech out of the ocean of the heart; the sun rises from the ocean, and Soma is mixed with the waters.

5. The loved one is Soma, immediately identified with the shining sun.

6. The women are either the voices and sacred speeches of the priests, calling to Soma (the womb of Order), or the streams of milk that mix with Soma. Both of these similes are extended in the next verse.

7. Soma is the buffalo who roars as he mingles with the waters.

8. The Gandharvas are the ones who reveal the secrets of the gods. Demigods associated with power and fertility, they are often identified with Soma, as is the case here, or the sun, as in the following verse.

9. The nymph, or Apsaras, as the beloved of the Gandharva, represents the Dawn, who loves the sun, or the waters or Speech, who love Soma.

10. Vena as the sun bears Soma on golden wings. The metaphor continues in the next verse.

11. 'Longing' (*venantas*), a pun on the name of Vena.

12. Here the divine youth (Gandharva) primarily represents the sun; in the second half of the verse, Soma is primary, the sun secondary.

13. By revealing his names, he reveals his forms.

14. Vena is Soma in the first half of the hymn, flying from the ocean through the wide expanse of space, to become the sun in the second half of the hymn, in the third realm that is heaven.

## 10.177 *The Bird*

The imagery of this hymn is closely tied to that of the Vena hymn. This is regarded as a magic-dispelling (*māyābheda*) incantation.

*1* The wise see in their heart, in their spirit, the bird anointed[1] with the magic of the Asura. The poets see him inside the ocean; the sages seek the footprints of his rays.[2]

*2* The bird carries in his heart Speech that the divine youth[3] spoke of inside the womb. The poets guard this revelation that shines like the sun in the footprint of Order.

*3* I have seen the cowherd who never tires, moving to and fro along the paths. Clothing himself in those that move towards the same centre but spread apart,[4] he rolls on and on inside the worlds.

### NOTES

1. The Asuras, noted for their magic, possess a miraculous balm which, placed upon the eyes, makes the bearer invisible to the eyes of others.

2. Vena as the sun is hidden inside the waters.

3. Here, as in 10.123.4, the Gandharva (the sun) 'reveals' the secrets of the gods. This secret is often told while the speaker is still in the womb. Cf. 4.27.1 and 4.18.1.

4. The waters and rays. This verse is taken from 1.164.31, which expands upon the riddle of the sun-bird.

## 1.42 *Pūṣan on the Road*

Pūṣan presides over roads and journeys. He is one of the Ādityas and therefore a solar god, though this aspect of his character is seldom emphasized.

*1* Traverse the ways, Pūṣan, and keep away anguish, O child of the unharnessing.[1] Stay with us, O god, going before us.

2 The evil, vicious wolf who threatens us, Pūṣan, chase him away from the path.

3 The notorious highwayman, the robber who plots in ambush, drive him far away from the track.

4 Trample with your foot the torch of the two-tongued slanderer, whoever he may be.

5 Worker of wonders,[2] full of good council, O Pūṣan, we beg you for that help with which you encouraged our fathers.

6 You bring every good fortune and are the best bearer of the golden sword. Make riches easy for us to win.

7 Lead us past our pursuers; make our paths pleasant and easy to travel. Find for us here, Pūṣan, the power of understanding.

8 Lead us to pastures rich in grass; let there be no sudden fever on the journey. Find for us here, Pūṣan, the power of understanding.

9 Use your powers, give fully and lavishly, give eagerly and fill the belly. Find for us here, Pūṣan, the power of understanding.

10 We do not reproach Pūṣan, but sing his praises with well-worded hymns. We pray to the worker of wonders to give us riches.

### NOTES

1. The releasing or unyoking of the horses at journey's end or at nightfall; by extension, perhaps, the release of the worshipper from evil or misfortune or exhaustion, the tight spot (*aṃhas*) or anguish.

2. An epithet usually given to the Aśvins, implying wonders wrought in order to be helpful to human worshippers.

## 6.55 *Pūṣan, Child of the Unharnessing*

1 Come, burning child of the unharnessing. Let the two of us be joined together. Be for us the charioteer of Order.[1]

2 Best of charioteers, lord of great wealth, friend with braided hair, we pray to you for riches.

3 You are a stream of riches, a heap of wealth, O burning one with goats for horses,[2] friend of this and that inspired singer.

4 Pūṣan with goats for horses, the prize-winner who is called the lover of his sister,[3] him we would praise.

5 I have spoken of him who is his mother's suitor; let him hear, he who is his sister's lover, the brother of Indra, and my friend.

6 Let the sure-footed goats who pull his chariot bring Pūṣan to us, carrying here the god who is the glory of the people.

### NOTES

1. Perhaps the one who carries us to Order (*ṛta*), or who drives Order to us.

2. The goat, sacred to Pūṣan (cf. 1.162.3–4), draws his chariot in place of the usual horse.

3. Apparently Dawn (Uṣas) was the sister of Pūṣan as well as his mother (v. 5), and, finally, the object of his (perhaps unrequited?) love. The Aśvins are also unsuccessful suitors and brothers of Sūryā (10.85). This incestuous tangle arises in part out of the fact that dusk, dawn, and twilight are natural siblings in close contact with the sun, and dawn 'gives birth' to the sun in one sense and is born from him in another.

## 2.38 *Savitṛ at Sunset*

Savitṛ 'the impeller', 'driver', or 'goader', is the god of the sun at morning and the setting sun, the latter aspect often emphasized in the hymns.

1 This god Savitṛ, the driver,[1] has risen up many times to goad us on – this is his work. Now he apportions to the gods the jewel,[2] and to those who offer the oblation he gives a share in happiness.

2 So that all will obey him, the god with broad hands
stands upright and stretches out his two arms before
him. Even the waters obey his command; even the wind
stops in his orbit.
3 Even the one who travels with swift horses[3] now un-
harnesses them; he[4] has stopped even the wanderer[5]
from going on. He has put an end to the voracious
hunger even of those who eat serpents.[6] Night has
come by Savitṛ's command.
4 She who weaves[7] has rolled up again what was stretched
out. The skilful worker has laid down the work half-
completed. He[8] stirs and stands up; he has set apart
the different times. With his thoughts gathered, the
god Savitṛ has come.
5 He who lives in a house[9] goes off into various dwellings,
all his life. The glow of fire springs up and spreads
out. The mother gives her son the best portion, be-
cause of the longing that Savitṛ has stirred up in him.[10]
6 He who went away because he wished to get something
has now come back; the desire of all who wander turns
to home. All of them, leaving their work uncompleted,
have followed the command of the divine Savitṛ.
7 Those whose portion you decreed to be water are in the
waters;[11] the hunters spread out over the dry land. The
trees belong to the birds; no one transgresses these
commands of this god Savitṛ.[12]
8 Varuṇa goes to the watery womb that he loves best,
after rushing about restlessly from one blink of the eye
to the next. Every bird and beast goes to his nest or
pen; Savitṛ has dispersed each creature to its proper
resting-place.
9 He whose law is not broken by Indra, nor by Varuṇa
or Mitra, nor by Aryaman or Rudra, nor even by the
forces of evil – that god Savitṛ I call upon for happiness,
bowing low.
10 Stirring up Good Luck[13] and Thought and Abundance –
and may Praise-of-Men,[14] the husband of goddesses,

help us – when blessings come and riches pile up let us be dear to the god Savitṛ.

*11* From the sky, from the waters, from the earth let there come to us that bounty that we long for and that you give, that brings happiness to those who praise and to your friend,[15] the singer whose praises reach far, O Savitṛ.

NOTES

1. That is, the driver of the chariot. The same epithet is also supplied to Agni in 3.31.1.

2. Both immortality and the sacrificial offering.

3. Simultaneously Savitṛ in his chariot and any man on earth, who unyokes now that night has come.

4. Only Savitṛ is meant here.

5. Either one who wanders about as he wishes to do, or one who has strayed from the path.

6. Probably birds of prey.

7. Both night, continued from verse 3, here 'rolling up' the sunlight, and the woman who takes up her weaving now that night has come.

8. Only Savitṛ here, who demarcates the different seasons and hours.

9. Both the householder who goes home at night, and the domestic fire (mentioned in the next part of the verse) that 'arrives' in the house at evening.

10. That is, the setting sun makes the boy hungry.

11. The animals who seek water-holes at the end of the day; the hunters, by contrast, are hunting on the dry land.

12. Several overlapping meanings: no one destroys the trees; no one, not even the trees, disobeys Savitṛ's command to rest at night.

13. Good Luck (Bhaga) is often personified as a god, but here he appears with other personifications regarded more as abstractions – thought (*dhī*) and abundance (Purandhi).

14. The praise that is bestowed upon men (Narāśaṃsa), rather than by them.

15. That is, the author of this hymn.

## 1.35 *Savitṛ at Night*

1 I call first to Agni for well-being; I call Mitra and Varuṇa
here to help. I call on Night[1] that gives rest to all that
moves; I call on the god Savitṛ for aid.
2 When he turns through the dark dust and gives rest
to the immortal and the mortal, the god Savitṛ who
watches all creatures comes with his golden chariot.
3 The god goes forward; he goes upward; he who is
worshipped goes with his two bright bay horses. The
god Savitṛ comes from the far distance, driving away
all evils.
4 The god Savitṛ, who is worshipped, mounts his high
chariot that is covered with pearls, painted with all
colours, fastened with golden pins; shining brightly,
he puts on his vital power for the dark dusts.[2]
5 The black horses with white feet have looked at the
people, pulling the chariot with the golden shafts in
front. All tribes, all worlds, rest always in the lap of
the divine Savitṛ.
6 There are three skies: two are the lap of Savitṛ, and
the last is the one that controls men, in the world of
Yama. Immortal things rest on him like a chariot wheel
on a lynch-pin. Let him who understands this proclaim
it here.
7 The eagle has looked over the middle realms of space;
he is the Asura who leads well and is spoken of in secret.
Where is the sun now? Who knows? To what sky has
his ray stretched?
8 He has looked upon the eight peaks of the earth, and on
the three plains a league wide, and the seven rivers.
The golden-eyed Savitṛ has come, bringing to the
worshipper the treasures that he longs for.
9 Golden-handed Savitṛ moves busily between the two,
between sky and earth. He drives away disease and bids
the sun approach; he reaches to the sky through the
dark dust.

10 Let the merciful and helpful Asura, the good leader with golden hands, come towards us. Routing the demons[3] and sorcerers, the god to whom we sing has taken his place against the evening.

11 On your ancient paths, Savitṛ, that are dustless and well made in the middle realm of space, on those paths that are good to go on come to us today, and protect us, and speak a blessing on us, O god.

NOTES

1. Here and in other verses of this hymn, Savitṛ appears in his nocturnal aspect (as Dawn often does), moving through the dark dust or haze of night.

2. That is, he uses his powers of brightness to cross the dark spaces of night.

3. Rakṣases, flesh-eating demons on earth, not the mighty Asuras of heaven.

## 10.127 *Night*

This is the only Rig Vedic hymn dedicated to the goddess of night, sister of Dawn and, like Dawn, a bright creature, full of coloured stars, in contrast with the feared darkness of black night that is banished (vv. 3 and 7).

1 The goddess Night has drawn near, looking about on many sides with her eyes.[1] She has put on all her glories.

2 The immortal goddess has filled the wide space,[2] the depths and the heights. She stems the tide of darkness with her light.

3 The goddess has drawn near, pushing aside her sister the twilight.[3] Darkness, too, will give way.

4 As you came near to us today, we turned homeward to rest, as birds go to their home in a tree.

5 People who live in villages have gone home to rest, and animals with feet, and animals with wings, even the ever-searching hawks.

6 Ward off the she-wolf and the wolf; ward off the thief.
O night full of waves, be easy for us to cross over.[4]
7 Darkness – palpable, black, and painted[5] – has come
upon me. O Dawn, banish it like a debt.[6]
8 I have driven this hymn to you as the herdsman drives
cows.[7] Choose and accept it, O Night, daughter of the
sky, like a song of praise to a conqueror.

NOTES

1. The stars.

2. Between sky and earth.

3. The actual term used here is dawn, but it probably indicates twilight in general, more specifically here the evening twilight, or even the entire day (as in the Vedic expression 'dawn and night' meaning 'day and night'). On the other hand, if one takes it literally as dawn, it may mean that the Night keeps dawn away because darkness must depart when dawn appears. Cf. 1.92.11, where Dawn pushes Night aside.

4. The verb 'to cross' is frequently applied to a transition from one period of time to another. Its primary meaning is to cross from one bank of a river to another, and here it may recall the epithet 'full of waves,' depicting Night as a dangerous body of water that one must cross. Cf. 1.92.6.

5. Night is here regarded as a material mass painted with stars or actually painting them herself.

6. The implication is that light (often compared to wealth) should banish darkness as money banishes the poet's debts; or Dawn may 'collect' the debt of the night, that is, make good what darkness had incurred or 'exact' the darkness from Night as one would exact money owing.

7. An elliptic image, but clear in the Vedic context that associates cows with light; the herdsman gives back at night the cows that he has kept all day.

# SKY AND EARTH

THE Sky (Dyaus) was an important god in Indo-European mythology and remained so in Greece, in the figure of Zeus. In India, his scope is greatly reduced, most aspects of his mythology being taken over by Indra, but he remains enshrined in several hymns as one half of the androgynous pair, Sky-and-Earth (often expressed as a single noun in the dual). This pair is essential not only to the cosmogony (1.160) but to the safety and well-being of mortals on earth, who invoke their help as one would ask parents for comfort (1.185). Like parents, too, they are described as being made of food and nourishment for mankind (6.70).

These divinities, referred to in the dual, are alternately characterized as male and female, parents of the sun, or as two sisters.

*1* Sky and earth, these two who are good for everyone, hold the Order and bear the poet of space.[1] Between the two goddesses, the two bowls that give birth magnificently, the pure sun god moves according to the laws of nature.

*2* Wide and roomy, strong and inexhaustible, the father and mother protect the universe. The two world-halves are as bold as two wonderful girls[2] when their father[3] dresses them in shapes and colours.

*3* The son of these parents,[4] their clever charioteer with the power to make things clear, purifies the universe by magic.[5] From the dappled milk-cow and the bull with good seed,[6] every day he milks the milk that is his[7] seed.

*4* Most artful of the artful gods, he[8] gave birth to the two world-halves that are good for everyone. He measured apart the two realms of space[9] with his power of inspiration and fixed them in place with undecaying pillars.

*5* Sky and earth, you mighty pair whose praises we have sung, grant us great fame and high sovereignty, by which we may extend our rule over the peoples for ever. Give us enormous force.

## NOTES

1. The sun, in the space between sky and earth.

2. These are the two goddesses of the previous verse, sky and earth as two bowls.

3. Tvaṣṭṛ or the creator.

4. The sun, child of sky and earth as parents again.

5. The sun's magic dispels darkness, thus both clarifying and purifying the world.

6. The dappled cow (Pṛśṇi) is the earth, the bull the sky.

7. The milker is the child, the sun; 'his' seed refers probably not merely to the bull but to the joint, androgynous creature that gives a fluid simultaneously milk (from her) and seed (from him).

8. Probably Tvaṣṭṛ or the creator. If it is the sun, he is giving birth to his own parents, an idea not without precedent in the *Rig Veda*. The sun is the subject of the second half of the verse.

9. Between sky and earth.

## 1.185 *Guard Us from the Monstrous Abyss*[1]

*1* Which of these two was first, and which came later? How were they born? Who, O poets, really knows? They themselves bear whatever has a name. The two halves of the day[2] roll past one another like two wheels.

*2* These two[3] who do not move, who have no feet, receive the teeming embryo[4] that moves and has feet, like a natural son in the parents' lap. Sky and earth, guard us from the monstrous abyss.

*3* I call upon Aditi's gift[5] that dispels evil and repels assault, the celestial, awe-inspiring gift that saves us from violent death. Sky and earth, guard us from the monstrous abyss.

*4* We wish to please the two world-halves whose sons are the gods, the two among the gods who free us from suffering and help the helpless, with the two rotating halves of the days. Sky and earth, guard us from the monstrous abyss.

*5* The two young women, true sisters who join in the lap of their parents,[6] share a common boundary[7] and kiss the navel of the world.[8] Sky and earth, guard us from the monstrous abyss.

*6* With truth I call upon the two wide and high mansions[9] who give birth[10] with the help of the gods, the two whose faces are lovely and who have received immortality. Sky and earth, guard us from the monstrous abyss.

*7* With reverence in this sacrifice I speak in prayer to the two who are wide, vast, and massive, whose boundaries are far distant, who having received immortality bring good fortune and dispel evil. Sky and earth, guard us from the monstrous abyss.

8 Whatever wrong we have ever done to the gods, or to an old friend, or to the master of the house, for all of these let the thought in this hymn be an apology. Sky and earth, guard us from the monstrous abyss.

9 Let both sides of the praise of heroes[11] be kind to me. Let both of them[12] stay near me with help and favour. There is plenty for the patron who is more generous than a stranger.[13] Let us become ecstatic, O gods, and invigorated by the drink of ecstasy.

10 I have in my wisdom spoken this truth[14] to heaven and earth, so that they will hear it first. Let them protect us from the blame and evil that we face. Let father and mother guard us with helping favours.

11 Let this come true,[15] what I have said here in prayer to you, sky and earth, father and mother. Become the closest of the gods with your helping favours. Let us find the drink whose luscious drops give strength and ecstasy.

## NOTES

1. The word (*abhvam*) designates a dark, formless, enormous and terrifying abyss, particularly associated with night (1.92.5) and the underworld, and hence opposed to the light of the worlds of sky and earth.

2. Day and night, loosely associated with heaven and earth through their duality rather than through a literal identification of day with heaven and night with earth.

3. Sky and earth.

4. The embryo, or seed (*garbha*), is the sun or Agni, here symbolic of all creatures (hence teeming).

5. As mother of the gods, Aditi gives the blessings of life and nature.

6. Cf. 1.160.2.

7. The line where sky and earth meet.

8. The *axis mundi*, here identified with the sun.

9. Sky and earth.

10. They give birth to the gods.

11. Praise given by the poet to heroes and gods, and praise given to him by heroes and gods.

12. Sky and earth, or both men and gods.

13. The stranger is the 'best enemy' or ritual competitor. Cf. 10.86.1.

14. The word for truth here (*ṛta*) designates actual reality and order, a statement *about* sky and earth as well as *to* them.

15. True here in the sense of physical actuality.

## 6.70 *The Two Full of Butter*

1 The two full of butter, beautiful masters of all creatures, broad and wide, milked of honey, beautifully adorned – sky and earth have been propped apart, by Varuṇa's law; unageing, they are rich in seed.

2 Inexhaustible, rich in streams, full of milk, the two whose vows are pure are milked of butter for the one who does good deeds. You two world-halves, rulers over this universe, pour out on us the seed that was the base for mankind.[1]

3 The mortal who makes an offering to you world-halves, sources of strength, so that he may walk on the right path, he succeeds: he is reborn through his progeny according to the law. Creatures with various forms but with a common vow have been poured out from you.

4 Enclosed in butter are sky and earth, beautiful in butter, gorged on butter, grown on butter. Broad and wide, they are the first priests[2] in the choice of the priest of the oblation. They are the ones that the priests invoke when they seek kindness.

5 Sky and earth that stream with honey, that are milked of honey, that have honey for their vow, let them soak us with honey, bringing sacrifice and wealth to the gods, great fame, the victory prize, and virility to us.

6 Sky and earth, the all-knowing father and mother who

achieve wondrous works – let them swell up with food to nourish us. Let the two world-halves, that work together to give benefits to all, together thrust toward us gain, and the victory prize, and wealth.

NOTES

1. The seed from which mankind (or Manu) originally grew.

2. The Purohitas who cast the first vote in choosing the oblation priest to assist them.

# VARUṆA

ALTHOUGH Varuṇa's original function was that of a sky god (like Ouranos, with whom his name is cognate), by the time of the *Rig Veda* he had developed into a god whose primary role was watching over the deeds of men (as a sky god is well placed to do) and punishing those who violated the sacred law (*ṛta*) of which Varuṇa was the most important custodian. He is also, like several other Vedic gods, credited with the archetypal acts of creation – finding the sun, propping apart the sky and earth, and so forth (5.85). His friendship, disaffection, and ultimate reconciliation with the sage Vasiṣṭha (7.86, 7.88, 7.89) form a paradigm for his stern but loving relationship with mankind in general. He is asked to protect the worshipper not only from his own avenging wrath but also from all dangers and hatreds (2.28), an all-encompassing role that was transferred to the gods Viṣṇu and Śiva in later Hinduism, when Varuṇa ceased to be worshipped any more.

## 5.85 *The Deeds of Varuṇa*

This hymn describes the great deeds of Varuṇa and closes with a wish that he will pardon the mistakes of the worshipper.

*1* For the emperor[1] I will sing a splendid, deep prayer, one that will be dear to the famous Varuṇa who struck apart the earth[2] and spread it beneath the sun as the priest who performs the slaughter spreads out the victim's skin.[3]

*2* He stretched out the middle realm of space in the trees; he laid victory in swift horses and milk in the dawn cows, intelligence in hearts and fire in the waters. Varuṇa placed the sun in the sky and Soma on the mountain.

*3* Over the two world-halves and the realm of space between them Varuṇa has poured out the cask,[4] turning its mouth downward. With it the king of the whole universe waters the soil as the rain waters the grain.

*4* He waters the soil, the earth,[5] and the sky. Whenever Varuṇa wishes for milk, the mountains dress themselves in cloud and the heroes,[6] brandishing their power, let them loose.[7]

*5* I will proclaim the great magic[8] of Varuṇa the famous Asura,[9] who stood up in the middle realm of space and measured apart the earth with the sun as with a measuring-stick.[10]

*6* No one has dared this great magic of the most inspired god: that these shimmering torrents, pouring down, do not fill the one single ocean with their water.[11]

*7* If we have committed an offence against a hospitable friend like Aryaman or a close friend like Mitra,[12] or against one who has always been a comrade, or a brother, or a neighbour – one of our own or a stranger – loosen that offence from us, Varuṇa.

*8* If we have cheated like gamblers in a game, whether we know it or really do not know it,[13] O god, cast all these offences away like loosened bonds.[14] Let us be dear to you, Varuṇa.

NOTES

1. Varuṇa who is the king over all kings.

2. That is, struck it and made it part from the sky.

3. The sacrificial priest (Śamitṛ) spreads the skin and places the limbs of the animal upon it. Cf. 1.162.19.

4. The overturned cask or leather bottle is a frequent metaphor for a torrent of rain. Cf. 5.83.7.

5. The earth here designates the whole world, in contrast with the surface (soil).

6. The Maruts.

7. The Maruts let loose the cloud – that is, the waters. The metaphor may also refer to other things loosed by the Maruts – their own horses or powers – or to the explicit simile, the garments.

8. Magic here in the sense of a miracle rather than an illusion.

9. Asura not in its later sense of 'demon' but in its early Vedic sense of sky god.

10. Cf. 1.154.1.

11. That is, although there are many rivers and rains, the ocean, though alone, contains them. No one dares this – no one dares to challenge it or to attempt it.

12. Aryaman is the god of formal hospitality to strangers, Mitra the god of intimate friendship among one's own kind.

13. Cf. 2.12.10 for a sin of which one is unaware.

14. The bonds are both the offences themselves and the bonds with which Varuṇa punishes those who offend. Cf. 7.86 and 7.89.

## 7.86 *Varuṇa Provoked to Anger*

According to one tradition, this hymn should be read together with 7.55, to which it is joined by a myth: In a dream (or in his sleep) one night the sage Vasiṣṭha came to the house of Varuṇa; as he entered, a dog ran at him, barking and trying to bite him, but Vasiṣṭha put him to sleep with several verses (7.55); then King Varuṇa bound Vasiṣṭha with his snares, and when Vasiṣṭha praised his father Varuṇa with more verses (7.86–9), he was released. One text says that Vasiṣṭha stole something (perhaps food), an episode that may be alluded to in the reference to Vasiṣṭha being like a cattle-thief; but it is precisely the unknown and indefinable nature of Vasiṣṭha's sin that gives this hymn its power. For the implication of someone else in one's own evil deed – an older brother, or a father, or the forces of wine and anger, or the cloud of sleep – tends to negate any possible sense of remorse; one can regret the results of an unknown act (visible in Varuṇa's punishment) but not repent of its motives.[1] One may be punished for the sins of other people; in this context, sin may be a misleading word to use, for although the worshipper wishes for expiation, he wishes to be 'free from sin' primarily in the sense of being free from the *effects* of sin. He wishes to serve Varuṇa in order to become free from sin, not to be free from sin in order to serve Varuṇa. 'The evil that sleep does not avert' may be a bad dream or a deed committed while a sleep;[2] this may be the source of the tradition that Vasiṣṭha composed this hymn while wandering in a dream (or in his sleep), but in any case it further highlights the tension between conscious evil (sin) and unconscious evil (for which there is no good term in English).

*1* The generations have become wise by the power of him who has propped apart the two world-halves even though they are so vast.[3] He has pushed away the dome of the sky to make it high and wide; he has set the sun on its double journey[4] and spread out the earth.

*2* And I ask my own heart, 'When shall I be close to Varuṇa? Will he enjoy my offering and not be provoked to anger? When shall I see his mercy and rejoice?'

*3* I ask myself what that transgression was, Varuṇa, for I wish to understand. I turn to the wise to ask them. The poets have told me the very same thing: 'Varuṇa has been provoked to anger against you.'

*4* O Varuṇa, what was the terrible crime for which you wish to destroy your friend who praises you? Proclaim it to me so that I may hasten to prostrate myself before you and be free from sin, for you are hard to deceive and are ruled by yourself alone.

5 Free us from the harmful deeds of our fathers, and from those that we have committed with our own bodies. O king, free Vasiṣṭha like a thief who has stolen cattle,[5] like a calf set free from a rope.

6 The mischief was not done by my own free will, Varuṇa; wine, anger, dice, or carelessness led me astray. The older shares in the mistake of the younger.[6] Even sleep does not avert evil.

7 As a slave serves a generous master, so would I serve the furious god and be free from sin. The noble god gave understanding to those who did not understand;[7] being yet wiser, he speeds the clever man to wealth.

8 O Varuṇa, you who are ruled by yourself alone, let this praise lodge in your very heart. Let it go well for us always with your blessings.

NOTES

1. Cf. 2.12.10 and 5.85.8.

2. Cf. 10.164.

3. Creation consists in the act (here attributed to Varuṇa, elsewhere to other gods) of propping apart heaven and earth and releasing the sun.

4. Either by day in the sky and under the earth by night, or, less likely, its daily and annual revolutions.

5. Varuṇa binds sinners with his snares of disease and misfortune. The thief is set free after doing expiation for his sin – or, perhaps, in order to be led to his punishment.

6. The elder brother may be implicated in his younger brother's lapse, or he may be the cause of it. 'Older' may also refer to an older generation, the ancestral sin mentioned in the previous verse.

7. The wisdom that Varuṇa gives to the generations is his own truth. Varuṇa himself is 'yet wiser' either than those to whom he gave understanding or than the clever man that he aids. Varuṇa is wise in a spiritual sense; the clever or 'sharp' man is merely worldly-wise.

## 7.88 *Varuṇa the Friend of Vasiṣṭha*

After an introductory verse spoken by the poet, Vasiṣṭha speaks of his bygone friendship with Varuṇa, a friendship now threatened by the possibility that Vasiṣṭha has committed some offence, which he does not know of, and incurred the punishing wrath of Varuṇa.

*1* Vasiṣṭha, bring a pure and most desirable poem to the bountiful Varuṇa, who draws toward us the great bull[1] who is worthy of sacrifice and thousands of gifts.

*2* 'Now that I have come into his[2] presence, I think the face of Varuṇa is Agni's. Let the Lord on High[3] lead me to the sun that is in the rock[4] and the darkness, so that I may see the marvel.

*3* 'When we two, Varuṇa, board the boat and sail forth to the middle of the ocean, when we skim along the crests of the waters, we will swing in the swing[5] and glitter.'

*4* Varuṇa set Vasiṣṭha right in the boat. The inspired master made him a seer, a poet, by his great powers, so that his days would be good days, so that his skies and dawns would stretch out.

*5* 'Where have those friendships of us two gone, when in the old times we could live together without becoming enemies? I went into your high palace, self-ruling Varuṇa, into your house with a thousand doors.[6]

*6* 'If your old friend and dear ally has committed sins against you, Varuṇa, do not make us who have offended you pay for that. Avenger, inspired one, give protection to the singer of praises.

*7* 'As we dwell in these solid dwelling-places, let Varuṇa set us free from the noose and help us win aid from the lap of Aditi. Protect us always with blessings.'

### NOTES

1. The sun, brought forth each day by Varuṇa.
2. Probably Varuṇa's presence, but perhaps that of the sun.

3. Varuṇa.

4. The sun rests in the rock of darkness all night; it is, moreover, trapped in the cliff until Indra sets it free (3.31), a feat also attributed to Varuṇa.

5. Varuṇa, as god of the waters, has a boat that glitters as it swings.

6. Vasiṣṭha's entry into Varuṇa's house is alluded to elsewhere in the *Rig Veda*; cf. 7.89.1 and the introduction to 7.86.

## 7.89 *The House of Clay*

Varuṇa casts his snares upon the offending worshipper in the form of dropsy; but he satisfies by the grace of his own nature the thirst of the man who suffers from physical or spiritual fever. Thus the waters in verse 4 refer to the feverish thirst and 'waters' of the dropsy and to the waters of Varuṇa himself. The concept of unconscious sin is implicit in verse 3 and clearly expressed in verse 5, which juxtaposes various levels of evil: offence, sin, and a violation of the cosmic law (*dharma*, Varuṇa's law, the 'true current' of verse 3). All of these are tempered by the possibility that they were done carelessly, unwittingly; for it is the duty of Varuṇa himself to make men thoughtful (to 'make the generations wise'),[1] and the duty of the repentant sinner to know his sin.

The house of clay is a metaphor for death on various planes: it is the urn used to store the ashes of the dead after cremation or to store their bones in burial; it is the earth, the house of the dead man; and it is the home of Varuṇa, to which Vasiṣṭha went one night.[2]

*1* Let me not go to the house of clay, O King Varuṇa, not yet. Have mercy, great ruler; be merciful.

*2* If I seem to stumble and tremble like a puffed up goat-skin,[3] O master of stones,[4] have mercy; great ruler, be merciful.

*3* If through weakness of will-power I have somehow gone against the true current, O pure one, have mercy; great ruler, be merciful.

4 Thirst has come upon the one who sings to you as he stands in the midst of waters; have mercy, great ruler, be merciful.

5 If we humans have committed some offence against the race of gods, O Varuṇa, or through carelessness have violated your laws, do not injure us, O god, for that sin.

NOTES

1. See 7.86.1.

2. Cf. 7.88.5 and introduction to 7.86. Cf. also n. 6 to 7.88.

3. The worshipper is palsied and swollen from dropsy, like a leather wine-bottle filled with air; and he trembles in fear of Varuṇa. For stumbling, cf. 8.48.5.

4. This epithet, usually applied to Indra, refers both to the mastery of stones used to press the Soma and to stones used as weapons in a sling.

## 2.28 *Varuṇa*

1 Let this song to the son of Aditi, the poet who rules himself, surpass in greatness all the songs that now exist. The god who is comfortable to sacrifice to, the abundant Varuṇa, is the one I beg for lasting fame.

2 Let us be happy in your command, having praised you, Varuṇa, with good intentions, awakening like kindled fires day after day at the approach of the dawns rich in cattle.

3 Let us be under your protection, for you have many heroes, Varuṇa our leader, and your word reaches far. You sons of Aditi, gods who cannot be deceived, consent to join us.

4 The son of Aditi set them free to flow and ordered them; the rivers go by the Order of Varuṇa. They do not tire, nor do they unharness themselves. They fly swiftly like birds in their orbit.

5 Loosen me from sin as from a sash; let us find the

fountainhead of your Order, Varuṇa. Do not let the
thread break while I am still weaving this thought, nor
let the measuring-stick of the workman shatter before
its time.
6 Keep fear far away from me, Varuṇa, and hold fast to
me, O emperor of Order. Set me free from anguish
as one would free a calf from a rope; I cannot bear to live
apart from you even for the blink of an eye.
7 Varuṇa the Asura, do not wound us with your weapons
that wound the man you seek when he has committed a
sin. Let us not be exiled from the light. Loosen clean
away from us our failures, so that we may live.
8 O Varuṇa born of strength, the homage to you that was
made in the past long ago we would speak now, and in
the time yet to come. Upon you who cannot be deceived
our vows are set, unshakeable, as if upon a mountain.
9 Abolish the debts for the things I have done, O king,
and do not make me pay for what has been done by
others. So many more dawns have not yet risen, Varuṇa;
make sure that we will live through them.
10 If someone I have met, O king, or a friend has spoken of
danger to me in a dream to frighten me, or if a thief
should waylay us, or a wolf – protect us from that,
Varuṇa.
11 Do not let me know the loss of a dear, generous, open-
handed friend, Varuṇa, nor let me lack the wealth that
makes a good reign, O king. Let us speak great words
as men of power in the sacrificial gathering.

## RUDRA AND VIṢṆU

RUDRA is a liminal figure in the *Rig Veda*, invoked with Vedic hymns but not invited to partake in the regular Vedic sacrifice; as the embodiment of wildness and unpredictable danger, he is addressed more with the hope of keeping him at bay than with the wish to bring him near (a form of worship that persists in Hinduism not in the cult of Rudra's successor, Śiva, but in the cult of the Goddess, who does not appear in the *Rig Veda* at all). Viṣṇu is a far more typically Vedic god, vaguely solar, benevolent, and procreative (cf. 10.184), often associated with Indra and prayed to jointly with him, but appearing alone in several hymns. The two gods are significant not merely for their roles in the *Rig Veda* but for the far more important roles they were destined to play in later sectarian Hinduism.

## 2.33 *Rudra, Father of the Maruts*

Though only three entire hymns in the *Rig Veda* are addressed to Rudra, the rich ambivalence of his character is the basis of an important line of Indian theology that culminates in the Hindu god Śiva. Rudra is fierce and destructive like a terrible beast, like a wild storm; the sage begs him to turn his malevolence elsewhere. Yet Rudra is not merely demonic, for he is the healer and cooler as well as the bringer of disease and destructive fever.

*1* Father of the Maruts,[1] send your kindness here. Do not cut us off from the sight of the sun. Let the hero spare our horses.[2] O Rudra, let us be born again through our children.

*2* By those most healing medicines that you give, Rudra, I would attain a hundred winters. Drive hatred far away from us, and anguish farther away; drive diseases away in all directions.

*3* Of what is born, you, Rudra, are the most glorious in glory, the strongest of the strong, with the thunderbolt in your hand.[1] Carry us safely to the farther shore of anguish;[3] ward off all attacks or injury.

*4* We would not wish to anger you, Rudra the bull,[1] by acts of homage or ill praise,[4] or by invoking you together with another god.[5] Raise up our heroes with your healing medicines; I hear that of all healers you are the best healer.

*5* If someone should call him with invocations and oblations, thinking, 'I will appease Rudra with songs of praise' – may the soft-hearted[6] god who is easy to invoke, the tawny god whose lips are full[7] – may he not suspect us of that and give us over into the power of his anger.[8]

*6* The bull[1] with the Maruts inspired me with his vital energy when I was in need of help. I long to win the

kindness of Rudra, as I would long to reach the shade
unharmed in the heat of the sun.
*7* Where is your merciful hand, Rudra, so healing and cool-
ing, that removes the injury that comes from the gods?
Have mercy on me, O bull.
*8* I send high praise to the high bull, tawny and white.
I bow low in homage to the radiant one. We praise
the dreaded name of Rudra.
*9* The fierce, tawny god of many forms has adorned his
firm limbs with shimmering gold. Never let the Asura
power[9] draw away from Rudra, the ruler of this vast
world.
*10* Rightly you carry the arrows and bow; rightly you
wear the precious golden necklace shaped with many
forms and colours; rightly you extend this terrible power
over everything.[10] There is nothing more powerful than
you, Rudra.
*11* Praise him, the famous young god who sits on the high
seat,[11] the fierce one who attacks like a ferocious wild
beast. O Rudra, have mercy on the singer, now that you
have been praised. Let your armies strike down someone
other than us.
*12* As a son bows to his father who greets him, so I bow to
you, Rudra, as you approach. I sing to the giver of
plenty, the true lord; being praised, give us healing
medicines.
*13* Your healing medicines, O Maruts, so pure, so strength-
ening, so comforting, that our father Manu[12] chose –
I desire these, O bulls, and happiness and health from
Rudra.
*14* Let the weapon of Rudra veer from us; let the great
malevolence of the dreaded god go past us. Loosen the
taut bows for the sake of our generous patrons; O
bountiful one, have mercy on our children and grand-
children.
*15* O tawny and amazing bull, O God, do not become in-
censed or kill us. Be here for us, Rudra, and hear our

call. Let us speak great words as men of power in the sacrificial gathering.

## NOTES

1. This hymn transfers to Rudra several attributes usually associated with Indra, such as the companionship of the Maruts, the thunderbolt, and the bull.

2. This verse may also imply a wish that Rudra will spare the worshipper when he is on horseback. Elsewhere in the *Rig Veda* (1.114.8), Rudra is asked not to harm horses.

3. For the image of crossing over danger, cf. 10.127.6 and 1.92.6.

4. The implication is that the worship may be given in an unsatisfactory way.

5. Many gods are invoked in pairs or groups in the *Rig Veda*, but never Rudra, who is given offerings separately from all other gods. The worshipper may also fear that he might offend Rudra by pairing him with an inferior god.

6. A vain hope or an optimistic euphemism, like calling the Greek Furies the Eumenides or 'well-disposed'.

7. The adjective, also applied to Indra, particularly indicates that his lips are ready to drink Soma.

8. The verse implies that the wrong-minded worshipper might think he could bribe Rudra and that such a man's thought might provoke Rudra to anger. The poet asks Rudra not to suspect *him* of such blasphemy. The verse turns upon the multiple meanings of *manā*: thought (the blasphemy), suspicion (Rudra's), and anger (also Rudra's).

9. Here the term '*asura*' still has its connotation of a class of divinities, though its later meaning, 'demonic', would also be appropriate to Rudra.

10. The power of chaos and darkness (*abhvam*). Cf. 1.185.

11. Probably the seat on a chariot, rather than a throne.

12. This may recall the time of original creation, when Manu, the father of mankind, first kindled the sacrificial fire and offered Soma to the gods; Soma may be the source of the 'healing medicines' given to Manu in return for sacrifice. For Rudra and Manu, cf. 1.114.2.

## 1.114 *Have Mercy on Us, Rudra*

1 We bring these thoughts to the mighty Rudra, the god
with braided hair,[1] who rules over heroes, so that it
will be well with our two-footed and four-footed
creatures, and in this village all will flourish unharmed.
2 Have mercy on us, Rudra, and give us life-force. We
wish to bow low in service to you who rule over heroes.
Whatever happiness and health Manu the father[2] won
by sacrifice, we wish to gain that with you to lead us
forth.
3 We wish to gain your kindness, Rudra, through sacrifice
to the gods, for you are generous. O ruler over heroes,
come to our families with kindness. Let us offer the
oblation to you with our heroes free from injury.
4 We call down for help the dreaded Rudra who com-
pletes the sacrifice, the sage who flies.[3] Let him repel far
from us the anger of the gods; it is his kindness that we
choose to have.
5 Tawny boar of the sky, dreaded form with braided
hair, we call you down and we bow low. Holding in his
hand the healing medicines that we long for, let him
grant us protection, shelter, refuge.
6 These words are spoken for Rudra, the father of the
Maruts, words sweeter than sweet, to strengthen him.
And grant us, O immortal, the food for mortals. Have
mercy on us, and on our children and grandchildren.
7 Do not slaughter the great one among us or the small
one among us, nor the growing or the grown. Rudra, do
not kill our father or our mother, nor harm the bodies
dear to us.[4]
8 Do not harm us in our children or grandchildren, nor in
our life-span, nor in our cows or in our horses. Rudra,
do not in fury slaughter our heroes. With oblations we
call you here for ever.
9 I have driven these praises to you as the herdsman
drives his cattle. Grant us kindness, father of the Maruts,

for your kindness brings blessings most merciful, and so it is your help that we choose to have.

10 Keep far away from us your cow-killing and man-killing power, O ruler of heroes. Have mercy on us and speak for us, O god, and grant us double protection.[5]

11 Seeking help, we have spoken in homage to him. Let Rudra with the Maruts hear our call. Let Mitra, Varuṇa, Aditi, Sindhu,[6] Earth and Sky grant this to us.

NOTES

1. Rudra's long hair is braided or piled on top of his head in a chignon.

2. As the primeval ancestor of man, Manu performed the first sacrifice by mortals for immortals.

3. Cf. 10.136.4 and 10.136.7.

4. Either our own bodies or the bodies of people we love.

5. Probably protection from his own wrath as well as from that of the other gods (before whom he is asked to speak on behalf of the worshipper), or from the killing of men and the killing of cattle.

6. A river goddess.

## 1.154 *The Three Strides of Viṣṇu*

Viṣṇu, like Rudra, seems prominent in the *Rig Veda* only through Hindu hindsight; though he is often invoked in conjunction with Indra (with whom Rudra also has close ties), he is merely one of several similar gods of a generally solar and beneficial character. This hymn is the basis of the later myth of the dwarf avatar who takes three steps to win the world from the demons.

Viṣṇu's three space-creating steps prop apart and thereby make the basic two-part Universe: the earthly regions and the 'upper dwelling-place' (v. 1) or 'highest footstep' (vv. 5–6), the seat of the immortal gods (vv. 5–6), particularly of Viṣṇu (or of Viṣṇu with Indra). It is significant that three steps are needed to accomplish this split into two; the paradox becomes strikingly explicit in verse 4, where Viṣṇu supports the threefold heaven and earth; the mediating third is Viṣṇu himself, who embodies 'all creatures'.

The three steps suggest many metaphorical levels. In the solar symbolism, they may be dawn, noon, and sunset, or three phases of the year that Viṣṇu 'measures apart' (vv. 1 and 3). These steps are called strides (*vikrama*, vv. 1–2 and 5) or steps (*pada*, vv. 3–6), the latter with many complex connotations that enlarge the metaphor. Its primary meaning is 'foot' (cognate with that word as with Latin *pes*, *pedis*); it then designates 'step' (the foot's action) and 'footprint' (the foot's after-image), as well as 'stand' or 'base' in the sense of dwelling-place (later devotional Hinduism makes much of the fact that the lowest part of god is the highest part of the universe). In the final verses, *pada* refers both to the actual place where men and gods dwell and the footstep which marks the place, in which the honey-fountain springs as water fills the mark made by a cow's hoof.[1]

*1* Let me now sing the heroic deeds[2] of Viṣṇu, who has measured apart the realms of earth, who propped up[3] the upper dwelling-place, striding far as he stepped forth three times.

*2* They praise for his heroic deeds Viṣṇu who lurks in the mountains, wandering like a ferocious wild beast,[4] in whose three wide strides all creatures dwell.

*3* Let this song of inspiration go forth to Viṣṇu, the wide-striding bull who lives in the mountains, who alone with but three steps measured apart this long, far-reaching dwelling-place.[5]

*4* His three footprints, inexhaustibly full of honey, rejoice[6] in the sacrificial drink. Alone, he supports threefold the earth and the sky – all creatures.

*5* Would that I might reach his dear place of refuge, where men who love the gods rejoice.[6] For there one draws close to the wide-striding Viṣṇu; there, in his highest footstep, is the fountain of honey.

*6* We wish to go to your[7] dwelling-places, where there are untiring, many-horned cattle.[8] There the highest footstep of the wide-stepping bull shines brightly down.

NOTES

1. Cf. the various uses of *pada* in 1.164.

2. Cf. 1.32.1, which begins with the same phrase.

3. The verb (*skambh*) is related to the noun for 'pillar', the *axis mundi* that props heaven apart so that creation may take place. This pillar is also a measuring-stick for Viṣṇu. Elsewhere this act is attributed to Varuṇa (5.85.5), who measures out the earth with the sun as with a measure.

4. The commentator suggests that this is a lion; this seems more likely, in view of the sinister characteristics attributed to Viṣṇu here, than to interpret it as a reference to the bull who is about to appear (vv. 3 and 6). Indeed, as bulls do not usually live in mountains, this may merely be an instance of the use of the word (*vṛṣan*) to denote any male full of seed, in this case a wild beast (as the Vedic gods are often said to be wild beasts).

5. This may refer to the entire triple world or to the earth as opposed to the upper dwelling-place.

6. The verb can be transitive or intransitive, to be or to make someone else happy or drunk. Here both meanings seem appropriate: the honey in the footprints acts like Soma, intoxicating the creatures who dwell there, the 'men who love the gods' specified in the next verse. The honey is in all three of his footsteps (v. 4), though the highest is the fountain of the nectar of immortality (v. 5).

7. The pronoun, in the dual, refers to both Indra and Viṣṇu.

8. Here, as elsewhere, the cattle may simply symbolize cattle (and, by extension, the riches of life), or something more. The commentator identifies them as rays of light (extensions of Viṣṇu as the sun); they may be stars. As cattle, they are untiring, as rays unfading; 'many-horned' would mean something like 'twinkling' (for stars) or 'widely diffused' (for sunbeams). (Cf. 1.163.11 for horns as rays.) But they may be just what the verse says, the cattle who abound in heaven.

# REALIA

THE *Rig Veda* is a sacred book, but it is a very worldly sacred book. Nowhere can we find the tiniest suspicion of a wish to renounce the material world in favour of some spiritual quest; religion is the handmaiden of worldly life. The gods are invoked to give the worshipper the things he wants – health, wealth, long life, and progeny. This is not to say that there is anything superficial about Vedic religious concerns, but merely that these meditations stem from a life-affirming, joyous celebration of human existence.

Almost every hymn in the *Rig Veda* expresses at some point a wish for the good things in life, but some are primarily devoted to a celebration of these things, with relatively little attention to the gods who are supposed to provide them, and in others such worldly concerns eclipse what leaven of theistic devotion remains in them. Several of these hymns are devoted to the waters, the fluid element or Dionysian element that looms so large throughout the *Rig Veda*; the waters give renewal of life (10.9) and are invoked as goddesses (7.49). Water is at the heart of another hymn that combines the profane appreciation of the rains with a satirical fondness for priests (7.103); the sacrificial arena also provides the setting for another paean to the things that make life worth living (9.112).

It thus becomes evident that, rather than characterizing the ritual world of the *Rig Veda* as worldly, one might do better to characterize the non-ritual Vedic world as sacred: religion extends out into every aspect of life, not merely the official religious moments. Thus blessings are sought for the warriors' arms (6.75) and for the gambler's wish to break away from his compulsion (10.34), as well as for the benighted traveller in the forest (10.146).

## 10.9 *The Waters of Life*

1 Waters, you are the ones who bring us the life force. Help us to find nourishment so that we may look upon great joy.
2 Let us share in the most delicious sap that you have, as if you were loving mothers.[1]
3 Let us go straight to the house of the one for whom you waters give us life[2] and give us birth.
4 For our well-being let the goddesses be an aid to us, the waters be for us to drink. Let them cause well-being and health to flow over us.
5 Mistresses of all the things that are chosen, rulers over all peoples, the waters are the ones I beg for a cure.
6 Soma has told me that within the waters are all cures and Agni who is salutary to all.[3]
7 Waters, yield your cure as an armour for my body, so that I may see the sun for a long time.
8 Waters, carry far away all of this that has gone bad in me, either what I have done in malicious deceit or whatever lie I have sworn to.
9 I have sought the waters today; we have joined with their sap. O Agni full of moisture, come and flood me with splendour.

### NOTES

1. That is, as mothers give milk to their children.

2. The travelling singer asks to be sent to a house whose owner has been blessed, so that by sacrificing for him the singer may be renewed.

3. Agni within the waters is a common theme, to which the hymn returns in the final verse. Cf. 10.51.

## 7.49 *The Waters, Who are Goddesses*

1 They who have the ocean as their eldest flow out of the sea,[1] purifying themselves, never resting. Indra, the bull with the thunderbolt, opened a way for them;[2] let the waters, who are goddesses, help me here and now.

2 The waters of the sky or those that flow,[3] those that are dug out or those that arise by themselves, those pure and clear waters that seek the ocean as their goal – let the waters, who are goddesses, help me here and now.

3 Those in whose midst King Varuṇa moves, looking down upon the truth and falsehood of people,[4] those pure and clear waters that drip honey – let the waters, who are goddesses, help me here and now.

4 Those among whom King Varuṇa, and Soma, and all the gods drink in ecstasy the exhilarating nourishment, those into whom Agni Of-all-men entered[5] – let the waters, who are goddesses, help me here and now.

### NOTES

1. A reference to the cosmic ocean that is their source, in contrast with the earthly ocean that is their resting-point.

2. Indra opened a way for the waters when he killed Vṛtra. Cf. 1.32.1.

3. That is, those that flow on earth, in contrast with the reservoirs of the sky.

4. Varuṇa is god of the waters and moves through the heavenly waters.

5. Cf. 10.51.

## 7.103 *The Frogs*

This unusual hymn moves on two parallel but sharply contrasting levels: as a naturalistic poem, it describes the frogs who are rejuvenated when the season of rains comes; as a sacerdotal hymn, it describes the Brahmins who begin to chant at the start of the rains. The point of comparison is the voice, a sacred and creative force throughout the *Rig Veda* (which is, of course, a book of songs). For years scholars have argued about whether or not the comparison is meant to satirize the Brahmins (a possibility probably first suggested by the analogue with Aristophanes). But although the mood of the hymn is indeed cheerful, it is unlikely that the *Rig Veda* would contain material in actual criticism of priests in general. On the other hand, it may well be satirizing *some* priests (as, for example, the priests on the 'other side' of the agonistic sacrifice). What makes the poem a *tour de force* is that every verse applies simultaneously to both frogs and Brahmins, a most elaborate and playful pun.

*1* After lying still for a year, Brahmins keeping their vow,[1] the frogs have raised their voice that Parjanya[2] has inspired.

*2* When the heavenly waters came upon him[3] dried out like a leather bag,[4] lying in the pool, then the cries of the frogs joined in chorus like the lowing of cows with calves.

*3* As soon as the season of rains has come, and it rains upon them who are longing, thirsting for it, one approaches another who calls to him, 'Akhkhala',[5] as a son approaches his father.[6]

*4* One of the two greets the other as they revel in the waters that burst forth, and the frog leaps about under the falling rain, the speckled mingling his voice with the green.

*5* When one of them repeats the speech of the other, as a pupil that of the teacher, every piece[7] of them is in unison, as with fine voices you chant over the waters.

*6* One lows like a cow, one bleats like a goat; one is speckled, one is green. They have the same name but they differ in form, and as they speak they ornament their voices in many ways.

*7* Like Brahmins at the over-night sacrifice[8] who speak around the full bowl of Soma, so you frogs around a pool celebrate the day of the year when the rains come.

*8* Brahmins with Soma raise their voices offering the prayer for the beginning of the year; the officiating priests[9] come forth heated[10] and sweating. None remain hidden.

9 They have kept the order of the twelve-month as ordained by the gods; these men do not neglect the season.[11] When the season of rains has come, after a year, the hot fires[10] come to an end.

10 He who lows like a cow has given, he who bleats like a goat has given, the speckled one, the green one has given us riches. By giving hundreds of cows, the frogs have prolonged life in a thousand Soma-pressings.[12]

## NOTES

1. A complex pun. Either a reference to the vow of silence which Brahmins (and frogs) have been keeping all year while estivating, or to their duty to chant (or croak) now.

2. Parjanya is the god of the rain-storm (cf. 5.83 and 7.101).

3. Most obviously a frog; but also with possible allusion to Vṛtra lying under the waters that Indra released on a parallel and auspicious occasion (1.32.10).

4. Cf. Parjanya's leather bag full of rains (5.83.7).

5. Sanskrit for 'Brekkekkekkek koax koax koax' (the sacred chant in *The Frogs* of Aristophanes).

6. He approaches him for instruction, for the father teaches his son the Vedic chants.

7. A pun. The word (*parvan*) means a piece of a text, or a chapter, the closing lines of which are chanted in harmony or unison; but with reference to the frogs, it means a limb, a piece of the body. Sāyaṇa says that in the hot dry season the frogs turn to earth, and in the rains they reappear with full-limbed bodies, every piece united.

8. An elaborate ceremony lasting through the night and involving Soma.

9. The Adhvaryus, who perform ritual in contrast with the Brahmins who offer prayer.

10. 'Heat' (in verse 8) refers specifically to the heated cauldron of milk offered in the Pravargya ceremony; when applied to the frogs, it retains its more general meaning of heat, particularly the heat of summer. The priests sweat over the cauldron, while the frogs appear to sweat as they are covered with drops of water. In

verse 9 the 'hot fires' refer to the heat of summer, not the sacrificial fires.

11. They perform the proper ritual at the proper season; now they chant the hymns appropriate to the beginning of the year (the rains).

12. The frogs are described with the phrases traditionally devoted to generous patrons, who extend their own life-spans as a reward for giving riches to the sages composing the hymns; or as priests extending the life-spans of the patrons. This is accomplished by means of a thousand Soma-pressings, or else it extends the life-span long enough to perform a thousand Soma-pressings.

## 9.112 *Human Diversity: A Hymn to Soma*

A humorous, ironic, and worldly hymn, whose straightforward message seems to be that we are all after the same thing: wealth. This thought recurs in more lofty tones throughout the *Rig Veda* (as in the references to wealth in the hymns to Varuṇa, Uṣas, and Viṣṇu). The hymn is loosely linked to Soma through the refrain; it may be a work-song, to be sung during the pressing of the Soma ('to divert the mind', says Sāyaṇa). It is quite diverting.

*1* Our thoughts bring us to diverse callings, setting people apart: the carpenter seeks what is broken, the physician a fracture, and the Brahmin priest seeks one who presses Soma.[1] O drop of Soma, flow for Indra.

*2* With his dried twigs, with feathers of large birds, and with stones, the smith seeks all his days a man with gold.[2] O drop of Soma, flow for Indra.

*3* I am a poet; my Dad's a physician and Mum[3] a miller with grinding-stones. With diverse thoughts we all strive for wealth, going after it like cattle. O drop of Soma, flow for Indra.

*4* The harnessed horse longs for a light cart; seducers long for a woman's smile; the penis for the two hairy lips, and the frog for water.[4] O drop of Soma, flow for Indra.

NOTES

1. All three seek patrons or customers. The Brahmin priest is the one who rectifies any errors that may have been committed in the course of the sacrifice; he is therefore a sacerdotal 'fixer' (or sacrificial physician) like the other two. 'Diverse callings' may also imply conflicting interests: it is to the physician's advantage when the patient sustains a fracture.

2. The plants, wings, and stones may be used for kindling, fanning the flames, and whetstones, or as sticks to make the shafts of arrows, feathers for their fletches, and stones for their arrowheads.

3. Highly vernacular words for father and mother are used here.

4. Sāyaṇa points out one more unexpressed longing implicit in the verse: the poet longs for Soma and for gold, for a generous patron, like all the others in the hymn.

## 6.75 *To Arms*

This is a benediction that the royal chaplain would recite over the arms of the king before a military expedition or to bless the warriors protecting the consecrated stallion in the horse sacrifice. Each item in the arsenal is described separately and praised.

*1* His face is like a thundercloud, when the armoured warrior goes into the lap of battles. Conquer with an unwounded body; let the power of armour[1] keep you safe.

*2* With the bow let us win cows, with the bow let us win the contest and violent battles with the bow. The bow ruins the enemy's pleasure; with the bow let us conquer all the corners of the world.

*3* She comes all the way up to your ear like a woman who wishes to say something, embracing her dear friend; humming like a woman, the bowstring stretched tight on the bow carries you safely across in the battle.

*4* These two who go forward like a woman going to an encounter[2] hold the arrow in their lap as a mother holds

a son. Let the two bow-tips, working together, pierce
our enemies and scatter our foes.
5 He is the father of many daughters, and many are his
sons.[3] He makes a rattling sound as he goes down into
battle. The quiver wins the attacks and all the skirmishes
when he is strapped on a back and set to work.
6 Standing in the chariot, the skilful charioteer drives his
prize-winning horses forward wherever he wishes to
go. Praise the power of the reins: the guides follow the
mind that is behind them.
7 Neighing violently, the horses with their showering hoofs
outstrip everyone with their chariots. Trampling down
the foes with the tips of their hoofs, they destroy their
enemies without veering away.
8 The wagon of transport – oblation is its name[4] – on which
the weapons and armour are placed, on it let us place
the working chariot and be of good heart all our days.
9 The fathers[5] have assembled around the sweet one,[6]
giving power, a refuge in time of need, powerful and
deep. With wondrous armies and the strength of arrows,
unfading and all with equal manly powers, they loom
immense as they storm the massed armies.
10 Fathers, Brahmins worthy of Soma, let the faultless
sky and earth be kind to us. Let Pūṣan keep us from going
the wrong way. O you who thrive on Order, guard us
so that no one who plots evil will have power over us.
11 Her robe is an eagle, and her tooth is a deer; bound with
cows, she flies as she is sent forward.[7] Let the arrows
give us shelter wherever men run together and run
apart.
12 Spare us, O weapon flying true to its mark; let our body
be stone. Let Soma speak a blessing upon us; let Aditi
give us shelter.
13 He beats them on the back and strikes them on the
haunches. O whip for horses, drive forward into battle
the horses who sense what is ahead.
14 It wraps itself around the arm like a serpent with its

coils, warding off the snap of the bowstring. Let the gauntlet,[8] knowing all the ways, protect on all sides, a man protecting a man.

15 The divine arrow is smeared with poison, with a head of antelope horn and a mouth of iron. To this seed of Parjanya[9] I bow low.

16 Once shot, fly far away, arrow, sharpened with prayer. Go straight to our foes, and do not leave a single one of them there.

17 Where the arrows fall as thick as boys with untrimmed locks of hair,[10] there let Brahmaṇaspati and Aditi give us shelter, give us shelter for all our days.

18 I cover with armour those places on you where a wound is mortal. Let Soma the king dress you in ambrosia.[11] Let Varuṇa make wider yet your wide realm. Let the gods rejoice in you as you are victorious.

19 Whoever would harm us, whether it be one of our own people, or a stranger, or someone from far away, let all the gods ruin him. My inner armour is prayer.

## NOTES

1. The armour is both the literal mail on the warrior and the armour implicit in the protection afforded by the present hymn, and by sacred power in general.

2. The word can mean both a battle and a meeting (either a rendezvous with a lover or a public meeting like a wedding or a festival).

3. The arrows are the sons and daughters of the quiver.

4. The transport wagon would carry not only the weapons and armour of the warrior, but his lighter war-chariot as well. Here it is further likened to the oblation that 'carries' the prayer to the gods (as Agni is said to be the 'transporter'), either through pure metaphor or as a reference to the actual use of the transport wagon to carry the oblation before and after battle.

5. The fathers are both prototypes of warriors (especially in their role in assisting Indra to set the cows free from the cave) and sources of power for their warrior descendants.

6. The Soma.

7. The arrow is robed in eagle feathers, tipped with deer-horn, and bound with leather thongs.

8. The leather protecting the forearm.

9. The arrow is made of reed, which is said to contain the seed (rain) of Parjanya.

10. The simile is based either upon the image of arrows falling as close together as strands of hair on the head of a boy whose hair is thick, or arrows whose feathers are like the strands of hair on the boys, or arrows falling helter-skelter like young boys at play.

11. Or in immortality, the effect of drinking ambrosia.

## 10.34 *The Gambler's Lament*

Tradition regards dice as the divinity to which this hymn is addressed, for the dice are praised in it, though they are also reviled: this is a monologue in which a gambler wrestles with his compulsive attraction to the dice. First, the dice are 'born' during a storm in which the brown nuts from which they are made cease to hang like pendant earrings from the nut tree and fall, to be made into dice. When the gambler loses his money, his wife is first alienated (v. 2) and then mistreated ('They touch her, pulling at her garments, hair, et cetera', says the commentator, perhaps thinking of the famous scene in the *Mahābhārata* where Draupadī, the wife of the brothers who have lost her at dice, is abused); she is ashamed and angry, rejected by him (probably when she tries to stop him from gambling) and in turn rejecting him (probably when he tries to get money from her). He enters houses at night to steal or to borrow money, but when he finally abjures the dice, he is advised to be happy with what he has and perhaps even to hope to win back his estranged wife and his lost cattle. Although this is basically a secular hymn (and in the monologue–dialogue form associated with non-liturgical hymns), one must bear in mind the religious significance of dice-playing in ancient India: the essential role played by the dice-game in the royal ceremony of consecration and the use of throws of the dice to represent the four Ages (or Yugas). Moreover, the hymn ends with a vow of repentance and a 'firm purpose of amendment' that express a fervent religious faith.

1 The trembling hazelnut eardrops of the great tree, born in a hurricane, intoxicate me as they roll on the furrowed board. The dice seem to me like a drink of Soma from Mount Mūjavant,[1] keeping me awake and excited.

2 She did not quarrel with me or get angry; she was kind to my friends and to me. Because of a losing throw of the dice I have driven away a devoted wife.

3 My wife's mother hates me, and my wife pushes me away; the man in trouble finds no one with sympathy. They all say, 'I find a gambler as useless as an old horse that someone wants to sell.'

4 Other men fondle the wife of a man whose possessions have been coveted by the plundering dice. His father, mother, and brothers all say of him, 'We do not know him. Tie him up and take him away.'

5 When I swear, 'I will not play with them',[2] I am left behind by my friends as they depart. But when the brown dice raise their voice as they are thrown down, I run at once to the rendezvous with them, like a woman to her lover.

6 The gambler goes to the meeting-hall, asking himself 'Will I win?', and trembling with hope. But the dice cross him and counter his desire, giving the winning throws to his opponent.

7 The dice goad like hooks and prick like whips; they enslave, deceive, and torment. They give presents as children do,[3] striking back at the winners. They are coated with honey – an irresistible power over the gambler.

8 Their army, three bands of fifty, plays by rules as immutable as those of the god Savitṛ.[4] They do not bow even to the wrath of those whose power is terrifying; the king himself bows down before them.

9 Down they roll, and up they spring. Handless, they master him that has hands. Unearthly coals thrown down on the gaming board, though they are cold they burn out the heart.

10 The deserted wife of the gambler grieves, and the mother grieves for her son who wanders anywhere, nowhere. In debt and in need of money, frightened, he goes at night to the houses of other men.

11 It torments the gambler to see his wife the woman of other men, in their comfortable rooms. But he yoked the brown horses[5] in the early morning, and at evening he fell down by the fire, no longer a man.

12 [*To the dice:*] To the general[6] of your great army, the first king of your band, to him I hold out my ten fingers[7] and swear this to be the truth: 'I am holding back no money.'

13 This is what the noble Savitṛ shows me: 'Play no longer with the dice, but till your field; enjoy what you possess, and value it highly. There are your cattle, and there is your wife, O gambler.'

14 [*To the dice:*] Grant us your friendship; have pity on us. Do not bewitch us with the force of your terrible sorcery. Lay to rest your anger, your hatred. Let someone else fall into the trap of the brown dice.

## NOTES

1. The Soma plant that grows on Mount Mūjavant is often said to prevent sleep.

2. The dice, or his friends.

3. That is, taking them back again.

4. Just as the rules of Savitṛ are fixed and binding over all creatures, even the other gods, so too the actions of the dice are incomprehensible and ineluctable. The commentator suggests that the dice play on the gaming board as Savitṛ plays in the universe.

5. Either actual horses, or a metaphor for the brown dice.

6. The general may be Kali, the losing throw, later personified as the spirit of gambling.

7. The ten fingers are extended both in the traditional gesture of submission and to show that the gambler is now literally empty-handed, that he has no more money for the dice to take.

## 10.146 *Lost in the Forest*

A traveller lost in the forest becomes frightened and succumbs to twilight mirages (vv. 3–4). He begs the female spirit of the forest (mentioned nowhere else in the *Rig Veda*) not to harm him.

*1* Spirit of the forest, spirit of the forest, who seem to melt away,[1] how is it that you do not ask about a village?[2] Doesn't a kind of fear grasp you?

*2* When the Chichika bird takes up the refrain from the droning cricket, the spirit of the forest is like a hunter startling the game with his noisy beaters.

*3* The spirit of the forest at evening: You think you see cows grazing; you think you see a house; you think a cart is rumbling.[3]

*4* Whoever stays in the forest at evening imagines: Someone is calling his cow; someone else is cutting wood; someone is crying out.

*5* The spirit of the forest does not kill – not if no one else approaches.[4] She eats sweet fruit and lies down wherever she pleases.[5]

*6* Mother of wild beasts, untilled by a plough but full of food, sweet-smelling of perfume and balm – to her, the spirit of the forest, I offer my praise.

### NOTES

1. The poet (the traveller lost in the forest) imagines that the spirit of the forest camouflages herself among the trees because she is afraid. He projects his fears upon her.

2. That is, why do you not ask where a village is, so that you can go there?

3. People would return in the evening with a cart laden with wood (v. 4); the small sounds of the forest imitate the creaking of such a cart.

4. A tiger or a robber might kill you, but this is not blamed upon the forest deity.

5. The spirit of the forest, being vegetarian, is harmless; she rests at night, in contrast with the demons and beasts who roam about.

# WOMEN

The *Rig Veda* is a book by men about male concerns in a world dominated by men; one of these concerns is women, who appear throughout the hymns as objects, though seldom as subjects. Though Aditi is the only Vedic goddess of true stature, many female nouns (often abstractions) are personified as female divinities: Dawn (1.92), Night (10.127), the Waters (10.9, 7.49), and the Forest (10.146); so, too, Destruction (Nirṛti) makes a sinister appearance quite often, and the bitch Saramā assists Indra (10.108). In addition, the *Rig Veda* presents several women who, if not goddesses, are at least immortal or quasi-immortal: Yamī (10.10), Urvaśī (10.95), Sūryā (10.85), and the wives of Indra and the monkey (10.86).

Moreover, several immortal or semi-mortal women appear in the *Rig Veda* in two groups of hymns that explore with surprisingly consistent detail and concept the relationships between men and women, mortal and immortal. The first is a group of conversation hymns (*ākhyānas*) and the second is a group of narratives centring around marriage: courtship, marriage, adultery, and estrangement.

The conversation hymns are a genre that is scattered throughout the *Rig Veda* (cf. 10.135, 10.51, 10.124, 4.26–7, 10.108, 10.28, etc.); it is particularly associated with hymns that relate to fertility, and may have been part of a special ritual performance involving actors and dancers. The dialogues with women all represent situations in which one member of the pair attempts to persuade the other to engage in some sort of sexual activity; sometimes it is the woman who takes the role of persuader (10.10, 1.179, 8.91), sometimes the man (10.95, 10.86); the mortal woman is successful (1.179, 8.91), while the immortal woman is not (10.10); the immortal man succeeds (10.86), while the mortal fails (10.95). The conversations between mortal men and immortal women (10.10, 10.95) end in the separation of the couple; between mortal men and women (1.179) or immortal men and mortal women (8.91), the result is union. The complex Vṛṣākapi hymn, involving two couples, seems to end in union (10.86).

The marriage hymns, like the conversation hymns, return again to the problem of sexual rejection: Yamī is rejected by Yama, Lopāmudrā by Agastya, Purūravas by Urvaśī. Apālā fears that she will be rejected by her husband because she is not beautiful, and this is a theme which haunts the marriage hymns; the woman wishes to be *subhagā*: beautiful, hence loved by her husband, hence fortunate. Ghoṣā invokes the Aśvins to help her find a husband because they are the most helpful of the gods, but also because they appreciate beauty and are known to restore impotent men; so, too, Mudgala's wife hopes that Indra will turn her husband from a steer to a bull. The woman is rejected, therefore, either because she lacks beauty or because her husband lacks virility, and the two reasons are causally intertwined in the hymns. The woman is also rejected because she is dangerous; the defloration of the bride endangers the groom, and the abducted wife is a source of danger to the abductor. This danger is, like the woman's ugliness, causally related to the problem of the husband's virility. *Subhagā* then assumes the further connotation of 'fortunate' in having a virile husband who lives long, so that the woman does not become a widow. Despite these dangers, the marriage hymns – unlike the conversation hymns – all have happy endings.

## Yama and Yamī

Yama, the first son of the sun, is regarded in later mythology as the first mortal man and king of the dead, while Manu, the sun's other son, is regarded as the ancestor of the human race. In Avestan mythology, the primeval incest of the twins, Yama and Yamī, remains an important episode in the procreation of the human race; in India, Yama rejects the erotic solicitations of his sister in the *Rig Veda* and is never again exposed to them, for later Indian mythology is significantly silent about the affair. The hymn is not, however, a commentary on a social charter ('Thou shalt not commit incest'), but rather a speculation – ultimately negative – on a possible cosmogony, the male and female twins functioning as a variant of the androgyne.

The hymn begins, as is usual with those of the 'conversation' genre, *in medias res*. Yamī invokes gods of procreation and argues that the human race must be preserved; Yama counters by invoking moral gods and their laws. Unlike the similar conversation between Agastya and Lopāmudrā (1.179), this hymn ends with the rejection of the woman, who finally loses her temper completely.

*1* [*Yamī:*] 'Would that I might draw my friend into intimate friendship, now that he has gone far across the ocean.[1] A man of foresight should receive a grandson from the father, thinking of what lies ahead on earth.'

*2* [*Yama:*] 'Your friend does not desire this friendship, in which a woman of his kind would behave like a stranger.[2] The heroes,[3] the sons of the great spirit,[4] supporters of the sky, see far and wide.'

*3* [*Yamī:*] 'The immortals desire this, that offspring should be left by the one mortal. Let your mind unite with my mind;[5] as a husband,[6] enter the body of your wife.'

*4* [*Yama:*] 'Shall we do now what we have not done before? Shall we who spoke truth out loud now whisper false-

hood?[7] The divine youth in the waters[8] and the woman
of the waters – such is our source, our highest birth.'[9]
5 [*Yamī:*] 'The god Tvaṣṭṛ,[10] the creator and impeller,
shaper of all forms, made us man and wife even when we
were still in the womb. No one disobeys his commands;
earth and sky are our witnesses for this.'[11]
6 [*Yama:*] 'Who was witness of that first day? Who has
seen it? Who can proclaim it here? The law of Mitra
and Varuṇa is high. Yet what will you say to men,
wanton woman, to seduce them?'
7 [*Yamī:*] 'Desire for Yama has come upon me, Yamī,
the desire to lie with him upon the same bed. Let me open
my body to him as a wife to her husband. Let us roll
about together like the two wheels of a chariot.'
8 [*Yama:*] 'These spies of the gods, who wander about here
below, do not stand still, nor do they blink their eyes.
Wanton woman, go away fast with another man, not
with me. Roll about with him like the two wheels of a
chariot.'
9 [*Yamī:*] 'She would do what he wished in the nights and
in the days; she would deceive the eye of the sun for
the instant of the blink of an eye. We twins are related in
the same way as sky and earth. Let Yamī behave to-
ward Yama as if she were not his sister.'
10 [*Yama:*] 'Later ages will come, indeed, when blood
relatives will act as if they were not related. Make a
pillow of your arm for some bull of a man.[12] Seek another
husband, lovely lady, not me.'
11 [*Yamī:*] 'What good is a brother, when there is no
protector?[13] What good is a sister, when destruction
breaks out?[14] Overcome with desire, I whisper this
again and again: mingle your body with my body.'
12 [*Yama:*] 'Never will I mingle my body with your body.
They call a man who unites with his sister a sinner.
Arrange your lustful pleasures with some other man,
not with me, lovely lady. Your brother does not want
this.'

13 [*Yamī:*] 'Dammit, Yama, how feeble you are. I have not been able to find any mind or heart in you. Some other woman will surely embrace you like a girth embracing a harnessed stallion or a creeper embracing a tree.'

14 [*Yama:*] 'You too, Yamī, will surely embrace another man, and he will embrace you, as a creeper embraces a tree. Seek *his* mind, and let him seek yours. Join with him in proper harmony.'

## NOTES

1. The ocean may be the metaphorical ocean separating mortals (like Yama) from immortals (as Yamī may be), in which case 'he' is Yama. But 'he' may be the avenging god whom Yama fears (vv. 2, 6, and 8), or the sun in the water (v. 4), in which case Yamī is assuring her brother that he need not fear, as the spy is absent across the ocean.

2. This may mean that Yama does not wish the woman of his kind (his sister) to act like a stranger (like a woman with whom sexual contact is allowed); in caste terms, he avoids marriage within the subgroup (*gotra*). Less likely, but possible, is the interpretation that Yama fears that a woman not like him (an immortal) will behave like one of his kind (a mortal woman, one who may have sexual contact with him). In caste terms, he avoids marriage outside the group (*varṇa*).

3. The gods, or perhaps just the Ādityas, the particular servants of Varuṇa.

4. Varuṇa, most likely, as guardian of the moral law; or Rudra, punisher of incest (in which case the 'heroes' would be the Maruts).

5. The word (*manas*) can designate mind or heart, the seat of both rational and emotional functions. But since it is later contrasted with a word for 'heart' (v. 13), it is here probably limited to the first connotation.

6. Here Yamī implies that Yama actually is her husband, a thought which she makes explicit in v. 5; later, however (v. 7), she merely asks him to behave *as if* he were her husband, as her resolve weakens.

7. The word, *anṛta,* means not merely to speak a lie but to say something that violates the moral order, to say something that may be true but should not be.

8. Probably the sun, born of the waters, but perhaps just any Gandharva.

9. Yama argues both that people born of such lofty parents should not break the moral law, and also that he and Yamī, having the *same* parents, cannot procreate together.

10. The god of procreation, and the artisan of the gods, fashioner of the embryo in the womb. Cf. 10.184.1, 4.18.3.

11. Here and in verse 9, Yamī argues that sky and earth are as closely related as she and Yama are, that their procreation was not only permitted but even archetypal.

12. 'Bull' is Vedic slang for a virile man, like 'stud' in American; cf. 1.179.1 and 1.179.4.

13. She argues that a brother should protect his sister, even if this involves incest, to keep her from going unsatisfied and unfertilized. Ironically, it is the brother who should find a husband for his sister and avenge her if she is rejected.

14. Destruction (*nirṛti*) both in the wider sense of the destruction of the human race (as she argues in verse 1) or in the more particular sense of the destruction that comes upon a man who dies sonless.

## 1.179 *Agastya and Lopāmudrā*

In this conversation, Lopāmudrā seeks to turn her husband Agastya, who has undertaken a vow of chastity, away from his asceticism so that he will beget a child upon her. Although he argues that there are two ways to achieve happiness (or immortality), she overpowers him (v. 4), and afterwards he wishes to atone for his lapse by drinking Soma (ingesting the divine form of the protean fluid that, in its human form, has just been 'sucked' from him). Finally the poet affirms that the two of them, by uniting after each had perfected a power (she eroticism, he asceticism), achieved both forms of immortality, spiritual and corporeal (through children).

*1* [*Lopāmudrā:*] 'For many autumns past I have toiled,[1] night and day, and each dawn has brought old age closer, age that distorts the glory of bodies. Virile men[2] should go to their wives.

2 'For even the men of the past, who acted according to the Law and talked about the Law with the gods, broke off when they did not find the end.[3] Women should unite with virile men.'[2]

3 [*Agastya:*] 'Not in vain is all this toil,[1] which the gods encourage. We two must always strive against each other, and by this we will win the race that is won by a hundred means,[4] when we merge together as a couple.'

4 [*Lopāmudrā:*] 'Desire has come upon me for the bull who roars and is held back,[5] desire engulfing me from this side, that side, all sides.'
[*The poet:*] Lopāmudrā draws out the virile bull:[2] the foolish woman sucks dry the panting[6] wise man.

5 [*Agastya:*] 'By this Soma which I have drunk, in my innermost heart I say: Let him forgive us if we have sinned, for a mortal is full of many desires.'

6 Agastya, digging with spades,[7] wishing for children, progeny, and strength, nourished both ways, for he was a powerful sage. He found fulfilment of his real hopes among the gods.

## NOTES

1. This word often refers to the exertion of religious activity. When she uses it, she may refer to her work as his wife or to her own asceticism (the commentator suggests that both of them practise asceticism), and when he uses it (v. 3) he refers to his asceticism.

2. This word (*vṛṣan*) recurs throughout this hymn (and elsewhere in the *Rig Veda*: cf. 1.32, 10.10.10). Its basic meaning is one who sheds rain or seed; it comes to mean a potent male animal, particularly a bull or a stallion.

3. The end of their asceticism; that is, they died childless and unsuccessful.

4. He argues that each of them should go his own way, as various strategies are needed to win the race for happiness and immortality, but he implies that he will ultimately accede to her importunities. By 'striving together' they will engage in the agonistic Vedic sacrifice, like two rival priests.

5. He holds back his seed. If this verse is placed in Agastya's mouth, it would mean: 'The desire of my swelling reed [phallus], which is held back, overwhelms me . . .'

6. He pants either with desire (before) or exhaustion (after); the verb merely indicates heavy breathing. This verse may follow an episode of mimed sexual intercourse.

7. A metaphor rare in the *Rig Veda* but widespread elsewhere, and obvious.

## 10.95 *Purūravas and Urvaśī*

This famous hymn takes the form of a conversation at a moment near the end of a complex myth. The myth is told in a later Brāhmaṇa text, with several details that may not be true to the original Vedic version but that provide a good background to the hymn: The water-nymph Urvaśī loved Purūravas; when she married him, she made him promise never to let her see him naked. She lived with him for a long time, and became pregnant by him, but the Gandharvas carried off the two lambs that were tied to her bed, and she cried out, 'They are taking away my son as if there were no hero or man here.' Then Purūravas, thinking, 'How can there be no hero here, when I am here?', sprang out of bed without taking the time to put anything on. The Gandharvas produced a flash of lightning, and she saw him naked in the light as clear as day. She vanished, and he wandered in sorrow until he came to a lake where there were nymphs swimming about in the shape of water-birds, Urvaśī and the other nymphs. They appeared to him at her request, and the conversation between Purūravas and Urvaśī took place, as in the Vedic hymn. The Brāhmaṇa goes on to say that Urvaśī took pity on Purūravas and lay with him for one night in a golden palace; after that the Gandharvas gave him a magic fire and taught him to kindle it in a special way and to make a special pot of rice with it, and in that way he became one of the Gandharvas.

The present hymn presents a rather different view of the

myth, implying that Urvaśī was not as happy with Purūravas as he was with her (and as he thought she was with him). She refuses to return to him, nor does she promise to make him immortal (though this might be read into the final verse).

*1* [*Purūravas:*] 'My wife, turn your heart and mind to me. Stay here, dangerous woman, and let us exchange words. If we do not speak out these thoughts of ours they will bring us no joy, even on the most distant day.'

*2* [*Urvaśī:*] 'What use to me are these words of yours? I have left you, like the first of the dawns. Go home again, Purūravas. I am hard to catch and hold, like the wind ...'

*3* [*Purūravas:*] '... or like an arrow shot from the quiver for a prize, or like a racehorse that wins cattle, that wins hundreds. As if there was no man with power there, they[1] made the lightning flash and in their frenzy thought to bleat like sheep.

*4* 'She[2] brought to her husband's father nourishing riches, and whenever her lover desired her she came to his home across from her dwelling-place and took her pleasure in him, pierced by his rod day and night.'[3]

*5* [*Urvaśī:*] 'Indeed, you pierced me with your rod three times a day, and filled me even when I had no desire. I followed your will, Purūravas; you were my man, king of my body.'

*6* [*Purūravas:*] 'Sujūrṇi, Śreṇi, Sumnaāpi, and Hradecakṣus, Granthinī, Caraṇyu[4] – they have all slipped away like the red colours of dawn, lowing one louder than the other, like milk cows.'

*7* [*Urvaśī:*] 'When he[5] was born, the goddesses[6] encircled him and the rivers that sing their own praises raised him, since the gods raised you, Purūravas, for the great battle, for the killing of enemies.'[7]

*8* [*Purūravas:*] 'When I, a mortal man, courted these immortal women who had laid aside their veils,[8] they shied away from me like excited[9] gazelles, like horses grazed by the chariot.'

9 [*Urvaśī:*] 'When a mortal man, wooing these immortal
women, unites with their group as they wish, make
your bodies beautiful,[10] like water birds, like horses
biting in their love-play.'
10 [*Purūravas:*] 'She of the waters flashed lightning like a
falling lightning-bolt and brought me the pleasures of
love. From the water was born a noble, manly son. Let
Urvaśī lengthen the span of his life.'
11 [*Urvaśī:*] 'You who were born to protect, Purūravas, have
turned that force against me.[11] I warned you on that
very day, for I knew, but you did not listen to me. Why do
you talk in vain?'
12 [*Purūravas:*] 'When will the son born of me seek his
father? He will shed tears, sobbing, when he learns. Who
would separate a man and wife who are of one heart,
when the fire still blazes in the house of the husband's
parents?'[12]
13 [*Urvaśī:*] 'I will answer: he will shed tears, crying,
sobbing, longing for tender care.[13] I will send you what I
have of yours. Go home; you will never have me, you
fool.'
14 [*Purūravas:*] 'What if your lover should vanish today,
never to return, going to the farthest distance? Or if
he should lie in the lap of Destruction, or if the ferocious
wolves should eat him?'
15 [*Urvaśī:*] 'Purūravas, do not die;[14] do not vanish; do
not let the vicious wolves eat you. There are no friend-
ships with women; they have the hearts of jackals.[15]
16 'When I wandered among mortals in another form, and
spent the nights with you for four years, once each day I
swallowed a drop of butter,[16] and even now I am sated
with that.'
17 [*Purūravas:*] 'I, the lover of Urvaśī, long to draw her to
me, though she fills the air and measures the middle
realm of space. Return and reap the reward for a good
deed. Fire consumes my heart.'
18 [*The poet:*] This is what these gods say to you, son of

Iḷā:[17] 'Since you are a kinsman of death, your descendants will sacrifice to the gods with the oblation,[18] but you shall taste joy in heaven.'

## NOTES

1. The Gandharvas, anxious to have her back in heaven, tricked Purūravas.

2. Purūravas speaks of Urvaśī in the third person, referring to a long time ago.

3. The *Śatapatha Brāhmaṇa* says that part of Urvaśī's contract with Purūravas included the stipulation that he must 'strike her with his rod' three times a day. Here he seems to boast of it, but she then complains that he did it against her will.

4. The nymphs apparently were with her during the marriage and vanished with her; they have reappeared now with her but apparently wish to vanish right away again.

5. Verses 6–7, 10, and 12–13 refer to a son of Purūravas and Urvaśī; Purūravas seems not to have known of him until this moment (a common motif in myths of the mortal lover of an immortal woman). Urvaśī implies that she and Purūravas united merely to produce the child, so that there is no longer any reason for them to remain together.

6. The Apsarases (water-nymphs, like the river goddesses). Urvaśī implies that they had to flee with her in order to care for the expected child of such a great father.

7. The enemies are demons. Kālidāsa's play based on this myth tells that Purūravas first met Urvaśī when he rescued her from demons; later, Indra allowed Purūravas to keep Urvaśī for ever in return for his services in arms against Indra's demonic enemies.

8. Either they had disrobed at night (as Purūravas had done), or they had laid aside their immortal forms; at the present moment, they may have taken off their waterbird forms so that he could speak with them or taken off their clothes to bathe.

9. The adjective may imply that they are in heat, and hence especially nervous.

10. She seems to be advising the Apsarases not to run away (as Purūravas has complained in the previous verse) if he approaches them properly (i.e. keeps his promise).

11. She accuses him of taking her against her will, and also re-

minds him of royal duties that he is neglecting in his pursuit of her.

12. The implication is that his parents are still alive, and will be saddened and ashamed to see them apart after so short a time.

13. She implies that the child will weep because he misses her, not him, when she has sent the boy to Purūravas; or else that he will weep for what he has missed when at last he finds his father.

14. Here she merely advises him not to kill himself as he threatens; in the Brāhmaṇa text, she actually gets the Gandharvas to teach him how to become immortal.

15. The word is actually 'jackal-wolves', echoing the previous image of wolves. The jackal later becomes the symbol of an unfaithful woman.

16. As a goddess, she is filled by the oblation and spurns her mortal lover; as a woman, she has had more than enough of his 'butter' (frequently a metaphor for semen).

17. The term, 'Aiḷa', could be son of either Iḷa or Iḷā, as Purūravas was born of a woman (Iḷā) who had been changed from her original form as a man (Iḷa).

18. Their mortal son will make offerings to him in the world of the dead, but Purūravas will be in the world of heaven.

## 8.91 *Apālā and Indra*

The first and last verses of this hymn narrate the story of Apālā; in between are verses spoken by her. The story is known from later commentaries: Apālā was a young woman hated by her husband (v. 4) because she had a skin disease (v. 7). She found Soma (v. 1), pressed it in her mouth and offered it to Indra (v. 2). Indra made love to her, which she at first resisted (v. 3) and then consented to (v. 4). She asked him to cure her and also to restore fertility to her father and to his fields (vv. 5–6). This triple boon is accomplished by an obscure triple ritual. Later tradition states that being drawn through three chariot holes caused her to slough her skin three times; the first skin became a hedgehog, the second an alligator, the third a chameleon. The Vedic verse merely states that her skin became sun-like (i.e. fair), and the ritual has obvious sexual symbolism. This symbolism provides a parallel to the motif of the cure: for while her skin is purified she is also given pubic hair, either because she had been hairless as a result of the skin disease or because she was an adolescent maiden (v. 1) who is made a woman by Indra.

*1* A maiden going for water found Soma by the way. She brought it home and said, 'I will press it for you, Indra; I will press it for you, mighty one.

*2* 'Dear man, you who go watchfully into house after house, drink this that I have pressed with my teeth, together with grain and gruel, cakes and praises.

*3* 'We do not wish to understand you, and yet we do not misunderstand you. Slowly and gently, ever more gently, flow for Indra, O drop of Soma.

*4* 'Surely he is able, surely he will do it, surely he will make us more fortunate.[1] Surely we who are hated by our husbands should flee and unite with Indra.

*5* 'Make these three places sprout, O Indra: my daddy's head and field, and this part of me below the waist.

*6* 'That field of ours, and this my body, and my daddy's head – make them all grow hair.'

*7* In the nave of the chariot, in the nave of the cart, in the nave of the yoke, O Indra of a hundred powers, you purified Apālā three times[2] and made her sun-skinned.

NOTES

1. The adjective has three closely linked meanings: beautiful, therefore loved by one's husband, therefore fortunate.

2. Cf. the three naves of the chariot wheel in 1.164.2 and 1.164.48.

## 10.86 *Indra and the Monkey*

This hymn, which Renou has called 'the strangest poem in the Rig Veda', deals with conflict and resolution on at least four levels, alluded to in a conversation between four people: Indra and his wife, and Vṛṣākapi (whose name means 'the monkey bursting with seed') and his wife. On the household level, there are crude arguments in which Indrāṇī accuses the monkey, a favourite of Indra, of having taken sexual liberties with her; Indra tries to calm her with flattery, and Vṛṣākapi's wife alternately flatters her, engages her in sexual banter about their husbands' powers, and insists either that Vṛṣākapi never touched Indrāṇī or that now, at least, he has ceased to do so; finally, Indrāṇī relents and asks the monkey couple to resume the *ménage à quatre*. This aspect of the myth places it among other bawdy and worldly hymns, usually set in the form of conversations.

The myth also suggests a chain of events involving sacrifice. At a time before the conversation in the hymn takes place, Indra has ceased to be worshipped or to be given the Soma; in the course of the hymn, he is then given in place of Soma another kind of offering, which he accepts, an offering of bulls (vv. 13 and 15), an oblation mixed with water (v. 12), or a 'pleasing mixture' (v. 15). Substitutes for Soma were common in Vedic and post-Vedic India, and any of these might have been used. These two levels, the household and the sacrifice, are linked by a third, which is merely implied: the substitute offering transfers the monkey's sexual powers to Indra, perhaps through the sacrifice or castration of the animal (referred to obliquely in v. 5) and the drinking of a 'mixture' (vv. 12 and 15 again) made from his genitals[1] (a ceremony that ensures that Indra will never die of old age – v. 11 – while simultaneously transferring Indra's sins to the monkey – v. 22). This aspect of the hymn suggests that it might be viewed in the context of a Vedic fertility ritual separate from the orthodox Soma tradition.

A fourth level, a variant of the second, is the agonistic banter between poets/priests sacrificing on behalf of two different gods (Indra and the demi-god Vṛṣākapi); each side mocks the god of the other faction. This would explain the refrain, which is unique to this hymn but is of a widely used general format; in answer to a series of challenges, Indra's supremacy is constantly reaffirmed.[2] Finally, if one accepts the tradition, following Sāyaṇa, that Vṛṣākapi is a son of Indra, yet another level of meaning arises, a variant of the first, in which the son challenges the father (unsuccessfully) for the sexual favours of the mother.[3]

*1* [*Indrāṇī:*] 'They no longer press the Soma, nor do they think of Indra as God, now that my friend Vṛṣākapi has gorged himself on the nourishments of the enemy.[4] Indra supreme above all!

*2* 'Indra, you pass over the erring ways of Vṛṣākapi. No, you will not find Soma to drink in any other place. Indra supreme above all!'

*3* [*Indra:*] 'What has this tawny animal, this Vṛṣākapi, done to you that you are so jealous of him – and begrudge him the nourishing wealth of the enemy? Indra supreme above all!'

*4* [*Indrāṇī:*] 'That beloved Vṛṣākapi whom you protect, Indra – let the dog who pants after the wild sow[5] bite him in the ear! Indra supreme above all!

*5* 'The ape has defiled the precious, well-made, anointed things[6] that are mine. I will cut off his "head", and I will not be good to that evil-doer. Indra supreme above all!'

*6* 'No woman has finer loins than I, or is better at making love. No woman thrusts against a man better than I, or raises and spreads her thighs more. Indra supreme above all!'

*7* [*Vṛṣākapi:*] 'O little mother,[7] so easily won, as it will surely be,[8] my loins, my thigh, my "head" seem to thrill and stiffen,[9] little mother. Indra supreme above all!'

*8* [*Indra:*] 'Your arms and fingers are so lovely, your hair so long, your buttocks so broad. You are the wife of a hero – so why do you attack our Vṛṣākapi? Indra supreme above all!'

*9* [*Indrāṇī:*] 'This impostor has set his sights on me as if I had no man.[10] But I *have* a real man, for I am the wife of

Indra, and the Maruts are my friends. Indra supreme
above all!'

10 [*Vṛṣākapi:*] 'In the past, this lady would go to the public festival or to a meeting-place.[11] There she would be praised as the one who sets all in order, the wife of Indra, a woman with a man. Indra supreme above all!'

11 [*Wife of Vṛṣākapi:*] 'Indrāṇī is the most fortunate[12] among women, I have heard, for her husband will never die of old age. Indra supreme above all!

12 [*Indra:*] 'I was not happy, Indrāṇī, without my friend Vṛṣākapi, whose offering of this oblation mixed with water goes to the gods and pleases them. Indra supreme above all!'

13 [*Vṛṣākapi:*] 'Wife of Vṛṣākapi, you are rich in wealth and in good sons and in your sons' wives. Let Indra eat your bulls and the oblation that is so pleasing and so powerful in effect. Indra supreme above all!'

14 [*Indra:*] 'They have cooked for me fifteen bulls, and twenty, so that I may eat the fat as well. Both sides of my belly are full. Indra supreme above all!'

15 [*Vṛṣākapi's wife:*] 'Like a sharp-horned bull bellowing among the herds of cows,[13] a mixture is being prepared for you, Indra, that will please your heart and refresh you. Indra supreme above all!'

16 [*Indrāṇī:*] 'That one is not powerful, whose penis hangs between his thighs; that one is powerful, for whom the hairy organ opens as it swells and sets to work.[14] Indra supreme above all!'

17 [*Vṛṣākapi's wife:*] 'That one is not powerful, for whom the hairy organ opens as it swells and sets to work; that one is powerful, whose penis hangs between his thighs. Indra supreme above all!

18 'Indra, this Vṛṣākapi found a wild ass that had been killed, a sword, a basket, a new pot, and a cart loaded with firewood.[15] Indra supreme above all!'

19 [*Indra:*] 'I am coming forward, looking about and distinguishing between enemy slave and noble ally.[16] I

am drinking with the one who has prepared a simple brew; I am looking for an expert. Indra supreme above all!

20 'How many miles separate the desert and the ploughed land.[17] Come home, Vṛṣākapi, to the closer houses. Indra supreme above all!'

21 [*Indrāṇī:*] 'Come back, Vṛṣākapi, and we two[18] will meet in agreement, so that you who destroy sleep[19] may come again on the homeward path. Indra supreme above all!'

22 [*The poet:*] As you went home to the north, Vṛṣākapi, where was the beast of many sins?[20] To whom, O Indra, did the inciter of people go? Indra supreme above all!

23 The daughter of Manu, named Parśu,[21] brought forth twenty children at once. Great happiness came to her whose womb felt the pains. Indra supreme above all!

## NOTES

1. This hypothesis, based rather loosely on the present hymn, is supported by correspondences between it and two important Vedic rituals. In the horse sacrifice, the horse is given the sword and several other articles here given to the monkey (v. 18; cf. 1.162.13–16); the stallion is killed and his virility transferred to the king after the queen has pantomimed ritual copulation with the stallion (corresponding to Vṛṣākapi's connection with Indrāṇī). A ritual in the *Atharva Veda* (20.136) contains a dialogue replete with banter about the size of sexual organs, verses that reverse those of the present hymn, and references to intercourse with a supernatural woman (the 'Great Naked Woman', Mahānāgnī) – all of which characterize both the horse sacrifice and the present hymn. In the *Atharva Veda* ritual, moreover, the Great Naked Woman is treated as a scapegoat, like Vṛṣākapi. These correspondences are intriguing, though by no means entirely convincing.

2. Cf. 2.12.

3. Cf. 10.28 and 4.18.

4. This word (*ari*) has an ambivalence based upon the agonistic sacrifice; it denotes one's 'best enemy', one's favourite rival; here it refers to the enemy of Indra and the friend of Vṛṣākapi, the pious

devotee of the latter rather than the former. (A similar juxtaposition occurs in v. 19.) Indrāṇī refers sarcastically to Vṛṣākapi as her 'friend', in contrast to the 'enemy' who is Vṛṣākapi's true ally.

5. The text has the unmarked sex (wild pig), but there may well be sexual overtones best conveyed by making the animal female.

6. A *double entendre*, for the private parts of the goddess and the sacred instruments of the ritual. The first meaning lends sexual overtones to the 'head' she threatens to cut off (an innuendo made explicit in v. 7), and the second places it in the context of a ritual beheading. That Indrāṇī is referring to her sexual charms is made clear by the following verse, in which she boasts that she is so consummate a bed-mate that she certainly need not stoop to a liaison with Vṛṣākapi.

7. A *triple entendre*: a term of respect for a mother goddess, a term often used for a whore, or a possible indication that Indrāṇī really is his mother. (It is also the term used in the sexual banter of the horse sacrifice.) These ambiguities carry over into the next phrase, for a woman 'easily won' is being insulted for her promiscuity, while a deity 'easily won' is praised for her generosity to the worshipper.

8. He may be bragging that he will soon have her again, or accepting either of the alternatives suggested by Indrāṇī: that she will kill him (v. 5) or allow him to have her (v. 6, in which Vṛṣākapi may misunderstand her implication that she is too good for him), an acceptance of the Liebestod that plays a part in later myths of the seductive, destructive goddess. He accepts her threat, and he lusts for her.

9. The verb connotes the rushing of blood to the surface of the skin, causing horripilation and erection. It indicates fear as well as desire, both relevant here: fear of the goddess and desire for the woman.

10. A pun: it may mean that she has no virile husband, or that she has no heroic sons. Indra is her husband, and the Maruts are sometimes said to be her sons. Here, Indrāṇī contests the previous assertion, that she has a husband to protect her.

11. *Double entendre*: sacrificial meeting-place or rendezvous. The public sacrifice is one made to gods with their wives (Indrāṇī with her man).

12. The word denotes a woman who is (a) beautiful, therefore (b) loved by her husband, therefore (c) fortunate in the most important way for a woman: her husband will live long.

13. This is a common metaphor for Soma. Vṛṣākapi's wife implies that even though her offering is not a Soma offering, it is just as good.

14. Verses 16–17 have inspired many imaginative interpretations. Apparently Indrāṇī refers first to Vṛṣākapi, whom she accuses of lacking power (both sexual and religious), and then to Indra, whom she praises for having this power; Vṛṣākapi's wife then retorts that Indra is *not* powerful, precisely because he is sexually active, while her husband *is* powerful, because he is (now, if not necessarily formerly) celibate and self-controlled (a statement that she then supports with v. 18). Moreover, Indra is sexually active because he represents potential power, while Vṛṣākapi, apparently having already *had* Indrāṇī, is now immune to sexual stimulation. The 'hairy organ' is most likely hers, which opens in response to him (cf. 9.112.4); the verb also serves to describe the male organ, which swells in its excitement, and thus the 'hairy organ' may be his; it is quite likely that the ambiguity is intentional. Sāyaṇa says that Indrāṇī speaks the first verse, wishing to have intercourse with Indra, and that Indra speaks the second, not wishing to have intercourse with her; in this gloss, the one who is (is not) powerful, respectively, is the woman, who does or does not excite her husband; Indra, in refusing her, argues that his power lies in the fact that he is immune to sexual stimulation. Finally, one may see the reversals between the two verses as a result of the transfer of virile powers rather than as a contrast between two static descriptions: in the first verse, Indra is not powerful, but the monkey is; in the second, the situation is reversed. The most likely interpretation, however, is that Indrāṇī praises the virile Indra and mocks the impotent Vṛṣākapi in the first verse, and Vṛṣākapi's wife praises the self-controlled Vṛṣākapi and mocks the priapic Indra in the second.

15. These are all items used in a sacrifice of expiation for one who has violated a vow of chastity. They are also used in the horse sacrifice, for the stallion breaks a year's vow of chastity in this ceremony.

16. The 'slave' is the indigenous inhabitant, regarded as demonic; the 'ally' is the conquering Āryan (cf. note 4). These two are further juxtaposed with the man who prepares a 'simple brew' (the Soma substitute), to whom Indra prefers the expert (the Soma-offerer).

17. The contrast seems to be between the non-Āryan desert,

where Vṛṣākapi has been performing his vow of expiation among non-Soma offerers, and the 'closer' houses of civilization under the plough; there may also be overtones of a contrast between a barren woman and one who has cropped.

18. She may be referring to herself and Indra, as a reconciled married couple, or to herself and Vṛṣākapi, as a reconciled illicit couple.

19. A possible allusion to the rape of Indrāṇī.

20. The beast may be Vṛṣākapi, the scapegoat who has taken Indra's many sins and given Indra his own fertile powers. Or it may be Vṛṣākapi's wife, accused of inciting Vṛṣākapi to his sacrilege against Indrāṇī.

21. Parśu's name means 'rib'; as the wife of the first man (and one who is said in many texts to be androgynous) she shares this anatomical description with Eve. Whether she is here identified with Vṛṣākapi's wife (or, indeed, with Indrāṇī), or merely stands for all womankind who benefit from the fertility of the gods, is an open question.

## 10.40 *The Courtship of Ghoṣā*

The hymn begins and ends with an invocation to the Aśvins. The central verses are set in the mouth of a woman, one of two instances in the entire *Rig Veda* where this occurs;[1] and according to Indian tradition, Ghoṣā is actually the author of this hymn. Though women do speak in some of the dialogue hymns,[2] they do not invoke the gods, and even here it is unlikely that Ghoṣā was in fact the author. In the hymn, Ghoṣā reminds the Aśvins of the many people they have helped in the past, including at least one (Siñjara) who has regained his virility. In this context it is relevant to note that the word for 'widow' is also interpreted by the commentaries, here and elsewhere, as referring to the wife of an impotent man. The hymn continues with Ghoṣā's image of a happy marriage (v. 9), at which the bride's parents weep and reminisce, and people wear wedding clothes rather than funeral clothes (v. 10). She asks them to bless her future husband (vv. 11–13), and the hymn ends, as it begins, with a question about where the Aśvins may be found, and the implied hope that they are going to the poet's house.

1 Where is your brilliant chariot going, O Heroes, and who has adorned it for its good journey as it comes, glorious at dawn, brought by thought and care morning after morning into house after house?

2 Where are the Aśvins in the evening, where in the morning, where do they stop and where have they spent the night? Who invites you as a widow takes her husband's brother to her bed, as a young woman takes a young man to a room?

3 Early in the morning you are awakened, like two old men praised by a bard, and worthy of sacrifice you go into house after house. For whom do you remain in shadow, O Heroes, and to whose Soma offerings do you come like two sons of kings?

4 Like hunters tracking wild elephants we summon you with the oblation at dawn and at dusk. To the man who offers the oblation at the right time, you who are heroes and husbands of beauty bring nourishment.

5 Ghoṣā, the daughter of a king, came to you, Aśvins, and said, 'I beg you, O Heroes; be with me by day and by night, as you give power to the racehorse to win the prize of horses and chariots.

6 'You wise Aśvins move about on your chariot, driving it like Kutsa[3] to the houses of the singers. Your bees bring raw honey by mouth, as a woman brings honey in a pot.

7 'You came to the aid of Bhujyu, you came to Vaśa, you came to Siñjara[4] and Uśanas. The sacrificer enjoys your friendship; I beg for a favour, with your help.

8 'You Aśvins rescue Kṛśa and Śaya, you rescue the worshipper and the widow. You Aśvins throw open the thundering cow-pen with seven mouths[5] to give rewards.

9 'She has become a young woman; the young man has run away to her. Plants wafting magic powers have

sprouted and flow to him as rivers flow to a valley. On
that day he becomes a husband.
10 'They mourn the living; they are transformed at the
sacrifice. Men have pondered deeply the long span. It is
a blessing for the fathers who have arranged this; the
wives are a joy for the husbands to embrace.
11 'We have not learned this – tell it to us – how a young
man rests in the lap of a young woman. Let us go to the
house of a bull full of seed and fond of cows. This we
desire, O Aśvins.
12 'Your favour has come, O Aśvins rich in prizes. Desires
are becoming firmly rooted in hearts.[6] As a pair, you
husbands of beauty have become our protectors; let
us go as loved ones to the home of a good friend.
13 'Grant to the eloquent wealth and strong sons, as you
rejoice in the house of a man. Husbands of beauty, make
a ford where one can drink well; clear away the hatred[7]
that stands like a post in the path.'
14 Where, and in whose houses, will they rejoice today, the
wondrous Aśvins, husbands of beauty? Who has detained
them? To the house of what inspired priest or sacrificer
have they gone?

## NOTES

1. The other is the Apālā song, 8.91.

2. Lopāmudrā (1.179), Yamī (10.10), Indrāṇī (10.86), Urvaśī (10.95), and Saramā (10.108).

3. Kutsa is a friend and charioteer of Indra. As charioteers who travel to the houses of many noble men, the Aśvins will be the ideal matchmakers.

4. The commentator identifies him with Atri. Cf. 1.116 and 5.78.

5. The Aśvins are asked to give cows as rewards, just as kings would reward Brahmins with cows taken from the royal cow-pens. The seven mouths are probably simply seven gates, seven being a recurrent number in the Vedas.

6. The lack of pronouns in this sentence leaves an ambiguity that may well have been intended in the original. One can speculate –

'our desires are rooted in your hearts' – but perhaps this goes against the force of the verse.

7. Perhaps the hatred of a rejecting husband. Cf. 8.91.4.

## 10.85 *The Marriage of Sūryā*

The divine prototype for human marriages is the hierogamy of Sūryā (daughter of Sūrya, the sun) and Soma (here, for the only time in the *Rig Veda*, regarded as the moon, as well as the sacred plant and its expressed juice). Later marriages are modelled upon this one, and the bride is called Sūryā. The first nineteen verses refer to the myth of the marriage of Sūryā and Soma; subsequent verses also refer back to Sūryā (vv. 20, 35 and 38) and to Soma (40–41), though the former seems merely to designate the bride and the latter is a reference to Soma in his other aspect, his *droit de seigneur* over all brides. Verses 20–47 present formulaic verses, some of a highly magical nature, to be recited at a wedding.

*1* The earth is propped up by truth; the sky is propped up by the sun. Through the Law the Ādityas stand firm and Soma is placed in the sky.

*2* Through Soma the Ādityas are mighty; through Soma the earth is great. And in the lap of these constellations Soma has been set.[1]

*3* One thinks he has drunk Soma when they press the plant. But the Soma that the Brahmins know – no one ever eats that.[2]

*4* Hidden by those charged with veiling you,[3] protected by those who live on high, O Soma, you stand listening to the pressing-stones. No earthling eats you.

*5* When they drink you who are a god, then you are filled up again. Vāyu is the guardian of Soma; the moon is the one that shapes the years.

*6* The Raibhī metre[4] was the woman who gave her away; the Nārāśāṃsī metre[4] was the girl who accompanied her.[5] The fine dress of Sūryā was adorned by the songs.[4]

7 Intelligence was the pillow; sight was the balm.
Heaven and Earth were the hope-chest when Sūryā
went to her husband.
8 The hymns of praise were the shafts[6] and metre was the
diadem and coiffure. The Aśvins[7] were the suitors of
Sūryā, and Agni was the one who went in front.[8]
9 Soma became the bridegroom and the two Aśvins were
the suitors, as Savitṛ[9] gave Sūryā to her husband and she
said 'Yes' in her heart.
10 Thought was her chariot and the sky was its canopy.
The two luminaries[10] were the two carriage animals
when Sūryā went to the house.
11 Your two cattle, yoked with the verse and the chant, went
with the same accord. You had hearing for your two
wheels. In the sky the path stretched on and on.
12 The two luminaries were your wheels as you journeyed;
the outward breath was made into the axle. Sūryā
mounted a chariot made of thought as she went to her
husband.
13 The wedding procession of Sūryā went forward as
Savitṛ sent it off. When the sun is in Aghā[11] they kill
the cattle,[12] and when it is in Arjunī[11] she is brought
home.
14 When you Aśvins came to the wedding in your three-
wheeled chariot, asking for Sūryā for yourselves, all
the gods gave you their consent, and Pūṣan, the son,
chose you as his two fathers.[13]
15 When you two husbands of beauty came as suitors for
Sūryā, where was your single wheel?[14] Where did you
two stand to point the way?[15]
16 Your two wheels, Sūryā, the Brahmins know in their
measured rounds. But the one wheel that is hidden, only
the inspired know that.
17 To Sūryā, to the gods, to Mitra and Varuṇa, who are
provident for all creation, to them I have bowed down.
18 These two[16] change places through their power of
illusion, now forward, now backward. Like two children

at play they circle the sacrificial ground. The one gazes
upon all creatures, and the other is born again and again
marking the order of the seasons.
19 He[17] becomes new and again new as he is born, going in
front of the dawns as the banner of the days. As he
arrives he apportions to the gods their share. The moon
stretches out the long span of life.[18]
20 Mount the world of immortality, O Sūryā,[19] that is
adorned with red flowers[20] and made of fragrant wood,[20]
carved with many forms and painted with gold, rolling
smoothly on its fine wheels. Prepare an exquisite wedding
voyage for your husband.
21 'Go away from here! For this woman has a husband.'
Thus I implore Viśvāvasu[21] with words of praise as I
bow to him. 'Look for another girl who is ripe and still
lives in her father's house. That is your birthright;
find it.
22 'Go away from here, Viśvāvasu, we implore you as we
bow. Look for another girl, willing and ready. Leave
the wife to unite with her husband.'
23 May the roads be straight and thornless on which our
friends go courting.[22] May Aryaman and Bhaga united
lead us together. O Gods, may the united household
be easy to manage.
24 I free you from Varuṇa's snare, with which the gentle
Savitṛ[23] bound you. In the seat of the Law, in the world
of good action, I place you unharmed with your husband.
25 I free her from here, but not from there.[24] I have bound
her firmly there, so that through the grace of Indra she
will have fine sons and be fortunate in her husband's
love.
26 Let Pūṣan lead you from here, taking you by the hand; let
the Aśvins carry you in their chariot. Go home to be
mistress of the house with the right to speak commands
to the gathered people.[25]
27 May happiness be fated for you here[26] through your
progeny. Watch over this house as mistress of the house.

Mingle your body with that of your husband, and even when you are grey with age you will have the right to speak to the gathered people.[25]

28 The purple and red appears, a magic spirit;[27] the stain is imprinted. Her family prospers, and her husband is bound in the bonds.[28]

29 Throw away the gown, and distribute wealth to the priests. It becomes a magic spirit walking on feet, and like the wife it draws near the husband.[29]

30 The body[30] becomes ugly and sinisterly pale, if the husband with evil desire covers his sexual limb with his wife's robe.

31 The diseases that come from her own people and follow after the glorious bridal procession, may the gods who receive sacrifices lead them back whence they have come.[31]

32 Let no highwaymen, lying in ambush, fall upon the wedding couple. Let the two of them on good paths avoid the dangerous path. Let all demonic powers run away.

33 This bride has auspicious signs; come and look at her. Wish her the good fortune of her husband's love, and depart, each to your own house.

34 It[32] burns, it bites, and it has claws, as dangerous as poison is to eat. Only the priest who knows the Sūryā hymn is able to receive the bridal gown.

35 Cutting, carving, and chopping into pieces[33] – see the colours of Sūryā,[34] which the priest alone purifies.

36 I take your hand for good fortune,[35] so that with me as your husband you will attain a ripe old age. Bhaga, Aryaman, Savitṛ, Purandhi[36] – the gods have given you to me to be mistress of the house.

37 Pūṣan,[37] rouse her to be most eager to please, the woman in whom men sow their seed, so that she will spread her thighs in her desire for us and we, in our desire, will plant our penis in her.

38 To you[38] first of all they led Sūryā, circling with the bridal procession. Give her back to her husbands, Agni, now as a wife with progeny.

39 Agni has given the wife back again, together with long life and beauty. Let her have a long life-span, and let her husband live for a hundred autumns.

40 Soma first possessed her, and the Gandharva possessed her second. Agni was your third husband, and the fourth was the son of a man.

41 Soma gave her to the Gandharva, and the Gandharva gave her to Agni. Agni gave me wealth and sons – and her.

42 Stay here and do not separate.[39] Enjoy your whole life-span playing with sons and grandsons and rejoicing in your own home.

43 Let Prajāpati create progeny for us; let Aryaman anoint[40] us into old age. Free from evil signs,[41] enter the world of your husband. Be good luck for our two-legged creatures and good luck for our four-legged creatures.

44 Have no evil eye; do not be a husband-killer. Be friendly to animals,[42] good-tempered and glowing with beauty. Bringing forth strong sons, prosper as one beloved of the gods and eager to please. Be good luck for our two-legged creatures and good luck for our four-legged creatures.

45 Generous Indra, give this woman fine sons and the good fortune of her husband's love. Place ten sons in her and make her husband the eleventh.[43]

46 Be an empress over your husband's father, an empress over your husband's mother; be an empress over your husband's sister and an empress over your husband's brothers.

47 Let all the gods and the waters together anoint our two hearts together. Let Mātariśvan[44] together with the Creator and together with her who shows the way[45] join the two of us together.

## NOTES

1. The first Soma in this verse is the drink that strengthens the gods; the second is the plant that grows on earth; and the third is the moon.

2. Verses 3–5 play upon the different Somas: the plant that is pressed, the god that the Brahmins know, the god protected in heaven, the plant between the pressing-stones, the juice that they drink, the moon that is drained of Soma and filled again, waxing and waning.

3. Seven gods guard Soma, among whom Vāyu is foremost (see verse 5).

4. Two Vedic metres used in the wedding hymn; their grammatical gender is feminine. The songs (*gāthās*) are feminine, like the metres. They may be personified as women helping Sūryā to dress or as adornments actually stitched upon the dress.

5. The word may refer to the dowry; cf. 10.135.5–6.

6. Of the chariot that takes the bride to the home of the bridegroom. Cf. the magical chariots in 10.135 and 1.164.

7. The Aśvins are elsewhere said to be the brothers and/or the husbands of Sūryā, but here they are the unsuccessful suitors. They are, in any case, her brothers.

8. Agni heads the procession and serves as the messenger, his usual function.

9. Savitṛ is here another name for Sūrya, the father of the bride.

10. Probably a designation for the two months of summer, regarded as particularly auspicious for marriages.

11. Two constellations of summer.

12. The cattle are slaughtered for the wedding feast.

13. Pūṣan is, like the Aśvins, both a brother and a lover of Sūryā; here he is the son of the Aśvins, who choose Sūryā for themselves instead of acting as intermediaries. Pūṣan is also, appropriately, as the god of safe roads and journeys, the one who supervises the wedding procession.

14. Here, and in verse 14, the two wheels of the solar chariot (identified by Sāyaṇa as the sun and moon) are contrasted with the mysterious single wheel, perhaps the nocturnal sun, or the year. Cf. 1.164.2.

15. The path to the secret sun in heaven, or the path to the groom's house.

16. After the verse of closing benediction (v. 17), two more

verses describe the sun and moon before turning to the human bridal couple. The heavenly bodies circle in the sky as the married couple will soon (v. 38) circle the fire. The second half of verse 18 refers first to the sun and then to the moon.

17. The moon.

18. His life, or the life of the gods, or of the sacrificer, or just time in general.

19. The bride is addressed as Sūryā, as is Sūryā herself, and the verse refers to both at once. The chariot that takes the bride to the house of the groom is here assimilated to the world of immortality that Sūryā wins in the sky.

20. *Kiṃśuka* flowers and *Śalmali* wood.

21. A Gandharva who possesses girls before their marriage. This verse and the next are an exorcism against his *droit de seigneur*, like that of Soma (cf. v. 40). Viśvāvasu, Soma, and the Aśvins are all rejected suitors.

22. This is a benediction to the families of the bride and groom, and perhaps in particular for the disappointed suitors.

23. Savitṛ is the father of Sūryā. In this verse the bride loosens her braids as a sign of release from her parents' house, a binding that is metaphorically attracted to the well-known bonds or snares of Varuṇa (see 7.86 and 7.89).

24. From her parents' house, but not from her husband's house.

25. This formula usually refers to the right of a man to speak in the assembly. It may mean that here, or refer to the wife's right to command servants.

26. This is a benediction as she enters the house of the groom.

27. Verses 28–30 and 34–5 concern the defloration of the bride and the staining of the bridal gown with her blood. This blood becomes a magic spirit, potent and dangerous though not necessarily evil; the defloration is an auspicious event but too powerful to allow its emblem to remain present afterwards. The power of the blood is transferred to the bride's family and to the husband, and though this is a good power it becomes evil if allowed to pollute the husband (v. 30) or to compete with the wife herself as an *alter ego* (v. 29). By exercising his *droit de seigneur*, Soma takes upon himself the first and most powerful stigma of the blood of defloration.

28. Double meaning: the bonds of marriage that unite them, and the magic lines drawn by the blood on the gown.

29. That is, it enters the groom when the bride enters the house.

30. Almost certainly the body of the husband.

31. This verse is to be spoken if the bridal party encounters a funeral procession on the road; verse 32 is to be spoken at a cross-roads.

32. The robe again, as in verses 28–30.

33. Literally, this verse describes the cutting up of the robe; but the words usually refer to the cutting up of the sacrificial animal, and there is a further overtone of the physical injury of the defloration itself, the sacrifice of the maidenhead on the altar of marriage.

34. A reference to the bride in terms of the paradigmatic Sūryā; the colours are the purple and red of the blood (v. 28).

35. The good fortune of being beautiful and therefore loved by her long-lived husband, as in verses 25 and 33.

36. Gods who are concerned with marriage. Purandhi is the bringer of abundance.

37. Here invoked not as the son of the Aśvins, as in the myth of Sūryā (v. 14), but as the god of safe roads and journeys and as the one who prepares the bride for the sexual act.

38. This may refer to the priests but more likely refers to the various divinities who possess the bride before her marriage – the Gandharvas (like Viśvāvasu in verses 21–2), Soma (vv. 40–41), and in particular, Agni.

39. This is addressed to the bridal couple.

40. Here and in verses 44 and 47, auspicious unguents are placed on the bridal couple to ensure good fortune and, perhaps, lubricity. Here the action is metaphorical and intended to bestow long life; in verse 44 the ointment is placed on the bride's eyes to prevent the evil eye, and in verse 47 it is placed over their two hearts to make them soften and fuse. Cf. the unguent on the widow's eyes in 10.18.7.

41. A general hope, as well as a reference to the particular evil sign represented by the blood of defloration (vv. 28–30, 34–5).

42. Domestic animals (*paśus*).

43. A strange wish. Later Hindu tradition regards the husband as being reborn as the son of his wife. This verse may merely imply that she should care for her husband as the eleventh male dependent upon her.

44. Assistant and messenger of Agni.

45. An unknown goddess, perhaps responsible for showing the bride the way to her husband's home and heart. Cf. *Atharva Veda* 11.4.12.

## 10.109 *The Rape and Return of the Brahmin's Wife*

This hymn exhorts the king to restore the Brahmin's abducted wife; it alludes to the parallel instance of the myth of Soma's abduction and return of the wife of Bṛhaspati. The two parallels are closely intertwined: Soma is called a king (an epithet that he has even when he is regarded as the incarnation of the sacred Soma plant and Soma drink, an aspect of the god not immediately relevant to this hymn), and so he is said to 'give back' the wife of Bṛhaspati both as the culprit (the adulterer returning the woman to her husband) and as the king (v. 2), whose responsibility it is to see justice done. Moreover, since the god whose wife Soma abducts is Bṛhaspati, 'Lord of Sacred Speech', the Brahmin of the gods, the poet is able to speak of Soma returning 'the Brahmin's wife'. Moreover, Soma 'gives back' all brides after he has exercised his *droit de seigneur* (see 10.85). Verse 2 is thus an extended pun: Soma returns the wife of Bṛhaspati as the king returns the wife of a human Brahmin.

An equivalent ambiguity may be seen in the question of the sin or offence for which the hymn seeks expiation. When the poet refers to such expiation, one assumes that it is meant to apply to Soma's offence. But later Hindu tradition regards the offence, and the expiation, as that of the husband or even of the wife. As Sāyaṇa tells the story: 'Speech was the wife of Bṛhaspati. One day she offended him because she was so ugly, and so he abandoned her. Then the gods, deliberating among themselves, made her free from offence [i.e. ugliness] and gave her back to Bṛhaspati.' The hymn allows of either interpretation, since the phrase 'Brahmin-offence' in the first verse could be either an offence *by* a Brahmin or one *against* him, and verse 7 does not say whose expiation is being performed. But the hymn itself does not blame the Brahmin or his wife, and one is inclined to think that the poet wishes to expiate the sin of the adulterer – and to purify the adulterous god Soma.

1 These were the first to speak about the sin against the Brahmin: the boundless ocean, Mātariśvan,[1] the fierce-flowing heat,[2] strong fire[3] that brings the force of life, and the divine waters who are first-born in the sacred order.

2 King Soma was the first who gave the Brahmin's wife back again, without a grudge; Varuṇa and Mitra agreed to go with her, and Agni, the summoning priest, took her by the hand and led her back.[4]

3 He[5] must be grasped by her own hand, as a token, when they have said, 'She is the Brahmin's wife.' She did not stay for a messenger to be sent. Thus is the kingdom of a ruler protected.

4 The gods and the seven sages who settled down to asceticism in the ancient time spoke about her: 'The wife of a Brahmin is dangerous, if she is taken away; she plants disorder in the highest heaven.'

5 He lives as a chaste student, a servant eagerly serving; he becomes a limb of the gods.[6] In that way, Bṛhaspati won back his wife again, when she had been carried off by Soma, just as the gods won back the sacrificial spoon taken by Soma.[7]

6 The gods gave back again, and men gave back. Kings, keeping their promises, should give back the Brahmin's wife.

7 When they gave back the Brahmin's wife and with the gods' aid erased the sin, they enjoyed the rich essence of the earth and then went on to the wide-striding realm.[8]

## NOTES

1. An assistant of Agni, sometimes identified with the wind.

2. *Tapas*, ritual or ascetic heat (cf. 10.190).

3. Fire as an element.

4. Soma, the Gandharva, and Agni are the three immortal husbands of the bride before she marries a mortal (10.85.40).

5. This verse seems to say that Bṛhaspati himself must take her by the hand, and not a messenger. But Sāyaṇa suggests that the gods

are here speaking to Bṛhaspati, and it may be that 'he' is her son, a token of their union. Later myths tell us that a son, Budha, was born to Soma and restored to his father in a similar way.

6. 'He' is probably Bṛhaspati, who lives in chastity because he lacks a wife; by serving the gods zealously, he obtains their aid in winning her back.

7. There is an elaborate pun in this verse. *Juhū* designates a special spoon used in the Soma sacrifice; it is therefore 'taken by Soma' (cf. 3.31.1–3). It also comes to mean 'speech', personified as the goddess of Speech who often leaves the gods and must be brought back again, like Bṛhaspati's wife. Sāyaṇa says that Juhū is the name of the wife of Bṛhaspati, but this renders the metaphor pointless.

8. Heaven, the realm of Viṣṇu who strides across it.

## 10.102 *Mudgala's Wife and the Bull in the Chariot*

This mysterious dialogue hymn conceals an erotic and procreative myth in the tale of a strange chariot race. Sāyaṇa tells two versions of the story in his introduction: 'Thieves stole away all of Mudgala's cattle but one old bull; yoking this remaining one to his cart, he yoked a wooden club [or, perhaps, a horse or bull named 'wooden club'][1] to the other side and went after the thieves, taking back his own cows.' The second version is shorter: 'Mudgala yoked a bull and a wooden club, went into battle, and won the combat.' These commentaries do not mention the central role of Mudgala's wife, nor do they tell us anything of the nature of this mysterious wooden club or how it could be harnessed to a chariot,[2] points which are somewhat (but not entirely) clarified by the hymn itself.

The central image of the hymn is the chariot race that is simultaneously a battle and a search for cattle; these frequently overlap in Vedic thought, for the chariot race is a formalization of battle (like hunting in England: all the glory of war and only seventy per cent of the danger); the sacrifice, too, included a mock cattle-raid. This particular battle/race/raid is unusual in having four transformations: the charioteer is a woman instead of a man (Mudgala's wife apparently riding beside him); the part of the first racehorse is played by an old bull; and the part of the second racehorse is played by a wooden club.[1] Much is made of the fourth transformation, that of an old cart into a racing chariot (a transformation which hinges upon the clever use of the piece of wood, in verse 7). The story as a whole, particularly the woman charioteer and the unusual chariot-animal, bears a striking resemblance to an old Irish myth;[3] this, together with notable parallels with Greek myths and Roman rituals, suggests an Indo-European origin for this strange tale.

The hymn opens with Mudgala's blessing on the race (vv. 1–3), and a description of the beginning of the race (v. 4) and its outcome (v. 2). The opponents try in vain to stop the bull (v. 5), but he races all the faster (v. 6). The wooden club is attached (vv. 7–8), amazing the onlookers (v. 9), and then it is led home in triumph (perhaps satirical) (v. 10). The hymn ends with a benediction from the onlookers (v. 11) and from Mudgala (v. 12).

*1* [*Mudgala:*] 'Let Indra boldly push forward your perversely transformed chariot.[4] O Indra, invoked by so many, help us in this race for fame and battle spoils.'[5]

*2* The wind whipped up her robe when she mounted the chariot and won a thousand cows. For Mudgala's wife was the charioteer in the contest for cattle; becoming the very army of Indra, she gambled and won the spoils.

*3* [*Mudgala:*] 'Hold back the thunderbolt[6] of the enemy who rushes against me to kill me, O generous Indra. Drive aside the missile of the Dāsa or the Ārya.'[7]

*4* The bull who was inspired to fight drank a lake of water. With a horn like a club he rushed against the enemy attack and crushed it. The animal with heavy testicles stretched forth his forefeet briskly, eager to win the race, longing for fame.

*5* The attackers excited the bull to bellow and to stale[8] right in the middle of the battle. Through him, Mudgala won as spoils of war a thousand and a hundred well-grazed cows.

6 The bull rumbled[9] as he was yoked; his long-haired charioteer[10] shouted. The droppings of the headstrong bull, who was running yoked to the wagon, struck Mudgala's wife.[11]

7 Cleverly he[12] struck off the rim of the chariot wheel and yoked the steer to it,[13] using all his force and skill. Indra aided the husband of cows; the humpbacked bull galloped with great leaps.

8 The man with a whip and braided hair[14] was successful in binding the wood to the rope. The bull performed the deeds of a hero for the great crowd, increasing in vigour as he looked at the cows.[15]

9 [*Bystanders:*] 'See over there the yoke-mate of the bull, the wooden club, lying in the middle of the racecourse. Through him Mudgala won a thousand cows, and a hundred, in the races.'

10 'Let all misfortunes stay far away!' 'Who has ever seen such a thing?' 'Hold on to the one that he yoked.' 'They are not bringing grass or water to him.'[16] 'Going above the yoking pole, he pulls as if he wished to command the drive forward.'[17]

11 'She has won, like a despised wife who wins back her husband, like a full-breasted woman who pours water even with a poor water-wheel.[18] Let us conquer with a charioteer who is so eager and nimble. Let her prize be rich and auspicious.'

12 [*Mudgala:*] 'You, Indra, are the eye of the eye of the whole world. For you are the bull who strives to win the race, driving a bull with a steer for his yoke-mate.'[19]

## NOTES

1. This is conjectural, as the term (*drughaṇa*) is a hapax, that might be the name of a racehorse or even an evil fiend of some sort; but it is explicitly called 'wooden' in verse 8.

2. Some farmers (in Bavaria and elsewhere) do yoke a horse to one shaft and a cow to the other, or even leave the second shaft empty. Cf. 1.116.18 for two strange and unmatched chariot animals, and 1.164 for a mysterious chariot.

3. The tale of the goddess Mácha harnessed to a chariot when she is pregnant.

4. The adjective 'perversely transformed' implies that it is perverted from its normal haulage function to that of a war chariot, for which it is unsuited.

5. These spoils are the cows taken by the thieves, Sāyaṇa suggests.

6. Indra is asked to repel the thunderbolt that is usually his own weapon but here apparently designates a missile hurled by the enemy. It may also stand for a club (a doublet of the club used by Mudgala) thrown by the enemy, perhaps to jam the spokes of the chariot wheel.

7. The Dāsa is the enemy who is a native inhabitant of the invaded country, the Ārya the enemy who is another member of the invading force.

8. Apparently the attackers try to make the bull roar and urinate because he must stand still to do this and so will be delayed. Since the bull has just drunk a lake of water in the previous verse, he might stale of his own accord anyway.

9. He may rumble as he stales; the verse is unclear, and it may be the cart or the wooden club that rumbles. Cf. the rumbling cart in 10.146.3.

10. The long hair here indicates that the charioteer is a woman, in contrast with the charioteer with braided hair in verse 8.

11. Apparently the droppings strike the charioteer because the bull is running so fast. The bull is excreting, as he staled in the previous verse, because he is furious, and since he does not have to stop to do this (as he must do to stale), Mudgala's wife is in the direct line of fire. One might see connotations of fertility in the manure, but it is certainly a most peculiar verse.

12. Mudgala.

13. Through parallel constructions, the verse describes the castrated bull (the steer) as a metaphor for the wooden club that is yoked by Mudgala, and contrasts him with the galloping bull (the husband of cows) who is aided by Indra and whose deeds are further described in verse 8. The contrast between the bull and the steer is repeated in verses 9 and 12.

14. This would appear to be Mudgala, if it is in fact he who is the

subject of the first part of verse 7, as seems most likely. But there may be a secondary reference to Pūṣan, the solar charioteer who is also said to have a whip and braided hair, and who may be imagined as the divine companion in the racing chariot, standing beside Mudgala's wife in the form of Mudgala himself.

15. The sight of the prize cows waiting to be given away at the end of the racecourse excites the bull.

16. While the bull is given fodder after the race, the wooden club is not, of course.

17. The wooden club, going in front, looks as if he feels himself to be the true driver, or so the onlookers joke.

18. This verse has complex overtones. The basic image is that of the dark horse overcoming obstacles (the improvised chariot) to win, as a neglected wife wins back her husband. Mudgala's wife may have been thus neglected, either because she had borne no children or perhaps because she was married to an old ascetic while she herself was young, 'eager and nimble' in more ways than as a charioteer. By becoming the woman charioteer, she becomes prosperous, full-blooming, like a full-breasted (i.e. lactating) woman with children. Thus she wins her way back into her husband's graces by winning the race, the prize substituting for the children she never had. She is then like the potent bull, and he is like the impotent piece of wood or the 'poor water-wheel'. In this race, as in the 'sexual race' won by Lopāmudrā and her old ascetic husband Agastya (1.179), they win together. The pouring of water supplies the basis of the simile: the full-blooming wife of Mudgala prospers like an earthenware wheel that sprinkles water, a patent sexual metaphor.

19. In the continued metaphor, Mudgala hopes to accomplish what the steer accomplished, while Indra helps his 'yoke-mate' the bull – Mudgala's wife.

# INCANTATIONS AND SPELLS

The *Atharva Veda* is the *locus classicus* for magic spells, but the later parts of the R*ig Veda* also contain many imprecations and chants. Some deal with white magic or medicine (10.97), some with bad dreams (10.164) or sleep (7.55), and some with the problem of black magic or sorcery (7.104). Many deal with the *rites de passage*: the wife hopes to overcome her rivals (10.145), succeeds in overcoming her rivals (10.159), wishes to become pregnant (10.184) and to have a healthy child (10.162). These life-affirming spells culminate in the wish that underlies so much of the R*ig Veda* – the wish that death will go elsewhere, at least for a little while longer (10.165).

## The Healing Plants

A doctor praises the healing herbs that supply his medicines and blesses the man whose illness he hopes to cure.

*1* The tawny plants were born in the ancient times, three ages before the gods; now I will meditate upon their hundred and seven forms.[1]

*2* Mothers, you have a hundred forms and a thousand growths. You who have a hundred ways of working, make this man whole for me.

*3* Be joyful, you plants that bear flowers and those that bear fruit. Like mares that win the race together, the growing plants will carry us across.

*4* You mothers who are called plants, I say to you who are goddesses: let me win a horse, a cow, a robe – and your very life, O man.[2]

*5* In the sacred fig-tree is your home; in the tree of leaves[3] your dwelling-place has been made. You will surely win a cow as your share if you win a man.[4]

*6* He in whom the plants gather like kings in the assembly, that priest is called a healer, a slayer of demons,[5] an expeller of disease.

*7* The one that brings horses, the one that brings Soma, the one that gives strength, the heightener of strength – all these plants I have found to stretch out the health of this man.

*8* Like cows from the cow-pen, out stream the powers of the plants that will win wealth – and your life, O man.

*9* Your mother's name is Reviver, and so you are the Restorers.[6] You are streams that fly on wings. Restore whatever has been injured.

*10* They have stepped over all barriers like a thief into a cow-pen. The plants have driven out whatever wound was in the body.

*11* When I take these plants in my hand, yearning for the

victory prize, the life of the disease[7] vanishes as if before a hunter grasping at his life.

12 He through whom you plants creep limb by limb, joint by joint, you banish disease from him like a huge man coming between fighters.[8]

13 Fly away, disease, along with the blue jay and the jay; disappear with the howl of the wind, with the rain storm.

14 Let one of you help the other; let one stand by the other. All of you working together, help this speech of mine to succeed.

15 Those that bear fruit and those without fruit, those without flower and those that bear flowers, sent by Bṛhaspati[9] let them free us from anguish.

16 Let them free me from the effects of a curse, and also from what comes from Varuṇa,[10] and from the fetter sent by Yama and from every offence of the gods.[11]

17 Flying down from the sky, the plants spoke: that man shall not be harmed whose life we join.

18 Of all the many plants in hundreds of forms, whose king is Soma, you[12] are supreme, a remedy for need and a blessing for the heart.

19 You plants whose king is Soma, spread out over the earth as you were sent by Bṛhaspati: unite your power in this plant.

20 Do not harm the man who digs you up, nor him for whom I dig you up; let all our two-footed and four-footed creatures be without sickness.

21 You growing plants who hear this, and those who have gone far away, all coming together unite your power in this plant.

22 The plants speak together with King Soma: 'Whomever the Brahmin priest treats, we will carry him across, O king.'

23 Plant, you are supreme; the trees are your subjects. Let the man who seeks to injure us be our subjects.

### NOTES

1. That is, the 107 types or species of healing herbs.

2. This, as in verse 8, is a direct address to the patient whose life is in danger.

3. The sacred fig is the Aśvattha; the tree of leaves is the Parṇa.

4. That is, if you win back the life of this man.

5. Rakṣases, local demons, not the grand Asuras of heaven.

6. A pun on Iṣkṛti and Niṣkṛti.

7. The curer is depicted as killing the disease to save the patient. The particular disease named here (*yakṣa*) is a kind of consumption.

8. The 'mediator' is a powerful king who remains neutral and intervenes between two warring kings.

9. Bṛhaspati is the deity who presides over spells.

10. Varuṇa sends a noose that consists in the disease of dropsy or other diseases.

11. Offences committed by men against the gods, bringing diseases down upon the offender, and offences committed by the gods against men, offences themselves consisting in diseases. Cf. 10.109.1.

12. The particular plant about to be used in the healing of the patient.

## 10.164 *Against Bad Dreams and Sins*

The evil thoughts that ruin waking life, that ruin the work of the poet, and that ruin peaceful sleep are all to be banished by an otherwise unknown god, the Master of Thought.

*1* Go away, Master of Thought, get out and wander in the far distance. In the far distance say to Destruction,[1] 'The thought of a living creature is of many kinds.'[2]

*2* 'They choose the boon that makes them happy; they yoke the lead horse that makes them happy; the eye of the son of Vivasvan[3] makes them happy. The thought of a living creature is of many kinds.'

*3* If we have done something bad on purpose or not on purpose, or with the wrong purpose, awake or asleep, let Agni place far away from us all these misdeeds that are displeasing.

4 If we commit an offence, O Indra, O Brahmaṇaspati, let the prophet descended from Angiras[4] protect us from oppression by those who hate us.

5 We have conquered today, and we have won; we have become free of sin. The waking dream, the evil intent – let it fall upon the one we hate; let it fall upon the one who hates us.

NOTES

1. The goddess Nirṛti, chaos and death.
2. Cf. 9.112.1.
3. Yama, king of the dead.
4. Probably Agni or Bṛhaspati.

## 7.55 *Sleeping Spell*

Several different suggestions have been made for the context of this hymn. Sāyaṇa relates it to Vasiṣṭha's hymns to Varuṇa:[1] Vasiṣṭha, having fasted for three days, entered Varuṇa's house to get food; he spoke this hymn to quiet the watch-dog. The hymn is also said to have been used by thieves and housebreakers, by lovers on secret nocturnal rendezvous in their mistresses' houses,[2] by mothers singing it as a lullaby to their children, or by the domestic priest (Purohita) praying for a peaceful slumber for the inhabitants of the house.

1 Lord of the House,[3] you who drive away diseases and permeate all forms,[4] be a gentle friend to us.

2 White and tawny son of Saramā,[5] when you bare your teeth they gleam like spears in your snapping jaws. Fall fast asleep!

3 Bark at the thief or at the marauder, as you run up and back again, O son of Saramā. But you are barking at those who sing Indra's praises; why do you threaten us? Fall fast asleep!

4 Tear apart the wild boar, for he would tear you apart. But you are barking at those who sing Indra's praises; why do you threaten us? Fall fast asleep!

5 Let the mother sleep; let the father sleep; let the dog sleep; let the master of the house sleep. Let all the kinsmen sleep; let our people all around sleep.

6 The one who rests and the one who moves, and whoever sees us – we close their eyes tightly as we close up this house.

7 The bull with a thousand horns,[6] who rises up out of the sea – with the help of that powerful one we put the people to sleep.

8 The women lying on benches or lying in chairs or lying in beds, the wives who smell good – we put all of them to sleep.

## NOTES

1. Cf. 7.86, 7.89, and 7.88.5.

2. This Rig Vedic hymn is specifically adapted to use by lovers in the *Atharva Veda* (4.5).

3. Vāstoṣpati, the Lord of the House, is a god to whom the previous hymn (7.54) is dedicated.

4. This is usually an epithet of Soma, sometimes of Agni.

5. Saramā is the eponymous ancestor of all brindled dogs. Cf. 10.108 and 10.14.10–11.

6. The moon, 'horned' both in the sense of resembling (when crescent) the horns of a bull and of having the rays of moonlight shooting away from him like horns from the head of an animal.

## 10.145 *Against Rival Wives*

This hymn is appropriately dedicated to Indrāṇī, wife of the notoriously womanizing Indra.

1 I dig up this plant,[1] the most powerful thing that grows, with which one drives out the rival wife and wins the husband entirely for oneself.

2 Broad-leaved plant sent by the gods to bring happiness and the power to triumph, blow my rival wife away and make my husband mine alone.

3 O highest one, I am the highest one, higher than all the highest women, and my rival wife is lower than the lowest women.

4 I will not even take her name into my mouth; he takes no pleasure in this person.[2] Far, far into the distance we make the rival wife go.

5 I have emerged triumphant, and you also[3] have triumphed. The two of us, full of the power to triumph, will triumph over my rival wife.

6 I have placed the plant of triumph on you,[4] and grasped you with my power to triumph. Let your heart run after me like a cow after a calf, like water running in its own bed.

### NOTES

1. The magic plant used in many Vedic spells.

2. That is, the husband does not really love the rival wife or co-wife (or other woman competing for the husband's love), who is not even worthy of being mentioned.

3. The magic plant is here directly addressed as an ally.

4. This verse is said to the husband, on whose head the plant is placed.

## 10.159 *The Triumphant Wife*

This hymn, which is connected with a dawn sacrifice (vv. 1 and 4), expresses a woman's triumphant conquest of her husband and banishing of her rival wives. Tradition associates it with Indrāṇī, though she is never mentioned in the hymn.

1 There the sun has risen, and here my good fortune[1] has risen. Being a clever woman, and able to triumph,[2] I have triumphed over my husband.

2 I am the banner; I am the head. I am the formidable one

who has the deciding word. My husband will obey my will alone, as I emerge triumphant.

3 My sons kill their enemies and my daughter is an empress, and I am completely victorious. My voice is supreme in my husband's ears.

4 The oblation that Indra made and so became glorious and supreme, this is what I have made for you, O gods. I have become truly without rival wives.

5 Without rival wives, killer of rival wives, victorious and pre-eminent, I have grabbed for myself the attraction of the other women as if it were the wealth of flighty women.

6 I have conquered and become pre-eminent over these rival wives, so that I may rule as empress over this hero and over the people.

### NOTES

1. *Bhaga*, the happiness that consists in being loved by one's husband.

2. That is, to win out against all the other women, as well as to win over the husband. Cf. 10.145.

## 10.184 *For a Safe Pregnancy and Birth*

1 Let Viṣṇu[1] prepare the womb; let Tvaṣṭṛ shape the forms. Let Prajāpati shed the seed; let Dhātṛ place the embryo in you.

2 Place the embryo, Sinīvalī;[2] place the embryo, Sarasvatī. Let the twin Aśvins, the lotus-garlanded gods, place the embryo in you.

3 With golden kindling woods the Aśvins churn out fire.[3] We invoke that embryo for you to bring forth in the tenth month.

### NOTES

1. The gods of this verse are all associated with various forms of begetting.

2. These are goddesses who assist at birth.

3. The churning of the fire-sticks is a sexual metaphor, resulting in the birth of a child, who is fire, born out of water (the fluids of the ocean or the sky) as the child is born out of the fluids of the womb.

## 10.162 *To Protect the Embryo*

*1* Let Agni the killer of demons[1] unite with this prayer and expel from here the one whose name is evil, who lies with disease upon your embryo, your womb.

*2* The one whose name is evil, who lies with disease upon your embryo, your womb, the flesh-eater – Agni has driven him away with prayer.

*3* The one who kills the embryo as it settles,[2] as it rests, as it stirs, who wishes to kill it when it is born – we will drive him away from here.

*4* The one who spreads apart your two thighs, who lies between the married pair, who licks the inside of your womb – we will drive him away from here.

*5* The one who by changing into your brother, or your husband, or your lover lies with you, who wishes to kill your offspring – we will drive him away from here.

*6* The one who bewitches[3] you with sleep or darkness and lies with you – we will drive him away from here.

### NOTES

1. Rakṣases, earthly demons.

2. The three stages of the embryo: just conceived, unmoving, and, in the third month, moving.

3. Literally, deludes.

## 7.104 *The Demons in Hell*

In banishing all evil spirits to a dark hole (a place that may prefigure the post-Vedic hell of the demons), the poet also takes the opportunity to wish evils upon the head of his rival priest, a 'sorcerer' who apparently accuses the author of the hymn of being a sorcerer.

1 Indra and Soma, burn the demon and crush him; bulls, hurl down those who thrive on darkness. Shatter those who lack good thoughts; scorch them, kill, drive out, cut down the devourers.
2 Indra and Soma, let evil heat boil up around him who plots evil, like a pot set on a fire. Set unrelenting hatred against the fiend,[1] the flesh-eating Brahmin-hater with the evil eye.
3 Indra and Soma, pierce the evil-doers and hurl them into the pit, the bottomless darkness, so that not a single one will come up from there again. Let this furious rage of yours overpower them.
4 Indra and Soma, together roll the shattering weapon from the sky, from the earth, upon the one who plots evil. Carve out of the mountains the hissing thing[2] with which you burn down the demon who thrives.
5 Indra and Soma, roll it from the sky. With unageing weapons of heat that burn like fire and strike like stone pierce the devourers and hurl them into the abyss. Let them go into silence.
6 Indra and Soma, let this prayer embrace you all around like the girth around two prize-winning horses. Like a pair of princes,[3] urge on these prayers, this invocation that I send to you by meditation.
7 Plot against them. Swooping down swiftly, kill the demons who hate us and would break us to bits. Indra and Soma, let nothing good happen to the evil-doer who has ever tried to injure me with his hatred.
8 Whoever has spoken against me with false words when I was acting with a pure heart, O Indra, let him become nothing even as he talks about nothing, like water grasped in one's fist.
9 Those who casually seduce the man of pure heart or who wilfully make the good man bad, let Soma deliver

them over to the serpent,[4] or let him set them in the lap of Destruction.[5]

10 Agni, whoever wants to injure the sap of our drink, of our horses, of our cows, of our own bodies, he is our enemy, a thief and a robber; let him fall upon hard times; let him perish with his own body and his offspring.

11 Let him with his own body and his offspring be beyond, let him be below all three earths. Gods, dry up the glory of the one who wants to injure us by day or by night.

12 For the clever man it is easy to distinguish: true and false words fight against one another. Soma favours the one of them that is true, that is straight; he kills the false.

13 Surely Soma does not push forward the one who is dishonest, nor the ruler who holds power falsely. He kills the demon, he kills the one who speaks lies.[6] Both of these lie in Indra's snare.

14 As if I worshipped false gods, or considered the gods useless – why, Agni knower of creatures, why are you angry with us?[7] Gather into your destruction those who speak hateful words.

15 Let me die at once if I am a sorcerer, or if I have burnt up a man's span of life. Let the one who falsely calls me a sorcerer be cut off from ten heroes.[8]

16 The one who calls me a sorcerer, though I am not a sorcerer, or the one who says he is pure, though he is demonic – let Indra strike him with his great weapon. Let him fall to the lowest depths under all creation.

17 She[9] who ranges about at night like an owl, hiding her body in a hateful disguise, let her fall into the endless pits. Let the pressing-stones slay the demons with their rumblings.

18 Maruts, scatter yourselves among all the peoples. Seek out, grab, and crush the demons who become birds and fly about at night, the ones who have injured the sacrifice of the gods.

19 Roll the stone from the sky, generous Indra. Sharpen it

completely when Soma has sharpened it. From in front, from behind, from below, from above, strike the demons with the mountain.

20 There they go! The dog-sorcerers[10] are flying away. Viciously they wish to harm Indra, who cannot be harmed. Indra sharpens his weapon against the slanderers. Now let him loose his bolt at the sorcerers.

21 Indra shattered the sorcerers who snatched away the oblation and waylaid him. Indra splits them as an axe splits a tree, bursting apart the demons as if they were clay pots.

22 Kill the owl-sorcerer, the owlet-sorcerer, the dog-sorcerer, the cuckoo-sorcerer, the eagle-sorcerer, the vulture-sorcerer.[11] Indra, crush the demon to powder as if with a millstone.

23 Do not let the demon of the sorcerers get close to us. Let the light[12] blot out the fiends who work in couples. Let the earth protect us from earthly anguish, and the middle realm of space protect us from the anguish of the sky.

24 Indra, kill the male sorcerer and the female who deceives by her power of illusion. Let the idol-worshippers sink down with broken necks; let them never see the rising sun.

25 Look here, look there, Indra and Soma; stay awake! Hurl the weapon at the demons; hurl the thunderbolt at the sorcerers!

## NOTES

1. A creature called Kimīdin, who, according to the commentator, goes about saying, 'What now?' (*kim-idānīm*). The other demons in this hymn are generally identified as Rakṣases.

2. The thunderbolt. Cf. 8.14.14.

3. Probably charioteers, like the Aśvins.

4. To death by serpents' bite, perhaps, or to the great serpent Vṛtra.

5. Nirṛti.

6. Or the one who speaks spells of black magic.

7. That is, I *don't* worship false gods, so why do you punish me as if I did?

8. Perhaps from ten generations of heroic sons, or from the assistance that ten heroes could render him in defence against the speaker.

9. A witch or sorceress.

10. Sorcerers who take the form of dogs, or werewolves.

11. Sorcerers in the forms of various animals.

12. The light of dawn, that will end the power of the night-roaming demons.

## 10.165 *The Dove of Death*

The dove, the messenger of the god of death, is driven from the house.

*1* Gods, a dove has come here seeking someone, sent as a messenger by Destruction.[1] We will sing against him; we will perform an expiation. Let all be well with our two-footed creatures, all be well with our four-footed creatures.

*2* Let the dove that has been sent to us be kind; gods, let the bird be harmless in our houses. Let the inspired Agni relish our oblation. Let the winged spear[2] spare us.

*3* Do not let the winged spear attack us; it settles by the fireplace in the kitchen. Let all be well with our cows and with our men; gods, do not let the dove harm us here.

*4* What the owl screeches is in vain; vain, too, the settling of the dove by the fire.[3] I bow low before Yama, before death, who sent this dove as a messenger.

*5* Drive the dove out, pushing him with a verse. Rejoicing in food, lead the cow around and wipe out all the evil traces. Let it[4] fly forth, flying its best, and leave us strength to live.

## NOTES

1. Nirṛti.
2. The dove is likened to a missile flying on wings.
3. The bad omen of the owl's screech and of the dove's entrance into the house are both made naught.
4. The dove, who is to leave behind it the strength of those in the house as well as, perhaps, of the dove.

## APPENDIX I
# *Abbreviations*

### *A. Authors of Translations* (T)

| | |
|---|---|
| B | W. Norman Brown, *India and Indology* |
| E | Tatyana Yakovlena Elizarenkova, *Rigveda: Izbrannye Gimny* |
| L | Charles Rockwell Lanman, *Sanskrit Reader* |
| M | Arthur A. Macdonell, *A Vedic Reader for Students* |
| MM | F. Max Müller, *Vedic Hymns* |
| N | Antonio T. de Nicolás, *Meditations through the Ṛg Veda* |
| OST | John Muir, *Original Sanskrit Texts* |
| P | Raimundo Panikkar, *The Vedic Experience* |
| R | Louis Renou, *Études védiques et pāṇinéennes* |
| RHS | Louis Renou, *Hymnes spéculatifs du Véda* |

### *B. Journals and Series Containing Articles with Commentaries* (C)

| | |
|---|---|
| *ABORI* | *Annals of the Bhandarkar Oriental Research Institute* |
| *AIOC* | *All India Oriental Conference* (SP: *Summary of Proceedings*) |
| *AJPh* | *American Journal of Philosophy* |
| *AO* | *Acta Orientalia* |
| *AOr* | *Archiv Orientalni* |
| *BDCRI* | *Bulletin of the Deccan College Research Institute* |
| *BSO(A)S* | *Bulletin of the School of Oriental (and African) Studies* |
| *HOS* | *Harvard Oriental Series* |
| *HR* | *History of Religions* |
| *IA* | *Indian Antiquary* |
| *IF* | *Indogermanische Forschungen* |
| *IIJ* | *Indo-Iranian Journal* |
| *JA* | *Journal asiatique* |
| *JAOS* | *Journal of the American Oriental Society* |
| *JAS* | *Journal of Asian Studies* |
| *JBomU* | *Journal of Bombay University* |
| *JBORS* | *Journal of the Bihar and Orissa Research Society* |

ABBREVIATIONS

| | |
|---|---|
| *JB(B)RS* | *Journal of the Bombay (Branch of the) Royal Society* |
| *JGJKSV* | *Journal of the Ganganatha Jha Kendriya Sanskrit Vidyapeeth* |
| *JIES* | *Journal of Indo-European Studies* |
| *JMSUB* | *Journal of the Maharaja Sayajirao University of Baroda* |
| *JOIB* | *Journal of the Oriental Institute of Baroda* |
| *JRAS* | *Journal of the Royal Asiatic Society* |
| *JRASB* | *Journal of the Royal Asiatic Society of Bengal* |
| *NIA* | *New Indian Antiquary* |
| *OLZ* | *Orientalische Literatur Zeitung* |
| *ON* | *Orientalia Neerlandica* |
| *PAPS* | *Proceedings of the American Philosophical Society* |
| *PrAOS* | *Proceedings of the American Oriental Society* |
| *ŚB* | *Śatapatha Brāhmaṇa* |
| *SBB* | *Sitzungenberichte der Böhmischen Akademie der Wissenschaften zu München* |
| *SBE* | *Sacred Books of the East* |
| *SP* | *See* AIOC |
| *WZKM* | *Wiener Zeitschrift zur Kunde des Morgenlandes* |
| *WZKSOA* | *Wiener Zeitschrift zur Kunde des Süd- und Ostasiens* |
| *ZDMG* | *Zeitschrift der Deutschen Morgenländischen Gesellschaft* |

APPENDIX 2

# *Dictionaries, Concordances, Bibliographies, and Selected General Studies of the* Rig Veda


Hermann Grassmann, *Wörterbuch zum* Rig *Veda* (Wiesbaden, 1955)

Maurice Bloomfield, *A Vedic Concordance* (HOS 10; Cambridge, Mass., 1906; reprinted Delhi, 1964)

A. A. Macdonell and A. B. Keith, *Vedic Index of Names and Subjects* (2 vols.; London, 1912; reprinted Delhi, 1958)

R. N. Dandekar, *Vedic Bibliography* (2 vols.; Bombay, 1946; Poona, 1961)

A. Hillebrandt, *Vedische Mythologie* (Breslau, 1902)

A. A. Macdonell, *Vedic Mythology* (Strassburg, 1897; reprinted Delhi, 1963)

Louis Renou, *Bibliographie Védique* (Paris, 1931)

A. Bergaigne, *La* R*eligion védique* (3 vols., Paris, 1878–83)

Jan Gonda, *The Vision of the Vedic Poets* (The Hague, 1963)

*Eye and Gaze in the Veda* (Amsterdam, London, 1969)

*Some Observations on the* Relations *between 'Gods' and 'Powers' in the Veda* ('s Gravenhage, 1957)

*Loka-World and Heaven in the Veda* (Amsterdam, 1966)

*The Epithets in the* R*gveda* ('s Gravenhage, 1959)

*Vedic Literature* (*Saṃhitās and Brāhmaṇas*) (vol. 1, fasc. 1 of *A History of Indian Literature*, ed. Jan Gonda, Wiesbaden, 1975)

A. B. Keith, *The Religion and Philosophy of the Veda and Upanishads* (HOS 31–2; Cambridge, Mass., 1925; reprinted Delhi, 1970)

A. D. Pusalker, *The Vedic Age* (London, 1957)

Louis Renou, *Vedic India* (Benares, 1971); trans. Philip Spratt, from vol. 3 of *L'Inde classique*, by L. Renou and Jean Filliozat (Paris, 1953)

Maurice Winternitz, *History of Indian Literature*, vol. 1 (Calcutta, 1927); trans. Mrs S. Ketkar, from *Geschichte der indischen Litteratur* (Prague, 1922)

APPENDIX 3

# *Translations of the* Rig Veda

*A. Complete Translations (hence not cited in Appendix 4 under specific hymns)*

Karl Friedrich Geldner, *Der Rig-Veda, aus dem Sanskrit ins Deutsche Übersetzt* (4 vols., HOS 33–6, Cambridge, Mass., 1951–7)

H. Grassmann, *Rig-Veda* (2 vols., Leipzig, 1876–7)

Ralph T. H. Griffith, *The Hymns of the* Rig *Veda* (London, 1889; reprinted Delhi, 1973)

A. Langlois, *Rig-Véda ou Livre des hymnes* (4 vols., Paris 1848–51)

A. Ludwig, *Der Rigveda oder Die heiligen Hymnen der Brāhmaṇa* (6 vols., Prag, Leipzig, 1876–88)

H. H. Wilson, *Ṛig-Veda-Sanhitā: A Collection of Ancient Hindu Hymns* (6 vols., London, 1850–88)

*B. Partial Translations, or Works Containing Selected Translations*

A. Bergaigne, *La Religion Védique* (3 vols., Paris, 1878–83)
*Quarante Hymns du* Rig*-Véda* (MSL 8: 1894, pp. 264ff.)

W. Norman Brown, *India and Indology: Selected Articles*, ed. Rosane Rocher (Delhi, 1978)

Franklin Edgerton, *The Beginnings of Indian Philosophy* (London, 1965)

Tatyana Yakovlena Elizarenkova, *Rigveda: Izbrannye Gimny* (Moscow, 1972)

P. Lal, *The Golden Womb of the Sun: Rigvedic Songs in a New Translation* (Calcutta, 1965–)

Charles Rockwell Lanman, *Sanskrit Reader* (Cambridge, Mass., 1884)

Jean Le Mée, *Hymns from the Rig-Veda* (New York, N.Y., 1975)

Hermann Lommel, *Gedichte des Rig-Veda* (München, 1955)

A. A. Macdonell, *A Vedic Reader for Students* (Oxford, 1917)
*Hymns from the Rigveda* (Calcutta, London, 1922)

John Muir, *Original Sanskrit Texts* (5 vols.; London, 1872; Amsterdam, 1976)

F. Max Müller, *Vedic Hymns* (Oxford, 1891; Delhi, 1964; SBE vols. 32 and 46)

Antonio T. de Nicolás, *Meditations through the Ṛg Veda* (Boulder, Colo., and London, 1978)

Raimundo Panikkar, *The Vedic Experience: Mantramañjarī* (Berkeley and Los Angeles, Calif., 1977)

Louis Renou, *Études védiques et pàṇinéennes* (17 fasc.; Paris, 1955–69)

*Hymnes spéculatifs du Véda* (Paris, 1956)

*Hymnes et prières du Véda* (Paris, 1938)

Paul Thieme, *Gedichte aus dem Rig-Veda* (Stuttgart, 1964)

E. J. Thomas, *Vedic Hymns* (London, 1923)

Jean Varenne, *Le Véda: Le Trésor spirituel de l'Humanité* (Paris, 1967)

APPENDIX 4

# *Bibliography of Translations and Commentaries on Hymns Translated in This Volume*

1.1 T: E 93 (270); L 69; M 3–10; MM 1.1–6; N 193; P 329–30; R 12.1 (12.71)

C: Sri Aurobindo, *Hymns to the Mystic Fire* (Pondicherry, 1952); Sri Aurobindo, 'The First Rik of the Rig Veda', *Sri Aurobindo Mandir Annual,* Jayanti, 11 (July 1952), 31–49; Sri Aurobindo, 'Riks of Madhucchandas (RV 1.1.1–5)', ibid., 12 (July 1953), 6–11; T. Benfey, 'Uebersetzung des Ṛg Veda (1.1–118)', *Orient and Occident* (1862–4)

1.26 T: MM 1.13–15; N 194; R 12.3 (12.72)

1.32 T: E 111 (284); L (70); N 195

C: E. Benveniste and L. Renou, *Vṛtra et Vṛthragna* (Paris, 1934); W. Norman Brown, 'The Creation Myth of the Rig Veda', *JAOS* 62 (1942), 85–98; W. Norman Brown, 'Theories of Creation in the Ṛg Veda', *JAOS* 85 (1965), 23–4; L. Buschardt, 'Vṛtra', in *Det Rituelle Daemon drab i den Vediske Somakult* (Kjøbenhavn, 1945); R. N. Dandekar, 'Vṛtraha Indra', *ABORI* 31 (1931); G. Dumézil, 'A propos de Verethrayna', *Annuaire de l'Institut de philologie* 9 (1949), 223–6; A. B. Keith, 'Indra et Vṛtra', *Indian Culture* 1 (1935); W. D. O'Flaherty, *Hindu Myths* (Penguin Books, 1975), 74–90; Walter Ruben, 'Indra's Fight against Vṛtra in the Mahābhārata', *Belvalkar Felicitation Volume* (Benares, 1957); V. N. Toporov, 'Parallels to Ancient Indo-Iranian Social and Mythological Concepts', in *Pratidānam: Indian, Iranian and Indo-European Studies Presented to F. B. J. Kuiper* (The Hague–Paris, 1968), 113–20; H. D. Velankar, 'Hymns to Indra in Maṇḍala I', *JBomU* 17:2 (September 1948), 1–22

1.35 T: M 10–21; P 139–41; R 15.14

1.42 T: E 191 (348); OST 1.174–5; P 804–5; R 15.139

C: S. D. Adkins, *Pūṣan in the Rig Veda* (Princeton,

N.J., 1941); S. D. Adkins, 'Pūṣan in the Sāma, Yajur, and Atharva Vedas', *JAOS* 67 (1947), 274–96; R. N. Dandekar, 'Pūṣan, the Pastoral God of the Veda', *NIA* 5 (1942), 57; W. Eidlitz, *Die vedische Gottesliebe* (Olten-Freiburg, 1955); N. Flensgurg, 'Bidrag til Rigvedas Mytologi Om Goden Pūṣan i Rig Veda', *Lunds Universitas Årsskrift* V (1909), 1–49; S. Kramrisch, 'Pūṣan', *JAOS* 81 (1961); V. Machek, *Origin of the Gods Rudra and Pūṣan*, 544–62

1.50 T: E 187 (346); L 71; P 320–23; N 199; OST 1.160; R 15.1

C: S. D. Adkins, 'RV. II, 38: a Problem Hymn', *JAOS* 81 (1961), 77–86; J. N. Banerjea, 'Sūrya, Ādityas and the Navagrahas', *Journal of the Indian Society of Oriental Studies* 19 (1948), 47–100; S. Bhattacharji, *The Indian Theogony* (Cambridge, 1970), 211–15; N. M. Chaudhuri, 'The Sun as a Folk-God', *Man in India* 21 (1941); R. N. Dandekar, 'New Light on Savitar', *ABORI* 20; G. Dumézil, *Mitra-Varuṇa*, 188–204; H. Oldenberg, 'Savitar', *ZDMG* 51 (1897), 59; D. P. Pandey, *Sūrya* (Leiden, 1939); H. von Stietencron, *Sāmba und die Śākadvīpīya-Brāhmaṇa* (München, 1965)

1.85 T: E 133 (297); M 21–30; MM 1.126–53; R 10.18 (10.66)

C: G. Dumézil, *L'Héritage indo-européen à Rome* (Paris, 1949), 62; G. Dumézil, 'Viṣṇu et les Marut à travers réforme zoroastrienne', *JA* (1953), 241; A. Giacalone-Ramat, 'Studi intorno ai nomi del dio Marte', *Archivio glottologico italiano* 47 (1962), 112–42; P. Thieme, 'Die Wurzel *vat*', *Asiatica. Festschrift F. Weller* (Leipzig, 1954)

1.92 T: OST 5.181; P 802–4; R 3.31 (16.17)

C: A. K. Coomaraswamy, *The Darker Side of Dawn*, Smithsonian Miscellaneous Collections, 94:1 (1935); A. A. Macdonell, 'The Uṣas Hymns of the Ṛgveda', *JRAS*, 1932

1.114 T: MM 1.422–5

1.116 T: R 16.12

C: W. D. O'Flaherty, *Women, Androgynes, and Other Mythical Beasts* (Chicago, Ill., 1980), 159–60, 218–20

1.154 T: E 170 (334); M 30–36; P 150–53; R 15.34

C: Jan Gonda, *Aspects of Early Viṣṇuism* (Utrecht, 1954), 55–72, 145–6; F. B. J. Kuiper, 'The Three Strides of Viṣṇu', *Indological Studies in Honor of W. Norman Brown* (New Haven, Conn., 1962), 137–51; W. D. O'Flaherty, *Hindu Myths* (Penguin Books, 1975), 175–9; Jaan Puhvel, '"Meadow of the Otherworld" in Indo-European Tradition', *Zeitschrift für vergleichende Sprachwissenschaft* 83 (1969), 64–9; P. Thieme, *Studien zur indogermanischen Wortkunde und Religionsgeschichte*, 46–50; Gaya Charan Tripathi, *Der Ursprung und die Entwicklung der Vāmana-legende in der Indischen Literatur* (Wiesbaden, 1968)

1.160 T: M 36–41; R 15.116

C: W. D. O'Flaherty, *Women, Androgynes, and Other Mythical Beasts* (Chicago, Ill., 1980), 21–4

1.162 T: R 16.84

C: A. Hillebrandt, 'Zu Rgveda I. 162', *ZDMG* 37, 521–4; P. Dumont, *L'Aśvamedha* (Paris, 1927); W. D. O'Flaherty, *Women, Androgynes, and Other Mythical Beasts* (Chicago, Ill., 1980), 154–64

1.163 T: P 377–8; R 16.87; RHS 17–19 (229)

C: W. D. O'Flaherty, *Women, Androgynes, and Other Mythical Beasts* (Chicago, Ill., 1980), 239–41

1.164 T: B 53–74; N 199–205; P 97–103, 660; R 16.88

C: V. S. Agrawala, 'Sanskrit, the Wish-fulfilling Mother of Wisdom and Culture', *JBORS* 45, 1959, 31–5; V. S. Agrawala, 'Vision in Long Darkness. The Thousand-syllabled Speech', fol. I. *Prithivi Prakashan* (Varanasi, 1963), 226; W. Norman Brown, 'Agni, Sun, Sacrifice, and Vāc: A Sacerdotal Ode by Dīrghatamas (Rig Veda 1.164)', *JAOS* 88 (2), (June 1968), 199–218; M. Haug, 'Vedische Rätselfragen und Rätselsprüche', *Sitzungsberichte der Bayerische Akademie der Wissenschaften* (Munich, 1875), 457ff.; Willard Johnson, 'On the Ṛg Vedic Riddle of the Two Birds in the Fig Tree (RV 1.164.20–2), and the Discovery of the Vedic Speculative Symposium', *JAOS* 96:2 (April–June 1976), 248–58 and *Poetry and Speculation of the Ṛg Veda* (Berkeley and Los Angeles, Calif., 1980); H. Lommel, 'Baumsymbolik beim altindischen Opfer', *Paideuma* Bd 6 (1958), 490–99; C. K. Raja, *Asya Vāmasya Hymn, with the Commentaries of Sāyana and Ātmānanda* (Madras, 1956); P. Regnaud, 'Études védiques et post-védiques', *Ann. Lyon* 38.1 (Paris, 1899); R. Roth, 'Zwei Sprüche über Leib und Seele: Rigveda I.164. 30.38', *ZDMG* 46, 759; Discussions of P. Regnaud and R. Roth, by O. Böhtlingk, *Ber. Lpz.* XLV 88, and H. Stumme, *ZDMG* 64, 485; P. S. Shastri, 'The Vision of Dīrghatamas', *Prabuddha Bhārata* 62 (February 1957), 63–6; P. Thieme, 'Untersuchungen zur Wortkunde', *Das Rätsel vom Baum*, 55; O. Viennot, *Le Culte de l'arbe dans l'Inde ancienne* (Paris, 1954); E. Windisch, 'Das Räthsel vom Jahre', *ZDMG* 48, 353

1.165 T: L 73; MM 1.179–208; R 10.54 (10.114)
C: H. D. Velankar, 'Hymns to Indra in Mandala I', *JBomU* 20 (2) (September 1951), 17–34; Emil Sieg, *Die Sagenstoffe des Ṛgveda* (Stuttgart, 1902), 108–19

1.170 T: E 135 (298); MM 1.286–8

1.171 T: MM 1.289–92
C: Aurobindo Ghose, 'Indra and the Thought-forces', *Arya* I (1914)

1.179 T: R 16.93
C: M. Mishra, 'On the Rgveda I.179.1, 4a, and 6c', *IA* (3rd ser.) 2 (3) (1969), 14–17; W. D. O'Flaherty, *Asceticism and Eroticism in the Mythology of Śiva* (Oxford, 1972), 52–5; Emil Sieg, *Die Sagenstoffe des Ṛgveda* (Stuttgart, 1902), 120–25; P. Thieme, 'Agastya und Lopāmudrā', *ZDMG* 113 (1963), 69–79

1.185 T: P 496–8; R 15.117

2.12 T: B 45–6; E 115 (288); M 45–56; P 199–204
C: W. Norman Brown, 'Theories of Creation in the Ṛg Veda', *JAOS* 85 (1965), 23–4; S. N. Shulka, 'A Fresh Interpretation of Ṛgveda II.12.3', *JGJKSV* 28:1–2 (January–April 1972), 615–36. Also in *SP* 26, *AIOC* (1972), 510–11; P. Thieme, *Der Fremdling im Ṛigveda* (Leipzig, 1938)

2.28 T: P 513–15; R 5.58 (7.15)

2.33 T: E 184 (344); M 56–67; MM 1.426–33; P 284–6; R 15.157

C: V. S. Agrawala, *Śiva Mahādeva, the Great God: An Exposition of the Symbolism of Śiva* (Benares, 1966); E. Arbman, *Rudra: Untersuchungen zum altindischen Glauben und Kultus* (Uppsala, 1922); S. Bhattacharji, *The Indian Theogony* (Cambridge, 1970), 109–210; J. Charpentier, 'Über Rudra-Siva', *WZKM* 23 (1909); R. N. Dandekar, 'Rudra in the Veda', *Journal of the University of Poona* 1 (1953), 94–148; H. Grégoire (avec la collaboration de R. Gossens et de M. Mathieu), *Asklèpios Apollon Smintheus et Rudra. Études sur le dieu à la taupe et le dieu au rat dans la Grèce et dans l'Inde* (Bruxelles, 1949); V. Machek, 'Origin of the Gods Rudra and Pūṣan', *AOr* 22 (1954), 544–62; M. Mayrhofer, 'Der Gottesname Rudra', *ZDMG* 103 (1953), 140–45; H. G. Narahari, 'Soma and Rudra in Vedic Mythology', *Bhāratīya Vidyā* 13 (1952) [1953]; W. D. O'Flaherty, 'Asceticism and Sexuality in the Mythology of Śiva', *HR* 8 (1969), 300–37, and 9 (1969), 1–41; V. Pisani, 'Und dennoch Rudra "Der Rote"', *ZDMG* 104 (1954), 136–9; S. Wikander, *Der arische Männerbund* (Lund, 1938), 69

2.35 T: M 67–79; R 14.33 (14.102)

C: H. W. Magoun, 'The Original Hindu Triad', *JAOS* 19:2 (1898), 145–50; 'Apāṃ Napat in the Rig-Veda', ibid., 137–44

2.38 T: R 15.10; RHS 21–3

C: S. D. Adkins, 'RV 2.38: A Problem Hymn', *JAOS* 81 (1961), 77–86; M. Winternitz, 'Ein Hymnus an Savitar', *AOr* 3 (1931), 296–302

3.31 T: E 117 (289)

C: J. C. Heesterman, 'Vala and Gomatī', *BDCRI* 19 (1958–9), 320–29; E. Harold, 'Social Significance of a Vedic Allegory (RV III, 31, 1–2)', *AOr* t. 26 (1958), 81–7

4.5 T: MM 2.335–9; P 626; R 13.9 (13.96)

4.18 T: B 37–9; E 227 (376)

C: K. Ammer, 'Tvaṣṭar, ein altindischer Schopfergott', *Die Sprache* Bd1 (1949), 68–77; M. Bloomfield, 'Contributions to the Interpretation of the Veda. III. The Marriage of Saraṇyū, Twaṣṭar's Daughter', *JAOS* 15 (1893), 172–88; W. Norman Brown, 'Indra's Infancy According to Rgveda IV, 18', *Siddhabharati* (Hoshiarpur, 1950), pt 1, 131–6; M. Leumann, 'Der indoiranische Bildnergott Twaṣṭar', *Asiatische Studien* Bd 12 (1959); W. D. O'Flaherty, *The Origins of Evil in Hindu Mythology* (Berkeley, Calif., 1976), 102–4; K. Rönnow, 'Viśvarūpa', *BSO(A)S* 6 (1931), 469–80; Emil Sieg, *Die Sagenstoffe des Ṛgveda* (Stuttgart, 1902), 82–6; P. Thieme, 'I Shall Make Peace', *BSO(A)S* 23 (1960), pt 2, 268

4.26–7 T: E 143 (305); N 209–10

C: David M. Knipe, 'The Heroic Theft: Myths from Ṛgveda IV and the Ancient Near East', *HR* 6:4 (1967), 328–60; Adalbert Kuhn, *Die Herabkunft des Feuers und des Göttertranks* (Gütersloh, 1886); R. Pischel, *Vedische Studien* (Stuttgart, 1889–92), 215; R. Roth, 'Der Adler mit dem Soma', *ZDMG* 36 (1882), 353–60; Ulrich Schneider, *Der Somaraub des Manu* (Wiesbaden, 1971); Emil Sieg, *Die Sagenstoffe des Ṛgveda* (Stuttgart, 1902), 88–96

4.58 T: R 16.105; RHS 33–5

5.2 T: MM 2.366–70; P 487; R 13.18 (13.104)

C: A. Hillebrandt, 'Zu *RV* V.2.1–6', *ZDMG* 33 (1879), 248; Emil Sieg, *Die Sagenstoffe*, 69–76.

5.40 T: L 76–7

5.78 T: R 16.42

C: Ludwig Alsdorf, 'Ṛgveda V.78: A Composite Legend Spell', *JBORS* 27 (3–5), 1971 (1972), 1–7; W. D. O'Flaherty, *Asceticism and Eroticism in the Mythology of Śiva* (Oxford, 1972), 57–64

5.83 T: E 180 (340); M 104–11; OST 5.140; P 274–6

C: V. Ivanov and V. Toporov, 'Le Mythe indoeuropéen du dieu de l'orage, poursuivant le serpent: reconstruction du schéma', in *Échanges et communications. Mélanges offerts à Claude Lévi-Strauss* (Paris–Le Haye, 1969), 1080; A. A. Macdonell, *Vedic*

*Mythology* (Strassburg, 1897), 83–5; J. Przyluski, 'Deux Noms Indiens du dieu soleil', *BSO(A)S* 6 (1931), 457

5.85 T: E 153 (317); N 211–12; R 5.69 (7.18)

C: G. Dumézil, *Ouranós-Varuṇa* (Paris, 1934); H. Lommel, 'Die Späher des Varuṇa und Mitra und das Auge des Königs', *Oriens* 6 (1953), 323–3; H. Lüders, *Varuṇa* (Göttingen, 1951, 1959); J. Przyluski, 'Varuṇa, God of the Sea and the Sky', *JRAS* (1931), 613–22

6.9 T: E 104 (278); P 330–33; R 13.42 (13.129); RHS 37–8

6.55 T: OST 5.177–8

6.70 T: E 177 (338); R 15.121

C: S. Bhattacharji, *The Indian Theogony* (Cambridge, 1970), 44–7, 160–61; A. A. Macdonell, *Vedic Mythology* (Strassburg, 1897), 21–2

6.75 T: R 16.109; RHS 39–42

7.49 T: M 115–18; P 118–19

7.55 T: E 244 (389); L 77; R 16.111

7.86 T: E 154 (318); L 78; M 134–41; N 214–15; P 515–17; R 5.70 (7.20); RHS 43–4

C: A. P. Karmarkar, 'Vasistha's Remorse over the Death of His Son', *ABORI* 22 (1941), 120–22; H. Oldenberg, 'Ueber die Liederfasser des Rigveda', *ZDMG* 42 (1888), 199–247; Emil Sieg, *Die Sagenstoffe des Rgveda* (Stuttgart, 1902), 105

7.88 T: E 156 (320); L 79; P 488; R 5.71 (7.24)

7.89 T: E 157 (321); L 80; P 517–18; R 5.72 (7.27)

7.101 T: B 11–12; R 15.113

C: W. Norman Brown, 'Some Notes on the Rain Charms', *NIA* 2 (1939), 115–19; W. D. O'Flaherty, *Women, Androgynes, and Other Mythical Beasts* (Chicago, Ill., 1980), 25–6

7.103 T: B 12–13; E 220 (369); M 141–7; OST 5.435; R 16.112; RHS 45–7

C: H. H. Bender, 'On the Naturalistic Background of the Frog-Hymn, Rig-Veda VII.103', *JAOS* 37, pt 3 (October 1917), 186–91; M. Bloomfield, 'On the "Frog-Hymn", Rig Veda vii.103, Together with Some Remarks on the Composition of the Vedic Hymns', *PrAOS* XVII (April 1896), 173–9; S. K. De, 'Wit, Humour, and Ancient Indian Literature', *Aspects of Sanskrit Literature* (Calcutta, 1959), 257–89; J. Gonda, 'The So-called Secular Hymns . . .', *ON* (1948), 312ff.; W. Norman Brown, 'Some Notes on the Rain Charms', *NIA* 2 (1939), 115–19

7.104 T: B 14–18; N 215–18; P 626; R 16.114
C: W. Norman Brown, 'The Rigvedic Equivalent for Hell', *JAOS* 61 (1941), 76–80; F. B. J. Kuiper, 'The Basic Concept of Vedic Religion', *HR* 15 (1975), 107–20; F. B. J. Kuiper, 'The Bliss of Aša', *IIJ* 8 (1964), 106–18

8.14 T: L 80
C: H. D. Velankar, 'Hymns to Indra in Mandala VIII', *JBomU* 15:2 (September 1946), 1–28

8.30 T: N 218; R 5.49 (4.110)

8.48 T: E 143 (306); M 152–64; P 364–9; R 9.69 (9.121)

8.79 T: N 219; R 9.70 (9.124)

8.91 T: L 82
C: A. K. Coomaraswamy, 'On the Loathly Bride', *Speculum* 20 (1945), reprinted in *Selected Papers*, ed. Roger Lipsey (Princeton, N.J., 1977), 353–70; G. Dumézil, *Mythe et épopée*, II (Paris, 1971), 342; Hanns Oertel, 'Contributions from the Jaiminīya Brāhmaṇa to the History of Brāhmaṇa Literature, pt 2, Indra Cures Apālā', *JAOS* 18 (1897), 26–31; L. von Schroeder, 'Das Apâlâlied', *WZKM* 22, 1908, 233–44; L. von Schroeder, 'Kleine Mitteilungen: Nachträge zum Apâlâlied', *WZKM* 23 (1909), 270–72

9.74 T: R 9.23 (9.85)
C: R. Gordon Wasson, *Soma: Divine Mushroom of Immortality* (New York, N.Y., 1968), 29–30

9.112 T: E 140 (303); N 221; OST 5.424; R 9.65 (9.118); RHS 279–80

9.113 T: E 141 (304); P 634–5; R 9.66 (9.118); RHS 51–3

10.5 T: N 221–2; R 14.4 (14.65)

10.9 T: L 83; P 119–20

10.10 T: E 222 (372); OST 5.288–90; P 544–51; R 16.122; RHS 55–7

C: T. Benfey, 'Rig Veda X.10.7', *Beiträge zur Kunde der indogermanischen Sprachen, herausgegeben von A. Bezzenberger* I, 47–51; V. A. Cadgil, 'Yama and Yamī', *JRAS* 20 (1944), 53–60; K. Geldner, 'Yama und Yamī', *Festgabe Albrecht Weber* (Leipzig, 1896), 18–22; R. Goldman, 'Mortal Man and Immortal Woman: An Interpretation of Three Ākhyāna Hymns of the Ṛg Veda', *JOIB* 18:4 (June 1969), 273–303; H. Heras, 'The Personality of Yama in the Ṛgveda', in H. R. Gupta (ed.), *Essays Presented to Sir Jadunath Sarkar* (Punjab University, 1958), 191–9; W. D. O'Flaherty, *Hindu Myths* (Penguin Books, 1975), 62–5; W. D. O'Flaherty, *Women, Androgynes, and Other Mythical Beasts* (Chicago, Ill., 1980), 176–84; U. Schneider, 'Yama and Yamī', *IIJ* 10 (1967), 1–32

10.14 T: E 198 (355); L 83; M 164–75; OST 5.291–5; P 575–9; R 16.124; RHS 59–62

C: S. S. Bhawa, 'Ṛgvedic pravát', *IA* I:1 (1964), 31–47; A. B. Keith, 'State of the Dead: Hindu', in Hastings's *Encyclopedia of Religion and Ethics II* (1920), 843–7; F. B. J. Kuiper, 'The Basic Concept of Vedic Religion', *HR* 15 (1975), 107–20; F. B. J. Kuiper, 'The Bliss of Aša', *IIJ* 8 (1964), 106–18; W. D. O'Flaherty, *The Origins of Evil in Hindu Mythology* (Berkeley, Calif., 1976), 212–21; H. I. Poleman, 'The Ritualistic Continuity of Ṛg Veda X.14–18', *JAOS* 54 (1934), 276–81

10.16 T: E 200 (356); L 84; OST 5.297–9; P 611–12; R 14.37 (14.107)

C: M. Bloomfield, 'On Vedic Agni Kravyavāhana and Agni Kavyavāhana', *Streitberg-Festgabe* (Leipzig, 1924), 12–14; Bruce Lincoln, 'Death and Resurrection in Indo-European Thought', *JIES* 5 (1977), 247–64; 'The Lord of the Dead', *HR* 20:3 (February 1981)

10.18 T: E 202 (357); L 86; P 609–10; R 16.127; RHS 63–5

10.28 T: E 229 (379)

C: V. S. Agrawala, 'The Riddles of Rsi Vasukra', *Bhārati* 5:1 (1961–2), 7–34; R. Pischel, 'Der Bock und das Messer', *ZDMG* 44 (1890), 497; R. Roth, 'Der Bock und das Messer', *ZDMG* 44 (1890), 371; H. D. Velankar, 'Hymns to Indra in Mandala X', *JBomU* 21:2 (September 1952), 1–20

10.33 T: E 245 (390); L 87

10.34 T: B 106–7; E 218 (368); M 186–95; OST 5.425; P 500–502; R 16.131; RHS 67–9

C: W. Norman Brown, 'Duty as Truth in Ancient India', *PAPS* 116 (1972), 252–68; H. Lüders, 'Das Wurfelspiel im alten Indien', *Abh. Götting. Ges. Wiss. (Phil.-hist. Kl.)* IX:2, *Neue Forschungen* (1907), 1–75

10.40 C: M. Bloomfield, 'On the Wedding Stanza, Rig-Veda X.40.10', *AJPh* 21, 411; M. Macnicol, *Poems by Indian Women* (New York, N.Y., 1923)

10.51 T: R 14.14 (14.79)

C: W. D. O'Flaherty, *Hindu Myths* (Penguin Books, 1975), 97–104

10:56 T: E 204 (358); R 16.133

10.58 T: P 579–82; R 16.134

10.71 T: B 75–9; E 246 (391); N 222–3; P 92–5; R 16.141; RHS 71–3

C: W. Norman Brown, 'The Creative Role of the Goddess Vāc in the Ṛg Veda', *Pratidānam: Indian, Iranian and Indo-European Studies Presented to F. B. J. Kuiper* (The Hague–Paris, 1968), 393–7; F. B. J. Kuiper, 'The Ancient Aryan Verbal Contest', *IIJ* 4:4 (1960); G. B. Palsule, 'Patañjali's Interpretation of ṚV 10.71.2', *Dandekar Felicitation Volume* (1969), 1–3; Manilel Patel, 'A Study of Ṛgveda X.71', *Viśvabharati Quarterly* 4 (August–October 1938); Frits Staal, 'RV 10.71 on the Origin of Language', in *Revelation in Indian Thought: A Festschrift in Honor of Professor T. R. V. Murti*, ed. Harald Concord and Krishna Sivaraman (Emeryville, Calif., 1977), 3–14

10.72 T: B 47–8; N 224; OST 5.48; P 801–2; R 16.142; RHS 75–6

C: W. Norman Brown, 'Theories of Creation in the Ṛg Veda', *JAOS* 85 (1965), 23–34; R. R. Bhagwat, 'Three Interesting Vedic Hymns', *JB(B)RS* 20

(1899), 234–56; W. D. O'Flaherty, *Women, Androgynes, and Other Mythical Beasts* (Chicago, Ill., 1980), 174–8

10:81 T: B 48; E 257 (400); P 807–8; R 15.167; RHS 77–8

C: S. Bhattacharji, *The Indian Theogony* (Cambridge, 1970), 320; W. Norman Brown, 'Theories of Creation in the Ṛg Veda', *JAOS* 85 (1965), 23–34; V. N. Deshpande, 'Some Reflections on the Two Viśvakarmā Hymns in the Ṛg Veda', *Journal of the Karnatak University* 6 (June 1962), 45–56

10.82 T: B 48–9; E 258 (401); P 812–13; R 15.170; RHS 79–80

10.85 T: E 206 (360); L 89; P 254–8; R 16.144; RHS 81–90

C: Ludwig Alsdorf, 'Bemerkungen zum Sūryāsūkta', *ZDMG* 111:2 (1961), 492–8; W. Caland, 'A Vaidic Wedding Song', *AO* 7 (1929), 305–11; J. Ehni, 'Rigv. X.85. Die Vermählung des Soma und der Sūryā', *ZDMG* 33 (1879), 166–76; A. Führer, 'Sanskrit-Rätsel', *ZDMG* 39 (1885), 99–100; J. Gonda, 'Notes on Atharvavedasamhita Book 14', *IIJ* 8:1 (1964), 1–24; R. Schmidt, *Beiträge zur Indischen Erotik* (Leipzig, 1902); R. Schmidt, *Liebe und Ehe im alten und modernen Indien* (Leipzig, 1904); M. Winternitz, *Das altindische Hochzeitsrituell* (Wien, 1892)

10.86 T: E 232 (380); R 16.147; RHS 91–6

C: Narāyan Aiyangār, *An Essay on the Vṛṣākapi Hymn of the Rigveda* (Madras, 1899); R. R. Bhagwat, 'Three Interesting Vedic Hymns', *JB(B)RS* 20 (1899), 234–56; K. Chattopadhyaya, *The Vṛṣākapi Hymn*, Allahabad University Studies I (1925); S. A. Dange, *Vedic Concept of 'Field' and the Divine Fructification* (Bombay, 1971), 49–67; W. D. O'Flaherty, 'The Post-Vedic History of the Soma Plant', pt 2 (pp. 95–147) of R. Gordon Wasson, *Soma: Divine Mushroom of Immortality* (New York, N.Y., 1968); Umakant P. Shah, 'Vṛṣākapi in Ṛgveda', *JMSUB* 8 (1958), 41–70; H. D. Velankar, 'Hymns to Indra in Mandala X', *JBomU* 22 (2) (September 1953), 6–26

10.90 T: B 4–10, 49–50; E 259 (403); M 195–203; N 225–6; OST 367–77; P 72–7; R 16.148; RHS 97–100

C: W. Norman Brown, 'The Sources and Nature of Puruṣa in the Puruṣasūkta', *JAOS* 51 (1931), 108–18;

'Theories of Creation in the Ṛg Veda', *JAOS* 85 (1965), 23–34; Ananda K. Coomaraswamy, 'Ṛgveda 10.90.1', *JAOS* 66 (1946), 145–61; V. Krishnamacharya, *Puruṣasūkta-bhāṣyam Śrīrangamunikṛtam* (Adyar Library, 1955); P. Mus, 'Du nouveau sur Ṛgveda 10.90?', in *Indological Studies in Honor of W. N. Brown* (New Haven, Conn., 1962), 165–85; 'Où finit Puruṣa?', in *Mélanges d'indianisme pour Louis Renou* (Paris, 1968), 539–64; W. D. O'Flaherty, *The Origins of Evil in Hindu Mythology* (Berkeley, Calif., 1976), 139–40; S. Schayer, 'A Note on the Old Russian Variants of the Purushasūkta', *AOr* 7 (1935), 319–29; Dieter Schlinghoff, 'Menschenopfer in Kausambī', *IIJ* 11 (1969), 176–89; Ganesh Umakant Thite, 'Animal Sacrifice in the Texts', *Numen* 17 (2) (August 1970), 151; A. Weber, 'Puruṣamedhakāndha', *ZDMG* 18 (1864), 277–84; *Indische Streifen* 1 (1868), 75–80; 'Ueber Menschenopfer bei den Indern der vedischen Zeit', *Indische Streifen* 1 (1868), 54

10.94 T: P 369–71; R 16.151; RHS 101–3

10.95 T: E 227 (374); R 16.152; RHS 105–8

C: J. Hertel, 'Die Geburt des Purūravas', *WZKM* 25 (1911), 153–86; K. R. Srinivasa Iyengar, 'Urvasi', *Sri Aurobindo Mandir Annual*, Jayanti 9 (15.8.1949), 46–84; A. B. Keith, 'The Birth of Purūravas', *JRAS*, January 1913, 412–17; D. D. Kosambi, 'Urvaśī and Purūravas', *JB(B)RS* 27 (1951), 1–30; A. Ludwig, 'Purūravas und Urvaśī', *SBB* 20 (1897), Zusätze und Berichtigungen; ibid. (1899), n. 4; M. A. Mehendale, 'On cakrán ná in the Ṛgveda X.95.12–13', *BDCRI* 14:2 (1955), 109–18; Indira Nalin, 'The Legend of Purūravas and Urvaśī', *JBomU* 19(2) (September 1950), 85–93; J. C. Wright, 'Purūravas and Urvaśī', *BSO(A)S* 30 (1967), 526–47; H. J. de Zwaart, 'RV X.95', *ON* (Leiden, 1948), 363–71

10.97 T: R 16.155

C: R. Roth, 'Das Lied des Artzes, Rigveda 10.97', *ZDMG* 25 (1871), 645

10.101 T: P 278–9; R 16.157; RHS 109–11; Sadashiv A. Dange,

'The Field and the Plough-share (a Ritual at Ṛgveda X.101)', *NIA* 17:2 (1967), 158–78

10.102 T: R 16.158

C: M. Bloomfield, 'Contributions to the Interpretation of the Veda: VI', *ZDMG* 48 (1894), 541–79; P. Bradke, 'Ein lustiges Wagenrennen in Altindien: RV 10.102', *ZDMG* 46 (1892), 445–62; Georges Dumézil, 'Le Iuges auspicium et les incongruités du taureau attelé de Mudgala', *La Nouvelle Clio* 5 (1953), 249–66; R. O. Franke, 'Der Drughaṇa des Mudgala-Liedes (ṚV X.102) und das Nandivisālajātaka', *WZKM* 8 (1894), 337–43; M. V. Henry, 'Mudgala, ou, l'hymne du marteau (suite d'énigmes védiques)', *JA* 1895, 516–58, and 1898, 329; H. D. Velankar, 'Hymns to Indra in Mandala X', *JBomU* 22:2 (September 1953), 6–26

10.108 T: E 236 (382)

C: R. R. Bhagwat, 'Three Interesting Vedic Hymns', *JB(B)RS* 20 (1899), 234–56; H. L. Hariyappa, *Ṛgvedic Legends through the Ages* (Poona, 1953), 148–83; G. Montesi, 'Il valore cosmico dell'Aurora nel pensiero mitologico del Rig-veda', *Studi e materiali de storia delle religioni* 24–5 (1953–4), 111–32; W. D. O'Flaherty, *Hindu Myths* (Penguin Books, 1975), 71–4; D. Srinivasan, 'The Myth of the Paṇis in the Rig-Veda', *JAOS* 93 (1973), 44–57

10.109 T: R 16.162

10.117 T: E 248 (392); OST 5.431; P 850–51; R 16.163; RHS 113–14

10.119 T: E 249 (393); OST 1.90; R 14.38 (14.110); RHS 115–17

C: R. Hauschild, 'Das Selbstlob (Ātmastuti) des somaberauschten Gottes Agni', *Asiatica. Festschrift F. Weller* (Leipzig, 1954), 247–88; H. D. Velankar, 'Hymns to Indra in Maṇḍala X', *JBomU* 22:2 (1954), 1–34

10.121 T: B 50–51; E 261 (405); MM 1.1–13; N 226–7; P 67–72; R 16.165; RHS 119–21

C: Chauncey J. Blair, *Heat in the Rig Veda and Atharva Veda* (New Haven, Conn., 1961); F. D. K. Bosch, *The Golden Germ* ('s Gravenhage, 1960); W. Norman Brown, 'Theories of Creation in the Ṛg Veda',

*JAOS* 85 (1965) 23–34; K. Hoffman, 'Bemerkungen zur vedischen Kosmologie', *OLZ* Jg. 49:9–10 (1954), 389–95; W. Kirfel, *Kosmographie der Inder nach den Quellen dargestellt* (Bonn-Leipzig, 1920); Stella Kramrisch, 'The Triple Structure of Creation in the ṚgVeda', *HR* 2:1 (1962), 140–75; F. B. J. Kuiper, 'The Bliss of Aša', *IIJ* 8 (1964), 106–18; H. Lommel, 'Der Welt-Ei Mythus im Rig Veda', in *Mélanges de linguistique offerts à Charles Bally* (Genève, 1939), 220; S. F. Michalski, 'Hymnes philosophiques du Ṛgveda', *Scientia* 46 (April 1952), 123–9; L. von Schroeder, 'Der siebente Aditya', *IF* 31 (1912), 178–93

10.123 T: E 251 (394); R 16.165

C: W. D. O'Flaherty, *The Origins of Evil in Hindu Mythology* (Berkeley, Calif., 1976), 321–3

10.124 T: B 3–4; R 14.29 (14.97)

C: W. Norman Brown, 'Proselyting the Asuras: A Note on Rig Veda 10.124', *JAOS* 39 (1919), 100–103; F. B. J. Kuiper, 'The Basic Concept of Vedic Religion', *HR* 15:2 (1975), 107–20; W. D. O'Flaherty, *The Origins of Evil in Hindu Mythology* (Berkeley, Calif., 1976), 113–15

10.125 T: B 51–2; E 252 (395); N 227–8; P 96–7; R 16.166; RHS 123–4

C: W. N. Brown, 'The Creative Role of the Goddess Vāc in the Rig Veda', *Pratidānam* (The Hague, 1968), 393–7; B. Essers, *Vāc, Het woord als godsgestalte in de Veda* (Groningen, 1952); C. A. Scharbau, *Die Idee der Schöpfung in der vedischen Literatur* (Stuttgart, 1932), 123

10.127 T: M 203–7; N 228–9; OST 4.497; P 839

10.129 T: B 17–19, 52; E 263 (407); M 207–12; N 229–30; P 54–9; R 16.168; RHS 125–6

C: W. Norman Brown, 'The Rigvedic Equivalent for Hell', *JAOS* 61 (1941), 76–80; 'Theories of Creation in the Ṛg Veda', *JAOS* 85 (1965), 23–34; F. B. J. Kuiper, 'The Basic Concept of Vedic Religion', *HR* 15 (1975), 107–20; A. Ludwig, 'Der Nāsadīya-hymnus, Rigveda X.129', *SBB* 1895, n. 14; Stanislao R. Michalski, 'Hymnes philosophiques du Ṛgveda',

*Scientia* 46 (April 1952), 123–9; Jwala Prasad, 'The Philosophical Significance of Ṛgveda X.129.5, and Verses of an Allied Nature', *JRAS* (1929), 586–98; W. D. Whitney, 'The Cosmogonic Hymn, Rig-Veda X.129', *PrAOS* 1882, 109

10.130 T: N 230; P 355–7; R 16.169; RHS 127–8

10.135 T: E 253 (397); M 212–16; P 551–4; R 16.170; RHS 129–30
C: M. R. Jambunathan, 'A Study of Ṛgveda 10.135', *AIOC* 15, *SP* (Bombay, 1949), 7

10.136 T: P 436–7; R 16.170; RHS 131–2

10.145 T: R 16.172

10.146 T: E 255 (398); N 231–2; OST 5.422; P 276; R 16.172; RHS 133–4
C: V. M. Apte, 'The Hymn to Araṇyānī (RV X.146)', *Chitramayajagat* (Poona, November 1942); S. G. Kantawala, 'A Comparative Study of the Hymn to Araṇyānī in the Ṛgveda and the Taittirīya Brāhmaṇa', *JOIB* 20:1 (September 1970), 1–11; P. Thieme, 'RV 10.146.2, āghāṭibhir iva dhāvayan', in *Pratidānam* (The Hague, 1968), 382–392

10.151 T: N 232; P 180; R 16.172

10.154 T: L 91; P 635–6

10.159 T: E 255 (398); R 16.173

10.162 T: R 16.174

10.164 T: E 216 (366); P 488; R 16.174; RHS 135–6
C: E. Abegg, 'Indische Traumtheorie und Traumdeutung', *Asiatische Studien* 1–4 (1959), 5; A. M. Esnoul, 'Les Songes et leur interprétation dans l'Inde', in *Sources orientales II: Les Songes et leur interprétation* (Paris, 1959), 215; Betty Heimann, *Die Tiefschlafspekulation der alten Upaniṣaden* (München, 1922)

10.165 T: E 216 (367); R 16.175

10.168 T: E 179 (339); M 216–19; MM 449–50; N 232–3; OST 1.145; P 131–2; R 15.109
C: S. Wikander, *Vāyu* (Uppsala–Leipzig, 1941)

10.171 C: H. D. Velankar, 'Hymns to Indra in Mandala X', *JBomU* 23:2 (September 1954), 1–18

10.173 T: E 217 (367); R 16.176
C: J. Gonda, *Ancient Indian Kingship from the Religious Point of View* (Leiden, 1969); J. C. Heesterman, *The Ancient Indian Royal Consecration* ('s Gravenhage, 1957)

10.177 T: R 16.176

10.184 T: R 16.177

10.190 T: E 264 (408); P 59–61; R 16.177; RHS 137

C: Chauncey J. Blair, *Heat in the Rig Veda and Atharva Veda* (New Haven, Conn., 1961)

## APPENDIX 5

## *Hymns Translated in This Volume, Listed in Numerical Order, with opening Sanskrit Phrase*

| | | |
|---|---|---|
| 1.1 | Oṁ Agnim īḷe | 99 |
| 1.26 | vasiṣvā hi miyedhya | 99 |
| 1.32 | Indrasya nu vīryāṇi pra vocam | 148 |
| 1.35 | hvayāmi Agniṃ prathamaṃ svastaye | 198 |
| 1.42 | saṃ Pūṣann adhvanas tira vy aṃho | 193 |
| 1.50 | ud u tyaṃ Jātavedasaṃ devaṃ vahanti ketavaḥ | 189 |
| 1.85 | pra ye śuṃbhante janayo na | 165 |
| 1.92 | etā u tyā Uṣasaḥ | 179 |
| 1.114 | imā rudrāya tavase | 224 |
| 1.116 | Nāsatyābhyāṃ barhir iva pra vṛṃje | 182 |
| 1.154 | Viṣṇor nu kaṃ vīryāṇi pra vocaṃ | 225 |
| 1.160 | te hi dyāvāpṛthivī | 203 |
| 1.162 | mā no Mitro Varuṇo Aryamāyur | 89 |
| 1.163 | yad akrandaḥ prathamaṃ jāyamāna | 87 |
| 1.164 | asya vāmasya palitasya hotus | 71 |
| 1.165 | kayā śubhā savayasaḥ sanīḷāḥ | 168 |
| 1.170 | na nūnam asti no śvaḥ | 170 |
| 1.171 | prati va enā namasāham emi | 171 |
| 1.179 | pūrvīr ahaṃ śaradaḥ śaśramāṇā | 250 |
| 1.185 | katarā pūrvā katarāparāyoḥ | 204 |
| 2.12 | yo jāta eva prathamo manasvān devo | 160 |
| 2.28 | idaṃ kaver ādityasya svarājo | 217 |
| 2.33 | ā te pitar Marutāṃ | 221 |
| 2.35 | upem asṛkṣi vājayur vacasyāṃ | 104 |
| 2.38 | ud u ṣya devaḥ Savitā | 195 |
| 3.31 | śāsad vahnir duhitur naptyaṃ gād | 151 |
| 4.5 | vaiśvānarāya mīḷhuṣe sajoṣāḥ kathā | 112 |
| 4.18 | ayaṃ panthā anuvittaḥ purāṇo | 141 |
| 4.26 | ahaṃ Manur abhavaṃ Sūryaścāham | 128 |
| 4.27 | garbhe nu sann anveṣām avedaṃ | 129 |
| 4.58 | samudrād ūrmir madhumān | 126 |

## APPENDIX 6

# *Index and Glossary*

## FOR THE BEST IN PAPERBACKS, LOOK FOR THE 

In every corner of the world, on every subject under the sun, Penguin represents quality and variety – the very best in publishing today.

For complete information about books available from Penguin – including Pelicans, Puffins, Peregrines and Penguin Classics – and how to order them, write to us at the appropriate address below. Please note that for copyright reasons the selection of books varies from country to country.

---

**In the United Kingdom:** Please write to *Dept E.P., Penguin Books Ltd, Harmondsworth, Middlesex, UB7 0DA*

If you have any difficulty in obtaining a title, please send your order with the correct money, plus ten per cent for postage and packaging, to *PO Box No 11, West Drayton, Middlesex*

**In the United States:** Please write to *Dept BA, Penguin, 299 Murray Hill Parkway, East Rutherford, New Jersey 07073*

**In Canada:** Please write to *Penguin Books Canada Ltd, 2801 John Street, Markham, Ontario L3R 1B4*

**In Australia:** Please write to the *Marketing Department, Penguin Books Australia Ltd, P.O. Box 257, Ringwood, Victoria 3134*

**In New Zealand:** Please write to the *Marketing Department, Penguin Books (NZ) Ltd, Private Bag, Takapuna, Auckland 9*

**In India:** Please write to *Penguin Overseas Ltd, 706 Eros Apartments, 56 Nehru Place, New Delhi, 110019*

**In Holland:** Please write to *Penguin Books Nederland B.V., Postbus 195, NL–1380AD Weesp, Netherlands*

**In Germany:** Please write to *Penguin Books Ltd, Friedrichstrasse 10–12, D–6000 Frankfurt Main 1, Federal Republic of Germany*

**In Spain:** Please write to *Longman Penguin España, Calle San Nicolas 15, E–28013 Madrid, Spain*

**In France:** Please write to *Penguin Books Ltd, 39 Rue de Montmorency, F-75003, Paris, France*

**In Japan:** Please write to *Longman Penguin Japan Co Ltd, Yamaguchi Building, 2–12–9 Kanda Jimbocho, Chiyoda-Ku, Tokyo 101, Japan*

PENGUIN CLASSICS

## THE BHAGAVAD GITA

*Translated by Juan Mascaró*

Sanskrit literature can boast some of the most beautiful and profoundly moving works of all times. It is essentially a romantic literature, interwoven with idealism and practical wisdom, expressing a passionate longing for spiritual vision. The eighteen chapters of the Bhagavad Gita (c. 500 B.C.) encompass the whole great struggle of a human soul. The three central themes of this immortal poem – Love, Light and Life – arise from the symphonic vision of God in all things and of all things in God

## THE UPANISHADS

*Translated and Selected by Juan Mascaró*

The Upanishads represent for the Hindu approximately what the New Testament represents for the Christian. The earliest of these spiritual treatises, which vary greatly in length, were put down in Sanskrit between 800 and 400 B.C. This selection from twelve Upanishads reveals the paradoxical variety and unity, the great questions and simple answers, the spiritual wisdom and romantic imagination of these 'Himalayas of the Soul'.

## HINDU MYTHS

*Translated by Wendy O'Flaherty*

These tales of Hindu gods and demons express in vivid symbols the metaphysical insights of ancient Indian priests and poets. This new selection and translation of seventy-five seminal myths spans the wide range of classical Indian sources, from the serpent-slaying Indra of the Vedas (c. 1200 B.C.) to the medieval pantheon – the phallic and ascetic Siva, the maternal and bloodthirsty Goddess, the mischievous child Krishna, the other avatars of Vishnu, and the many minor gods, demons, rivers and animals sacred to Hinduism. The traditional themes of life and death are set forth and interwoven with many complex variations which give a kaleidoscopic picture of the development of almost three thousand years of Indian mythology.

## SPEAKING OF ŚIVA

*Translated by A. K. Ramanujan*

*Speaking of Śiva* is a collection of *vacanas* or free-verse lyrics written by four major saints of the great *bhakti* protest movement which originated in the tenth century A.D.

Composed in Kannada, a Dravidian language of South India, the poems are lyrical expressions of love for the god Śiva. They mirror the urge to by-pass tradition and ritual, to concentrate on the subject rather than the object of worship, and to express kinship with all living things in moving terms. Passionate, personal, fiercely monotheistic, these free verses possess an appeal which is timeless and universal.

## POEMS FROM THE SANSKRIT

*Translated by John Brough*

For many readers in the West, Indian literature means the Bhagavad Gita or the Kamasutra: this anthology of secular poems from the classical Sanskrit redresses the balance. These poems were written between the fourth and tenth centuries A.D. and illustrate the great diversity of subject-matter, style and imagination in a highly-artistic aspect of Indian culture. A purely literary language by the fourth century, Sanskrit contains a wealth of synonyms and tends itself to a strict metrical form with complex and subtle sound patterns. In his introduction, John Brough confesses his affection for Sanskrit poems – an affection which is reflected in his verse translations.

## THREE SANSKRIT PLAYS

*Translated by Michael Coulson*

The three plays translated here are leading examples of Classical Sanskrit drama and were probably written between 350 and 750 A.D.

*Sakuntalā* by Kālindāsa, India's most celebrated poet, and *Rākshasa's Ring* by Visākhadatta, are epic legends of heroic drama. Elegantly and serenely retold, they create the atmosphere of a highly sophisticated fairy tale. The third play, *Mālatī and Mādhava* by Bhavabhuti, leaves the subject of kings and gods and turns to everyday life, featuring the activities of ministers, merchants and courtesans.

It is the skilful blend of gentleness, grace and fantasy with a calm maturity and wisdom that places each of these plays at the summit of Sanskrit literary achievement.

In addition to the general introduction and guide to pronunciation, the volume contains an introduction to each play.

## BUDDHIST SCRIPTURES

*Translated by Edward Conze*

Most of the writings chosen for this anthology were recorded between 100 and 400 A.D., the Golden Age of Buddhist literature. They include passages from the *Dhammapada*, the *Buddhacarita*, the *Questions of King Milinda*, and the *Tibetan Book of the Dead.* Dr Conze has concentrated on texts intended for the layman rather than for the monk and his selection exhibits more of the humanity than the profundity of the Scriptures. His translation shows a respect for the characteristic diction of Buddhist teachings and manages to preserve much of the original flavour.

## THE DHAMMAPADA

*Translated by Juan Mascaró*

The *Dhammapada* is a collection of aphorisms which illustrate the Buddhist *dhamma* or moral system. Probably compiled in the third century B.C., the verses encompass the struggle towards Nirvana – the supreme goal for the Buddhist – and point out the narrow Path of Perfection which leads to it. 'In the *Dhammapada* we can hear the voice of Buddha,' writes Juan Mascaró, translator of the *Bhagavad Gita* and the *Upanishads.* 'The gospel of light and of love is amongst the greatest spiritual works of man. Each verse is like a small star and the whole has the radiance of eternity.'

## WANG WEI: POEMS

*Translated by G. W. Robinson*

Wang Wei (A.D. 699–761), though sometimes eclipsed by his contemporaries, Li Po and Tu Fu, is nevertheless one of the greatest poets in Chinese literature. During his life he survived several political upheavals, dividing his time between the court and his country estate, where he drew inspiration from the mountains and solitude. His poetry affirms his belief in a whole natural order, which includes mankind, and thus his delicately observed – though generalized – descriptions of landscapes are rendered especially moving by the sense of unity expressed by the unseen poet's presence. A devoted Buddhist, Wang Wei was still prey to life's pleasures, and many of his poems reflect an unresolved conflict between the worldly and the mystical sides of his nature.

## POEMS OF THE LATE T'ANG

*Translated by A. C. Graham*

Chinese poetry achieved an unsurpassed greatness in the eighth and ninth centuries A.D. Its most famous poets, from the widely established Tu Fu to Li Shang-yin (one of the first of Chinese poets to make love his central theme), explore their language to its utmost limits in poems that have a sharp definition of outline and yet a complexity and allusiveness unknown to Western writers.

The seven poets of this anthology include Han Yü, who has the power, it is said, to create beauty out of ugliness and Li Ho, whose morbid sensitivity relates him to Baudelaire. The brilliant political allegory *The Eclipse* by Lu T'ung, the bold imagery of Meng Chiao, and the swift elegant poems of Tu Mu complete the volume.